IMPACTS OF WAR

1914 & 1918

also by John Terraine

MONS
DOUGLAS HAIG: THE EDUCATED SOLDIER
THE WESTERN FRONT 1914-1918
THE GREAT WAR 1914-1918
THE LIFE AND TIMES OF LORD MOUNTBATTEN
PASSCHENDAELE: A STUDY IN INEVITABILITY
TO WIN A WAR
1918: THE YEAR OF VICTORY
WHITE HEAT: THE NEW WARFARE 1914-1918
THE RIGHT OF THE LINE: THE RAF IN THE EUROPEAN WAR 1939-45
BUSINESS IN GREAT WATERS: THE U-BOAT WARS 1916-45
THE SMOKE AND THE FIRE: MYTHS AND ANTI-MYTHS OF WAR 1861-1945

Editor:
GENERAL JACK'S DIARY

IMPACTS OF WAR

1914 & 1918

JOHN TERRAINE

Why, my dear Hankey, do we worry
about history?… Obviously history
is written for schoolmasters and
armchair strategists. Statesmen and
warriors pick their way through the
dusk.

*Lord Esher to Lieutenant-Colonel
M.P. Hankey, March 15th, 1915*

LEO COOPER

LONDON

First published in Great Britain in 1970 by
Hutchinson & Co (Publishers) Ltd.

Revised edition published in Great Britain in 1993 by
LEO COOPER
190 Shaftesbury Avenue, London WC2H 8JL
an imprint of
Pen & Sword Books Ltd
47 Church Street, Barnsley, South Yorkshire S70 2AS

Copyright © John Terraine 1970, 1993

A CIP catalogue record for this book is available
from the British Library

ISBN 0 85052 317 6

Printed by Redwood Books
Trowbridge, Wiltshire

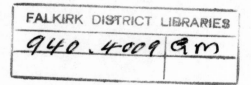

ACKNOWLEDGEMENTS

My thanks are due to those who have given permission for quotations from the following books:

Memory Holds The Door (1940) by John Buchan, by kind permission of The Tweedsmuir Estate and Hodder and Stoughton. *Rudyard Kipling's Definitive Verse* (1940) by kind permission of Mrs. Bambridge. *The Battles of the Somme* (1917) by Sir Philip Gibbs, with acknowledgement to William Heinemann Ltd., *Realities of War* (1920) by Sir Philip Gibbs by kind permission of Anthony Gibbs Esq. *Ordeal by Battle* (1915) and *Anvil of War* (1936) by F. S. Oliver, with acknowledgement to Macmillan & Co. *Peacemaking* (1933) and *King George V* (1952) by Sir Harold Nicolson, by kind permission of Nigel Nicolson. *Vestigia* (1919) and *The First World War* (1920) by Colonel Repington, with acknowledgement to Constable and Co. Ltd. *The World Crisis* (1938) by Sir Winston Churchill, with acknowledgement to the Hamlyn Publishing Group Ltd. *Grey of Falloden* (1937) by G. M. Trevelyan, with acknowledgement to Longman Group Ltd. *Great Britain and the War 1914-1918* (1967) by Sir Llewellyn Woodward, with acknowledgement to Methuen and Co. *From the Dreadnought to Scapa Flow* by Arthur J. Marder, with acknowledgement to the Oxford University Press. *Eyewitness* (1932) by Sir Ernest Swinton, with acknowledgement to Hodder and Stoughton Ltd. *The Autobiography of Richard Burdon Haldane* (1929) with acknowledgement to Hodder and Stoughton Ltd. *War Memoirs* Of Lloyd George (1938) by kind permission of Beaverbrook Newspapers Ltd.

Every effort has been made to clear the relevant copyright in quotations included in the text.

M

CONTENTS

INTRODUCTION TO ORIGINAL EDITION, 1970

The impacts of war are limitless, and in many respects unfathomable. In the First World War, four broad levels of impact upon Britain may be discerned: impact upon the soldiers and sailors in the battle line—the most severe; impact upon the military leaders (the generals above all) who directed them—this also could be severe; impact upon politicians who directed the generals and admirals—and here the severities begin to change their substance; impact upon the people whom the politicians represented—this is where generalisation must always be taken with large pinches of salt. The patriotic widow who loses all her sons is a part of Public Opinion; so is the Conscientious Objector; so is the profiteer. One cannot make forty million separate statements; yet one cannot ignore the weight of Public Opinion in a democracy merely because it is bound to be diverse. The short cut which I have used for the purposes of this book is to treat Public Opinion in terms of the guidance it received, i.e. the Press, and in particular the Press which was influential with people who were influential.

I am, then, concerned in Part I with the impact of war in 1914, mainly at several removes from the battlefield, on a Government and people ill-prepared for such a trial; and in Part II with its impact in 1918 (when, because of the enemy's action, the battlefield became the only place that mattered) chiefly upon soldiers and generals.

INTRODUCTION TO THIS EDITION

I am particularly pleased to see this book back in print at last. For far too long I have been uneasily aware that it has been "hard done by"—a fate that can befall a book as well as an author.

It was written during an interval between two television experiences—the fiasco of the BBC's *British Empire*, with which I fortunately severed connection before the series was screened, and the promise of *The Mighty Continent*, only partly fulfilled. These were distractions which could not fail to affect a serious work of history.

It was also affected by the misfortunes of its editor at Hutchinson's. He was the late Ronald Lewin, who had also emerged from the BBC, where he had been Head of the Home Service in those distant days, and would shortly also emerge from publishing to embark on his own very distinguished writing career, culminating (though not ending) with his superb *Slim: The Standard-Bearer* (Leo Cooper, 1976).

At the end of the sixties, when he was editing *Impacts of War*, Ronald was passing through a period of bereavement and ill-health which distracted him too, sufficiently to deprive me of the full value of his experience and advice, and probably also deprive the book of the professional thrust which every book needs. So it fell by the wayside. This was a pity, because if nothing else, *Impacts of War* contains the products of some fresh research and some material which had never seen the light of day. In Part 1 Mr. A.C. Ainger's "*Marching Songs for Soldiers*" (1914) and in Part II the extracts from soldiers' letters in 1918 could stand by themselves to illustrate the great gulf of consciousness which divides the beginning from the end of the First World War.

John Terraine
March 1993

PART I

HOME FRONT

I

What happened between 1914 and 1918 provided, for everyone and every country that shared the experience of war (and this goes far beyond the list of belligerents) a succession of dreadful novelties. In every country the equanimity of all classes of the population was deeply and permanently disturbed. It is probably true that this disturbance affected Britain more than any other nation. This is not a matter of loss of life during the war; by comparison with the other great powers of Europe, Britain got off lightly in that respect. It was not a matter of loss of 'wealth' (that curious national 'wealth' which so often seems to bear little relation to the actual wealth of the majority of people who comprise the nation); Britain lost wealth, certainly—a great deal of it—but as a second war and its aftermath were to reveal, she had a lot left. And it was certainly not a matter of physical destruction, such as Belgium suffered through enemy occupation, or France, in the man-made desert known as the 'zone of the armies'—an area larger than the whole of Holland. It was very much to do with equanimity: the dislocation of a state of mind.

This, no doubt, is the explanation of Sir Harold Nicolson's critical verdict after the experience of a second world war:

> Public opinion, it must be recalled, was less stable in the first than in the second war. The civilian population, faced as they were with the unprecedented horror of a major catastrophe, did not in 1914 display the same patience, charity, confidence or sense of proportion as were so stolidly manifested by their successors of 1939. In all wars rumours ramp and individuals are unjustly maligned; but the suspiciousness, credulity and inequity of the civilians during the first war were in excess of any similar emotions provoked by the even greater and more immediate perils of 1940.[1]

All this is very true—except the reason which Harold Nicolson supplies from hindsight: 'the unprecedented horror of a major catastrophe'. That the war of 1914–1918 was a major catastrophe was fairly evident before it ended, and very evident shortly afterwards. But it

[1] Harold Nicolson: *King George V: His Life and Reign;* Constable 1952; ch. xvi.

3

was not evident at the beginning; and yet the symptoms of which he speaks began to make themselves felt very early indeed. What *was* unprecedented was the shock of a new experience, of new demands upon the whole nation after a long period of immunity from such demands. And very soon there was also the shock of receiving bad news, which was not only unexpected, but also very badly handled. By 1939 at least *some* lessons had been learnt, and if follies persisted, fewer people were taken in by them.

In 1914 the British were very naive. It is a myth that the Edwardian period was a halcyon age of calm and grandeur. It was a period, at home, of increasing social and industrial unrest, culminating, in the reign of George V, in a dire and immediate threat of civil war. Abroad, the reign of Edward VII, and the early years of his successor, were marked by a series of dangerous international crises—dangerous enough to alter foreign policy fundamentally, and with it military policy. The naiveté consisted in a steady refusal to recognise these facts, and an even more resolute refusal to draw conclusions from them. In this respect the British people undoubtedly had 'the government they deserved'; neither government nor people had the slightest desire to face such uncomfortable realities.

It becomes with each passing year more difficult to recapture the British frame of mind at the beginning of the Twentieth Century. The actual turn of the century marked a zenith of Victorian imperial complacency: a true zenith because the downward turn then became visible—if anyone cared to look. At the turn of the century Britain was at war with the Boer republics of South Africa. It has been estimated that the total military force which the two republics together (Transvaal and Orange Free State) could put into the field was about 60,000 burghers: armed, mounted farmers loosely organised on a territorial Commando system.[1] As a challenge to the might of the British Empire, such a force seemed laughable, or pitiable. Yet the challenge was maintained from October 1899 to

[1] The adoption of the name 'Commando' by the British Army in 1940, its subsequent retention, and its great popularity with the Press, have led to some confusion. A Boer Commando in 1899 was merely the assembly of fighting men of a particular district, e.g. the Jacobsdal Commando, Boshof Commando, Lichtenburg Commando, etc. Later, when the two republics were overrun by the British, but many Boers continued to fight on, the name was used somewhat differently: it now referred to the leader, not to a geographical area, e.g. Christian de Wet's Commando, De la Rey's Commando, etc. It remains a mystery, only explicable in terms of the British national habit of ignorance and inexactitude about military affairs, why it should have been adopted forty years later for highly-trained specialist formations recruited at first from the cream of our Regular Army, and continue to be used by that ancient amphibious corps, the Royal Marines.

May 1902; and by the time the Boers at last sued for peace, the Empire had been forced to deploy against them a total of 448,435 officers and men.[1] These facts alone reveal a reality of weakness behind a façade of strength; added to the more specific shocks of 'Black Week'[2] and the incidental setbacks which continued to afflict the Imperial forces right up to the end of the war, they had a salutary impact on British complacency.

The Army's misfortunes, however, are only a part of the story, and not the more important part. These could be corrected—and *were* very largely corrected—by duly considered reforms. Less appreciated, but far more disturbing where it was appreciated, was a sense of naval weakness. During the South African War Britain became the butt of almost universally hostile reaction abroad. A Franco–Russo–German alliance was even mooted against her, but was rejected by the German Kaiser Wilhelm II. Nevertheless, in 1900 there was an invasion scare which caused serious misgivings about the state of the Navy. The Government tended to brush these aside: this, after all, was still the age of the 'two-power' standard, the doctrine that the British Fleet 'should be equal to the combination of the two next strongest Navies in Europe'. In 1900 that meant France and Russia, and the 'two-power standard' was effective.

Yet the critics had a point—indeed, many points. They questioned the tempo of naval construction. Britain, they said, was approaching a point where no work was going to be done in any given year upon that year's programme. And this point was, in fact, reached in 1901–1902. They criticised the Reserve Fleet as being useless for war; the 1901 manoeuvres illustrated their point, and Admiral Sir John Fisher underlined it when, as First Sea Lord (1904–1910) he scrapped 150 obsolete vessels. The critics attacked the Navy's weapons, concentrating on gun-sights, the continuing use of relatively inefficient black powder, and muzzle-loading guns. Sixteen battleships were armed with muzzle-loaders; admittedly, only two of them were in commission, but was there a case for retaining any, in the twentieth century? They urged the need for more battleships (at that time still the hard core of naval strength). They questioned the deployment of the Fleet, asserting that both the Channel and the Mediterranean Fleets were inadequate for their vital tasks. They criticised gunnery; again the official returns gave them backing—in 1902 British ships were missing their targets on average more than

[1] Adjutant-General's Return, laid before the Royal Commission on the South African War, 1903.
[2] The British defeats at Stormberg, Dec. 10th 1899, Magersfontein, Dec. 11th and Colenso, Dec. 15th. The public reaction was out of all proportion to the casualties sustained, which totalled about 3,000 for all three actions.

twice out of every three rounds.[1] Long-range gunnery, at a time when gun ranges were constantly increasing, was virtually unknown. And finally, the critics attacked the training of officers and seamen. Practically, they said, it was still far too much based on the days of sail; theoretically (strategy and tactics) it scarcely existed at all. This was a formidable indictment.[2]

During the next decade sweeping naval reforms took place, initiated by Fisher, and continued by Winston Churchill as First Lord of the Admiralty with Prince Louis of Battenberg as First Sea Lord. Most of the points of criticism of 1900 were met; the Fleet was transformed, as the Army was being transformed by the Haldane Reforms. But long before this programme was even halfway complete, a new point had arisen, a new context of naval power itself, and a new rating of British naval power which could scarcely have been predicted in 1900. Then, the Two-power Standard, and the degree of naval supremacy which it implied, were fundamentals of British political and strategic thinking. It did not seriously matter, it was not perilous to the nation, that the Army should be in difficulties in a war at the far end of Africa. That was something that could be put right. It did not seriously matter that world opinion was bitterly anti-British. What could world opinion do, in the face of the Two-power Standard? It did not even matter that Britain herself was deeply divided about the war; behind the shield of the Two-power Standard she could afford the luxury of internal divisions and other preoccupations. What *was* serious was the demise of the Standard itself.

So magical was the sense of this inheritance of power—itself the product of over two hundred years of tradition, of which the climax was Trafalgar, since when for 95 years the Navy had scarcely been challenged—that even now it is hard to grasp that the 'two-power' doctrine only existed effectively for twenty years, or rather less. The

[1] cf. Admiral Sir Andrew Cunningham's alleged signal to the Admiralty in 1941, on being reminded that his report on 'Progress in Naval Gunnery' was overdue:

There has been NO progress in gunnery in the Mediterranean in the years 1940 and 1941, but certain old lessons well known to Noah and the Armada have been re-learned at much trouble and expense. The most notable lesson is that the right range for any ship of the Mediterranean Fleet, from a battleship to a submarine, to engage an enemy ship with gunfire is POINT BLANK (nowadays 2,000 yards or less) AT WHICH RANGE EVEN A GUNNERY OFFICER CANNOT MISS.

(Quoted in *Matapan* by S. W. C. Pack, Batsford 1961.)

[2] This summary is drawn from Professor A. J. Marder's *Anatomy of British Sea Power* (*1880–1905*), ch. xviii, in which the pros and cons will be found set out in far greater detail and balance. I am only concerned here with the critics' case.

famous Standard was laid down in 1889, and reaffirmed with emphasis and clarity by the Gladstone government of 1893. As we have seen, it applied to a possible threat from France and Russia. In 1903 occurred the last active flutter of 'two-power' philosophy—a scare ('brief alarm' is a better description) about an unexpected enlargement of the Russian battleship-building programme. Just over a year later, the destruction of the Russian Fleet by the Japanese at Tsushima (May 1905) displayed to all the irrelevance of this fear. It was already even more irrelevant for a quite different reason.

In 1905 a new portent was seen. In that year, by the terms of reckoning then adopted, Germany and the United States of America tied for third place in the list of world naval powers. This was a formidable combination, deeply significant for Britain's future. These two countries were her greatest commercial and industrial rivals, with economic growth rates and potential which Britain could no longer hope to match. A Standard which might be maintained in relation to France and Russia could certainly not be maintained in relation to these two countries, unless they permitted it; and this they clearly would not do.

Fortunately, their combination was merely statistical; it was not in any sense political, and the British response to their emergence as naval powers was different for each of them. As regards America, there was even a disposition to welcome the new development. Sentimentality played its part in this; Professor Marder quotes T. A. Brassey (editor of the *Naval Annual*) in 1903:

> In her political relations with the United States, old England may confidently reckon that the claims of kinship will always prevail. Blood is thicker than water.

Twelve years later the strength of the kinship and the thickness of the blood were considerably more open to doubt. *The Spectator* (1904) was rather more realistic:

> We do not mean to fight with America, nor she with us; and if war should break out between the two branches of the race, it will be in the nature of a civil war, and against civil wars it is impossible to prepare.[1]

There were even proposals for joint exercises by Royal Navy and U.S. Navy squadrons—but that was too much for a Service which, even at its lowest ebbs, guarded its technical secrets jealously. On the other hand, naval opinion in Britain, as threats developed in European waters, tended to regard an increasing American presence

[1] Quoted in Marder, *Anatomy of British Sea Power*, p. 443.

B

in the Pacific as an asset (despite the Anglo-Japanese alliance, and the advantages already accruing from it).

Germany was a different matter altogether. It could not be known that the 'Very Secret' Memorandum drawn up by Admiral Tirpitz in June 1897 contained the explicit statement:

> For Germany the most dangerous naval enemy at the present time is England. It is also the enemy against which we most urgently require a certain measure of naval force as a political power factor.

The insanity of this passage would be its own protection: the proposition that England was Germany's 'most dangerous naval enemy' in 1897 is so bizarre that, even had the document been discovered and published, almost no-one in Britain would have believed it. Yet this was Tirpitz's belief and dominating principle. This was what he insisted upon while his staff were working on the details of the Memorandum:

> Again and again, Tirpitz pressed home to his subordinates the fact that the relationship to England must always be their guiding motif. In a marginal comment on an older memorandum, he criticized his predecessor's arguments in favour of short building periods and early replacement provisions. 'The main point is missing,' he wrote. 'The private dockyards must learn to build *quickly* in order to be competitive *against England*.'[1]

The significance of the Memorandum is that it formed the basis of the German Navy Law of 1898. It planned for a fleet of 19 battleships, 12 large cruisers, 30 small cruisers and 12 torpedo-boat divisions, to be completed by 1905, and, of course, concentrated in European waters. As these vessels began to come down the slipways, with the regularity and efficiency to be expected from German industry, it began also to be recognised in Britain that here was a new potential enemy and a grave new threat. Even before 1905, this recognition had produced a fundamental change in British policy: the *Entente Cordiale*. Thus the policy of Admiral Tirpitz, warmly supported by his Navy-minded Emperor, produced exactly the opposite result to that intended. What it did *not* produce was an understanding in Britain of the consequences of a step which, at the time, had the air of a settling of differences, a smoothing-out of unnecessary disputes (Newfoundland fishery rights, and the Suez Canal Convention were also subjects of the *Entente Cordiale*) rather than a commitment to immense undertakings.

[1] Jonathan Steinberg: *Yesterday's Deterrent: Tirpitz and the Birth of the German Battle Fleet;* Macdonald 1965.

The tempo of events—or the rhythm of crises—now became very much faster. In 1905 the power-balance of Europe was dangerously disturbed. Russia sustained a series of heavy defeats at the hands of the Japanese which caused her to accept a loser's peace in September. Meanwhile, the Tsarist régime was shaken by the revolution which brought into existence the first Soviet, and ended with a capitulation by the government to liberal demands for more representative government. Russia was France's ally—her only offset to the growing power of Germany, her only solid guarantee against a repetition of the events of 1870–1871 which still haunted her dreams. Tsarist autocracy was distasteful to most Frenchmen of the Third Republic, but beggars cannot be choosers; the decline of Russian power was an alarming matter for the French.

Their alarm was well-founded. The temptation to profit by the shift in the power balance proved too strong for Germany's rulers. Jealousy of France's empire and influence in North Africa provided the spur, and Morocco the arena of conflict. As a German newspaper said in 1904:

> Morocco is a German concern owing to our increasing population and need of naval bases. If Germany does not peg out claims, she will retire empty-handed from the partition of the world. Is the German man-in-the-street to get nothing? The time has come when Germany must secure Morocco from the Atlas to the sea.[1]

Whether the Kaiser himself really believed that a provocative policy in Morocco was wise is uncertain; yet his person was the instrument of that policy. In March 1905 he visited Tangier and announced that he proposed to deal with the Sultan of Morocco as an independent ruler without reference to France, and that he wanted free trade and equal rights for Germany in Morocco. This was a direct challenge to France; if she resisted it, and the Germans did not back down, there would almost certainly be war—a war which Germany would probably win with ease. How did the *Entente Cordiale* (less than a year old) stand in such a situation? Would it prove to be a reality, or not?

To the surprise of the Germans, the British Government (Lord Lansdowne was Foreign Secretary in Balfour's Administration) indicated that they would stand by France; they also urged discussions, negotiations and arbitration between the disputants. The Germans maintained pressure, and the French Foreign Minister, Delcassé, was forced to resign—an apparent German victory. At the same time, Germany sought by all possible means to restore her 'image' of

m *The Kaiser and His Times*, by Michael Balfour; Cresset Press 1964.

respectability, especially in Britain. Colonel Repington, newly-appointed Military Correspondent of the *Times*, wrote:

> We were great fools in those days. We were as blind as bats. ....
> The Germans used every means to ingratiate themselves with us,
> and there began that series of mutual visits and fawnings of Anglo–
> German statesmen, philanthropists, editors, and Chambers of
> Commerce which are part of the stock-in-trade of German militant
> diplomacy and appeal so readily to easy-going, unsuspecting
> Britishers.[1]

A veil of wilful ignorance continued to conceal both from the leaders
and the people of Britain the true significance of the assurance which
had so softly been uttered to the French. In any case, they had other
things to think about.

Many things now happened in rapid succession. In December 1905
Balfour resigned, and a Liberal Ministry was formed. In that
Ministry, Sir Edward Grey was Foreign Secretary, and Mr. R. B.
Haldane was Secretary of State for War. In that same month (Dec.
27th) Colonel Repington wrote an important article in the *Times*:

> I asked our innocents whether they really served the cause of peace
> by falling on the necks of our German cousins and embracing them.
> I said that the restoration of friendship between England and
> Germany was a desirable consummation in itself, but could only be
> sanctioned and guaranteed by the re-establishment of normal
> relations between France and Germany, and that this, in its turn,
> would not be in sight until Germany, at the then approaching
> Conference of Algeçiras, had given convincing proofs that she
> harboured no designs of aggression, and did not venture to contest the
> validity of the Anglo–French *entente cordiale* by striking at us with a
> poisoned Moorish arrow through France. I said that protestations
> of our regard for Germany would come better later when they had
> been deserved. I described them to be, at that moment, inoppor-
> tune and even dangerous, since they weakened France and were
> exploited in Germany to encourage German Chauvinism, and
> added that, far from fulfilling the laudable intentions of their
> British promoters, they were an indirect incentive to war.[2]

Strong words; the question was (and one of the first people to ask it
was the French Military Attaché in London, Major Huguet), did
the new British Government agree with these sentiments?

[1] Col. Repington: *Vestigia;* Constable 1919.
[2] Ibid.

In January 1906 there was a General Election, and the Liberals won by a landslide. The new Prime Minister was Sir Henry Campbell-Bannerman; the Party behind him was still very much the party of Cobden and Gladstone.

> Both these statesmen had been convinced that the world was moving steadily towards a settled peace, and that before another century had passed away—possibly even in a single generation— their dreams of general disarmament would be approaching fulfilment.[1]

The Liberal Party of 1906 was deeply imbued with pacifism, or at the least, anti-militarism.

> They had made the excessive cost of the Army one of the planks of their electioneering platform and were bound to press for military economies.[2]

This was not a reassuring turn of events, at a period when the Moroccan crisis was reaching its peak. Sir Edward Grey had stated privately that he had no intention of going back on Lord Lansdowne's assurance to France; this was something—would it be enough?

It was during the strange interval between Campbell-Bannerman taking office and the ratification of this step by the electors that the next significant move occurred. Once more Colonel Repington played a key part; associated with him were Lord Esher and Sir George Clarke (Secretary of the Committee of Imperial Defence), but since both of them 'were serving in an official capacity and I was a free lance' it was Repington who actually handled the delicate transaction which now followed. He put to the French Government, through the Military Attaché, a series of questions about the form of aid, military and naval, which the French would hope to receive from Britain if war should break out. From this démarche there ensued what might and should have been foreseen:

> On Jan. 17 Major Huguet informed me that Grierson (Director of Military Operations at the War Office) had opened relations with him that morning, and that he felt himself entitled to consider that Grierson would not have done so without authority from the Minister of War and the Government. I thought that he was perfectly justified in arriving at this conclusion, and informed

---

[1] F. S. Oliver: *Ordeal by Battle;* Macmillan 1915.
[2] *Vestigia.*

Huguet that my share in the conversations was now at an end, and that it remained for the French Staff and ours to get to work and go ahead.[1]

So, with perfect inevitability, the *Entente Cordiale* advanced out of the broad political sphere into the specific military sphere, and with equal inevitability produced a military understanding and a war-plan based on it. What remains almost incredible is that this course of events, sanctioned by responsible Ministers, was not recognised by them for what it was, not impressed by them upon their Cabinet colleagues, and least of all explained to the British people.

---

[1] Repington: *The First World War 1914–1918;* Constable 1920. For details of the negotiations and their military consequences see *The Western Front* (John Terraine); Hutchinson 1964, pp. 46–57.

I I

Whatever may have been the origins of the Great War, the origin of the manner in which it was fought by Great Britain lies in the highly secret activities of the month of January, 1906. And the psychological shocks later sustained by British Public Opinion, when it discovered what it had been let in for, are due to the careful preservation of this secrecy—obviously necessary up to a point for security reasons, but far less acceptable in terms of the personal and doctrinal reasons which also operated.

As I have said, many things happened in rapid succession, or indeed, simultaneously, during this turn of the year, 1905–1906. We have noted the development of the Moroccan crisis to a dangerous pitch; the change of Government in Britain, immediately followed by a General Election which in those days took some weeks, and dispersed Ministers and Members to their constituencies all over the country, where they plunged into electioneering—a dangerous enough hiatus in itself; then the Liberal victory, and while it was happening the institution of Staff talks. Two further developments may now be mentioned; their consequences will be our topic for some time. The coming to power of the Liberals brought Haldane to the War Office; he came with well-formulated ideas of what he should be about, but has freely admitted the influence of the Anglo– French Staff talks on his work of reform:

> Without the guidance we derived through the conversations we could not have been ready in July 1914. The Expeditionary Force was shaped to meet the demands so defined. In military organisation the form must always be determined by what is the most likely use to which the Army may have to be put.[1]

So we perceive that the most far-reaching Army reforms ever undertaken (until the virtual destruction of the Army in the 1960s) were shaped by the 1905 crisis. Haldane began work at once; but the Office on the other side of Whitehall was ahead of him. On February 10th 1906, King Edward VII launched the new battleship H.M.S.

[1] R. B. Haldane: *Autobiography;* Hodder & Stoughton 1919.

Dreadnought, the first all-big-gun, turbine-driven capital ship. She was the fruit of a policy relentlessly driven forward by Sir John Fisher, and the effect of her launching, bitterly proclaimed by Fisher's many enemies and critics, was that she

> rendered all existing battleships obsolete, so sweeping away Britain's overwhelming preponderance in pre-dreadnoughts (about three to one over Germany) and giving the Germans a level, or nearly level, start in the competition for naval supremacy.[1]

It was a remarkable conjunction of events which brought together a new government with strong pacifist traditions, a severe international crisis, and revolutionary changes in both the military and naval sides of national defence. Evidently, great issues would now depend upon the men who would have to deal with this conjunction: the key figures in the new Liberal Administration. The three men immediately and chiefly affected were Campbell-Bannerman, Haldane and Grey. This is not the place for any attempt at 'studies in depth' of these important statesmen; but it is necessary to note how each of them reacted to the untoward situation of 1906.

Campbell-Bannerman did not long survive his accession to power. He died in 1908, and his memory has been largely overshadowed by that of his successor, H. H. Asquith, during whose premiership so many large issues came to a head. But it was Campbell-Bannerman who first had to grasp the nettle, and the manner in which he did it proved to have lasting consequences. Writing of him as Leader of the Liberal Party, Haldane agreed that Campbell-Bannerman was 'genial and popular' and respected for political courage shown during the South African War; but, somewhat cruelly, Haldane added:

> he was not identified in the public mind with any fresh ideas, for indeed he had none.[2]

This may have been a source of strength in the special circumstances of the 1906 crisis. J. A. Spender, Editor of *The Westminster Gazette*, and later his biographer, wrote:

> There never was in fact a more miraculous change in the *form* of a public man than from Campbell-Bannerman as leader of the Opposition, to Campbell-Bannerman as Prime Minister.[3]

---

[1] Marder: *From the Dreadnought to Scapa Flow*, vol. i; O.U.P.
[2] Haldane: *Autobiography*, pp. 156–157.
[3] J. A. Spender: *Life of Campbell-Bannerman*, vol. ii.

In fact, contrary to many expectations, Campbell-Bannerman acted as a stabilizing force at a time when sweeping electoral success (a majority of 84 over all parties) might well have gone to the heads of the Liberals. No admirer of Liberalism, Colonel Repington concedes this, and at the same time points to Campbell-Bannerman's most serious weakness (in this context), saying:

> C.-B. was a fine old Tory in Army matters. He was also a warm friend of the French, and quickly realised the whole position. How he explained matters to certain members of the new Cabinet I did not ask, *and it did not matter*. I believe that he considered it a departmental affair, and did not bring it before the Cabinet at all at the time.[1]

The italics above are mine; it *did* matter; it mattered very much indeed. We shall return to this when we come to speak of Grey.

Haldane defies any brief analysis: a many-sided man, of great talent and energy—a leader in the campaign for red-brick universities, a philosopher who tried hard to bring philosophy and science to terms with each other, a great legal mind, an outstanding reformer of the Army ... and yet, to this day, somewhat shadowy, an enigma. John Buchan has left perhaps the most telling short statement about him:

> His personality was so unlike those of other public men that he became the centre of a myth. The impression got abroad that his methods were of a subtlety which was almost devious. It was wholly false. He was a practical man, and was always prepared 'by indirections to find directions out', but he was eminently single-minded and sincere. As a friend said of him, you could hear him 'tramping up the back stairs'. What he had in a full degree was the gift of persuasion, the power of wearing down opposition by sheer patience and reasonableness; and he had also that chief of diplomatic talents, the ability to read an opponent's mind and shape his arguments accordingly. His old affection for Germany made him slow to give up hope of peace, but it never blinded him, and he probably understood the German spirit better than any man in Britain.[2]

Haldane was not a very obvious choice for the War Office in 1906, and has left in his autobiography an amusing and instructive account of how he arrived there. Yet there were some who were perceptive enough to appreciate the significance of his appointment—among them Beatrice Webb:

[1] Repington: *The First World War*, i, p. 13.
[2] John Buchan: *Memory Hold-the-Door;* Hodder & Stoughton 1940.

... the great coup is to get Haldane to take the War Office—the
courtly lawyer with a great capacity for dealing with men and
affairs, and a real understanding of the function of an expert, and
skill in using him.[1]

One of Haldane's most important experts was General Haig, whom
he summoned from India to help him with his work at the War
Office in 1906. Haig recorded:

Mr. Haldane is a fat, big man, but with a kind, genial face. One
seemed to like the man at once. . . . He seems a most clear-headed
and practical man, most ready to listen to and weigh carefully all
that is said to him.[2]

A little later Haig illustrated what this clear-headedness and practi-
cality meant:

We discussed objects for which Army and Expeditionary Force
exist. He is in no doubt—viz. to organise to support France and
Russia against Germany, and perhaps Austria. By organising war
may be prevented.[3]

Haldane remained Secretary of State for War until 1912; during
that time a modern, efficient British Expeditionary Force was
created; the Territorial Army was founded and brought to an efficient
condition as the 'second line' behind the Regulars; the functions of
the General Staff were clarified and fulfilled; the concept of Imperial
Defence was enunciated and given reality. It is an impressive performance; what makes it most impressive, however, is the unfaltering
recognition of the purpose of it all—war with Germany. We shall see
that the gap between recognition and avowal would somewhat mar
the achievement.

And now for Sir Edward Grey; one of the most skilled assassins
of other men's reputations, David Lloyd George, has dealt according
to his manner with Grey, and while not accepting his verdict as
final (or even entirely truthful) it may be as well to give it, if only
because in the application of cruel definitions, if nothing else,
Lloyd George was an artist.

Just before 1914 the vogue of the taciturn was still prevalent and
no man profited as much by it as Grey. His striking physiognomy
with the thin lips, the firmly closed mouth, and the chiselled
features gave the impression of cold hammered steel. Add to this

[1] Beatrice Webb's Diary, Dec. 15th 1905.
[2] Haig: Diary, June 1906.
[3] Ibid.

exterior the reticence of speech and the calm level utterance on the rare occasions when he spoke, and you were led to expect imperturbable strength in an emergency. He did not command the flaming phrase that illumines but sometimes also scorches and leaves behind an irritating burn. On the other hand he possessed to perfection that correctitude of phrase and demeanour which passes for—and sometimes is—diplomacy, and that serene flow of unexceptionable diction which is apt to be reckoned as states-manship until a crisis comes to put these urbanities to the test. . . .

Sir Edward Grey belonged to a class which, through heredity and tradition, expects to find a place on the magisterial bench to sit in judgment upon and above their fellow-men, before they ever have any opportunity to make themselves acquainted with the tasks and trials of mankind. . . . Grey stepped into generalship without ever doing any soldiering—not a good training for facing real danger. It was all right when things went smoothly, and all you had to do was to put forward a soldierly appearance on parade. It is a different thing when you are suddenly confronted with the greatest and most deadly diplomatic struggle ever seen between great nations. . . .

He was the most insular of our statesmen, and knew less of foreigners through contact with them than any Minister in the Government. He rarely, if ever, crossed the seas. Northumberland was good enough for him, and if he could not get there and needed a change, there was his fishing lodge in Hampshire. This was a weakness—and it was a definite weakness in a Foreign Secretary, and especially in a Foreign Secretary with no imagination—which accounted for some of his most conspicuous failures. He had no real understanding of foreigners—I am not at all sure that for his purpose he would not include Scotland, Ireland and Wales as foreign parts. Moreover, when a conference in some foreign capital might have saved the situation, his dislike of leaving England stood in the way. . . .[1]

Lloyd George could be lethal—in more ways than one. Perhaps, as he wrote this, there was an uneasy murmur at the back of his mind saying that Grey, whom he considered a failure, had always commanded more trust and respect among his associates than he, Lloyd George, had ever known. Nevertheless, within his ruthless analysis, there was more than a germ of truth.

With little imagination or personality, slow to move and a creature of habit, imbued with a few ideas which have become part of him

---

[1] Lloyd George: *War Memoirs*, ch. iii.

as a result of time, the Englishman drifts from day to day without looking beyond the needs of the moment.[1]

Writing in 1928, after souring experiences of liaison with the British in peace and war, General Huguet was being somewhat less than kind or fair. Ten years after a war which had stretched British imagination and personality (and that of many others) to unforeseen limits, his comment is not very sound. In 1906 and the years which followed, it came closer to the truth. The fault of Grey, of Campbell-Bannerman, even of Haldane, was indeed this tendency to drift and shy away from the logic of events. All three are to blame for imprecision, and for taking refuge behind a form of words—an alibi—which could never stand up in the court of practical politics. But Grey must be blamed most, because as Foreign Secretary it was his duty to point out and insist that what might seem adequate and desirable to Liberal Englishmen would unfailingly have a different look abroad. Lloyd George's accusation that he had 'no real understanding of foreigners' would seem to be borne out by his failure to do this.

What *had* they done, together, these three men? What *was* their interpretation of the Staff talks which they had endorsed? First, Repington's evidence:

> The matter was not fully *en train*, of course, until the approval of the new Prime Minister, Sir Henry Campbell-Bannerman, had been secured. I had some doubt about the manner in which he would view it, but in his talk with Mr. Haldane he was very firm and clear on the point that we should be prepared for all emergencies, and that conversations between the two Staffs, *without any binding agreement between the Governments*, were permissible measures of prudence. It was arranged that a paper should be signed by Grierson and Huguet *stipulating that the conversations should not commit either Government*, and this was done[2].

Haldane confirms this:

> The Prime Minister asked whether it could be made clear that the conversations were purely for military General Staff purposes and were not to prejudice the complete freedom of the two Governments should the situation the French dreaded arise. *I undertook to see that this was put in writing.* . . . That the conversations were to leave us wholly free was expressed in a letter which was signed.[3]

[1] Huguet: *Britain and the War: A French Indictment;* Cassell 1928.
[2] Repington: *The First World War.* (My italics.)
[3] Haldane: *Autobiography.* (My italics.)

There is something pathetic, even at this distance, in this belief in the virtues of putting peculiar arrangements 'in writing'—something odd in the fact that an acumen like Haldane's should accept such a device. No amount of 'writing', no signature to a piece of paper, could alter the impression of the transaction on the second party—France. Huguet does his best to be fair to Britain about it:

> It was understood that the (British Government) retained full liberty of action and that—if the likelihood of war between France and Germany were realised—the Government of the day would be the sole judge of the line of action to be taken, without being tied in any sense by the studies which might have been previously undertaken. There was nothing surprising in this reservation which conforms to the traditional British attitude to foreign affairs—a policy which has always and which will always consist in finding a means to keep the balance of power between any and every possible Continental alliance or agreement so that in this way her own security may be guaranteed. Since, therefore, the conditions effecting this balance are likely to change, England has never been willing to commit herself in advance to promises which altered conditions might make impossible of realisation when the day of reckoning came.
>
> Nevertheless, we were somewhat surprised in 1906 to see the readiness with which the authorisation asked for by the French Government was granted. Sir Henry Campbell-Bannerman, Sir Edward Grey and Mr. Haldane were all three, as politicians, too shrewd and wary not to realise that *the studies which were being entered upon—no matter what the reservations—constituted nevertheless an undertaking of sorts, at any rate a moral one.*[1]

Huguet's conclusion is the heart of the matter. Staff Talks *must* constitute an undertaking, practical *and* moral, because (as Britain discovered with surprise and some horror in August 1914) if they are at all fruitful they must inevitably dictate actual plans. In 1914 this also meant that they dictated the scheme of mobilisation and a whole complex of movement timetables which could not be changed without creating chaos. The indictment against the Liberal leaders, then, is threefold: first, their failure to perceive the real meaning of the step they had taken prevented them from recognising its significance abroad—which in turn prevented them from exploiting it. They had firmly placed their country in one of two opposing camps—but could never bring themselves to say so firmly. Secondly, arising from this, they did not (*could* not) alert the nation to what had been

---

[1] Huguet: *Britain and the War.* (My italics.)

done and what it might mean. Eight years elapsed before the thing
was put to the test, and if, in that time, British Public Opinion
underwent any useful change, this was never thanks to any leadership by the party in power. The instability of Public Opinion throughout the 1914–1918 war, and the lack of faith of successive governments during it in the people they were leading, stem from this.
Finally, and again due to the same original fault, the great defence
programmes of the next few years (Fisher's modernisation of the
Navy, Haldane's of the Army) were robbed of their full fruition.
Much was being done, but because the nation was never frankly
told for what reason it was being done, the work was carried out
not in an atmosphere of patriotic urgency, but in one of materialist
complacency.

It is hard to exonerate Grey. His sympathetic biographer, Professor
G. M. Trevelyan, does his best:

> Grey appears to have underestimated the diplomatic significance
> which France and Germany were likely to attach to those Con-
> versations, and, as he himself later admitted, the Cabinet ought to
> have been informed of them at once. But Campbell-Bannerman,
> as Prime Minister, was even more responsible than Grey for the
> neglect to bring the Conversations before the Cabinet of which
> he was Chairman, a fact which some of Grey's critics studiously
> ignore.[1]

Of course the Prime Minister was at fault; in such a matter the chief
responsibility must always be his. But it is precisely to guide Prime
Ministers away from such faults that a Foreign Secretary is necessary.
Trevelyan displays Grey's weakness again when he says:

> The Military Conversations had ... a greater diplomatic effect
> abroad than Grey supposed; but that effect was to the good, for
> German knowledge that our soldiers were in consultation with
> those of France and Belgium was probably one of the reasons
> why the Algeçiras Conference of 1906 reached a peaceful con-
> clusion.[2]

In other words, the Grey–Campbell-Bannerman policy was really
the policy of a Deterrent. In relation to the immediate crisis of 1906
it appears to have worked, because at the Algeçiras Conference
which opened in January and ended in April, Germany suffered a
diplomatic defeat, and was compelled to abandon the demands which
had precipitated the whole affair. In fact,

[1] G. M. Trevelyan: *Grey of Falloden;* Longmans, Green & Co. 1937,
pp. 133–134.
[2] Ibid., p. 135.

The German Government achieved in the Moroccan episode the exact opposite of what it intended for, instead of disrupting the *Entente*, it drew France and Britain closer together and . . . the ultimate climb-down was too obviously the result of firm opposition to earn any gratitude.[1]

Yet the chief effectiveness of a deterrent lies in the acknowledgment of its existence by those who wish to deter and those who are to be deterred. No one can doubt that it was a desire to preserve peace which prompted Campbell-Bannerman and Grey to open Staff Talks with the French. The irony is that the Liberal revulsion from anything (no matter how pure its motive) smacking of militarism finally defeated its own object. The deterrent was prevented from deterring, and when the inevitable happened the price, for Britain, was in important respects far higher than it need have been.

The military consequences of this self-delusion were, of course, disastrous. I have discussed them in detail elsewhere,[2] but there can be no harm in quoting again the penetrating conclusion of one of the men upon whose shoulders the burden of inheritance fell. Field-Marshal Sir William Robertson, who became C.I.G.S. in 1915, had no hesitation in tracing back the many difficulties of framing war policy which he encountered to the lack of understanding of the Staff Talks of 1906:

> Not only was the Cabinet unaware of the conversations, but even the Foreign Secretary, who gave permission for them, knew nothing of their results. Writing to the Prime Minister[3] on the subject in 1911 he said: 'What they (the General Staffs) settled I never knew—the position being that the Government was quite free, but the military people knew what to do, if the word was given.' It was, however, of little use for the 'military people' to 'know what to do' unless adequate means were available for doing it, and this they could not be if the Cabinet knew nothing about what was taking place. On the principle that half a loaf is better than no bread the conversations were useful, but a more unsatisfactory method of ensuring co-operative action can hardly be imagined than that of leaving the two General Staffs to patch together a plan which the British Government, as such, declined to endorse with its formal approval. As the British Official History of the war says, although there was an 'obligation of honour', there was no actual undertaking to send the Expeditionary Force, or any part of it, 'to any particular point or, in fact, anywhere at all'.

---

[1] Balfour: *The Kaiser and His Times.*
[2] Terraine: *The Western Front.*
[3] Asquith.

Moreover, since there was no such undertaking the French authorities were forced to frame their plan of campaign not knowing whether they would or would not receive British assistance, while we, on our side, were not able to insist upon our right to examine the French plan in return for our co-operation. When the crisis arose there was no time to examine it, and consequently our military policy was for long wholly subordinate to the French policy, of which we knew very little.[1]

In effect, the Liberal leaders were making certain of having the worst of all bargains. The British citizen, of course, was ignorant of all this. What he would have made of it, had he known, is a speculation; what he did make of it when he began to experience the results does not make pretty reading.

[1] Field-Marshal, Sir William Robertson: *Soldiers and Statesmen 1914–1918;* Cassell 1926, vol. i, pp. 48–49.

I I I

Punctuated by spells of unhealthy panic, but, for the majority of people, not illuminated by better understanding of their increasing danger, the remaining years ticked by towards the outbreak of the Great War. The Liberal preoccupation was social reform. The birth of the Labour Party and the growth of the Trade Union movement supplied a new accompaniment to the harmony of Progress. The activities of the Militant Suffragettes, the bitterness of industrial warfare, the intractabilities of the Irish Question, supplied all the necessary discords. In 1911 a nation-wide dock strike provided the focus of agitation, but, as Ben Tillett, the dockers' leader, wrote, this was only the outward sign of a vast disturbance:

A strange, hectic period of our economic history! It was a great upsurge of elemental forces. It seemed as if the dispossessed and disinherited class in various parts of the country were all simultaneously moved to assert their claims upon society.[1]

In 1914 Ireland had the limelight, and Britain came to the very edge of civil war over Home Rule and the problem of Ulster. Professor Gilbert Murray, after attending the House of Commons on a day of high passion, wrote:

The debate was exciting, but deplorable. It seemed as if nobody cared for the community as a whole; it was all party or class.[2]

International affairs and their military counterpart proceeded through all this in an atmosphere of delusive irrelevance. The *Entente Cordiale* asserted its compulsive logic: in August 1907 Britain came to an agreement with France's ally, Russia, and the Triple *Entente* came into being as a counterpoise to the Triple Alliance of Germany, Austria and Italy. The event is worth more than a mention: it ran against the whole grain of previous British thought and policy. The Liberals detested Imperial Russia because of the harshness of Tsarist autocracy. The Tories were anti-Russian

[1] Ben Tillett: *Memories and Reflections.*
[2] From Asa Briggs: *They Saw it Happen 1897–1940;* Blackwell 1960.

23   c

because of the real or supposed Russian threats to India which had
recurred at intervals ever since the Crimean War. In 1897 the whole
North-West Frontier of India had been ablaze and Britain had been
obliged to put forth her largest military effort in that region to date;
Russian intrigue and provocation were widely suspected. In 1904
Russian warships, on their way from the Baltic to their dismal fate
at Tsushima, had fired on British trawlers off the Dogger Bank, and
there was even a risk of war. In 1905, while Russia and Japan were
still at war, the Anglo–Japanese Treaty was renewed for ten years.
And now, in 1907, without a murmur, as though it was a matter of
no significance, Britain and Russia became allies. Admiral Tirpitz
and the Kaiser had indeed sown the wind.

In the following year their policies and personalities succeeded,
at least briefly, in awakening the British public. On October 28th
1908 the *Daily Telegraph* published an interview with Kaiser Wilhelm
II on Anglo–German relations. Through staggering incompetence
and foolishness, the text of this interview had not been approved by
any member of the German Government; it had merely been vetted
for inaccuracies by a minor Foreign Office official. In view of the
Kaiser's well-known impulsiveness and indiscretion, this seems
almost incredible; yet it is a fact. Vainglorious, opinionated and often
dangerously insensitive to other people's feelings though he might
be, on this occasion the Kaiser undoubtedly thought that what he
had to say would actually improve the deteriorating relations between
Britain and Germany. Instead, he achieved a curious and distasteful
mixture of patronization and hectoring. He complained of being
misrepresented; he told the British that he and his government
desired good relations—but that Public Opinion in his country was
turning against them; he boasted that he had protected Britain
against France and Russia during the South African War; he even
claimed that that war had been won by adopting his advice; and he
added for good measure not only that the growing German Fleet
was not a threat to Britain, but that one day she would be glad
of it.

Had he not been the Emperor, it would have been difficult to take
this seriously; and had it not been for further developments shortly
afterwards, it is doubtful whether anyone of note in Britain *would*
have paid attention to it. The British were startled, of course, and
irritated; but the main outcry against the interview was in Germany
herself, in the Reichstag. The Left blamed the Kaiser for being
provocative, and the Right accused him of being too pro-British. In
fact, in every way, the unfortunate man procured the opposite effects
to those he had intended. Lord Esher summed up the incident in
his journal:

He sets all Europe by the ears—or would if he could—in a rage
of egoistic chatter. . . . He fails to see that he could have furnished
us with no more telling argument for 'keeping our powder dry'.
A feckless man.[1]

Far more to the point than any of the Kaiser's ill-considered words
were his deeds—and as far as serious British opinion was concerned
these were to be seen coming down the slipways of the German
shipyards in the form of battleships. The *Daily Telegraph* interview
was only the curtain-raiser for the scare of 1909.

German naval programmes were stated at intervals in the Navy
Laws. What happened, in the spring of 1909, was a sudden grave
fear in the Admiralty that Germany was building secretly in addition
to what was promulgated in the latest Navy Law. To maintain
superiority over this suspected clandestine activity, the Admiralty
demanded the construction of six new battleships. The Liberal
Party was deeply shaken by this; the Chancellor of the Exchequer,
Lloyd George, and the President of the Board of Trade, Winston
Churchill, took the lead in opposing what they claimed was an
entirely exaggerated fear and a needless expense. Four new British
ships, they said, would be quite ample. At once there was a storm.
Navalists and Conservatives, in righteous indignation, went beyond
the Admiralty's proposal, and demanded eight ships. A Conservative
M.P. coined the phrase which became a national slogan: 'We want
eight and we won't wait.'

Battle was joined between the 'panicmongers', or patriots, as they
preferred to be called, and the 'pacifists' or 'Little Englanders'.
Declared the *Daily News* (23 March), 'Panic, always infectious, is
spreading like the plague'. Around the four contingent ships the
two sides fought like Greeks and Trojans over the body of
Patroclus. The *National Review* (April) blamed the transfer of
naval supremacy to Germany on Fisher, 'the reincarnation of
Marshal Leboeuf—the French War Minister who had boasted,
on the eve of Metz and Sedan, that the French Army was ready
"to the last gaiter button".' The *Saturday Review* (20 March)
termed McKenna's[2] speech of the 16th 'the most miserable,
humiliating piece of news that the public have read since the time
of Stormberg and Magersfontein.' The *Observer* (21 March)
advised Englishmen to 'insist on the Eight the whole Eight, and
nothing but the Eight, with more to follow, and break any man
or faction that now stands in the way'.[3]

[1] Esher: *Journal*, Oct. 28th 1908.
[2] Reginald McKenna, First Lord of the Admiralty.
[3] Marder: *From the Dreadnought to Scapa Flow*, i, pp. 167–168.

The outcome of the uproar has been entertainingly described by Churchill, who was on the losing side:

> In the end a curious and characteristic solution was reached. The Admiralty had demanded six ships: the economists offered four: and we finally compromised on eight.[1]

As it turned out, the scare of German secret building was ill-founded: the Navy Law of 1908 meant what it said. But the significance of the agitation lies elsewhere. As Churchill also said: 'Genuine alarm was excited throughout the country by what was *for the first time* widely recognized as a German menace.' The italics are mine. We have seen (Ch. I) that as far back as 1897 Admiral Tirpitz had designated England as the enemy against whom the German battle-fleet was to be built. Only now, in 1909, did the fact sink into the minds of any large number of Englishmen, and the full truth of what had already happened was concealed from the general public. As Churchill handsomely admitted:

> . . . although the Chancellor of the Exchequer and I were right in the narrow sense, we were absolutely wrong in relation to the deep tides of destiny.[2]

By 1909, in naval terms, the deep tides had flowed a long way. The Two-power Standard had ceased to exist. In November 1908 the Prime Minister, Mr. Asquith, had had no difficulty in asserting the survival of the Standard, and defining it as 'a preponderance of 10% over the combined strengths in capital ships of the two next strongest Powers, whatever those Powers might be.' By May 1909, Asquith was saying that the Two-power Standard was not to be understood as a 'transcendant dogma', but as a convenient rule-of-thumb, whose application might vary according to 'political and strategic conditions'.

Behind the smokescreen of the Prime Minister's verbiage, it was apparent that the traditional standard was no longer valid. Although the question of the naval standard was subsequently discussed periodically in Parliament, the Government's statements were not very clear or precise down to 28 March 1912. It was then that Churchill, as First Lord, told the House of Commons that *the official standard was one of 60% superiority in dreadnoughts over Germany*. Later, in March 1914, Churchill told the Commons that the Admiralty had adopted this standard 'in 1908 or 1909'.

---

[1] Churchill: *The World Crisis*, ch. ii.
[2] Ibid.

The date was April 1909, and the standard was originally suggested by Jellicoe, the Third Sea Lord and Controller.[1]

So what had for long been regarded as the very foundation of Britain's naval (and imperial) position slipped quietly away. It is small wonder if the man-in-the-street was altogether unaware of what had happened. Prince Louis of Battenberg, one of the Navy's most educated officers, became First Sea Lord in December 1912. His younger son, now Admiral of the Fleet the Earl Mountbatten of Burma, asked his father what his job was.

He said, 'My boy, my job is to keep the fleets of the Royal Navy at operational strength, efficiency and immediate readiness so as to be able to take on the combined might of the next two greatest powers in the world and be certain of defeating them in battle.' I said to him I thought that was rather a stiff job.[2]

Fifty-three years later the gist of Prince Louis's message remained quite clearly fixed in Lord Mountbatten's memory, as well it might. This is indicative of the strength of the tradition which it expressed. Prince Louis must have known what Churchill knew, but even within a trustful family circle, to a son already in the Navy himself, was reluctant to state bluntly what had been happening. No wonder the public remained blithely ignorant; no wonder it found naval proceedings somewhat unfathomable in 1914.

Lord Fisher's work of naval reform was carried out against a background of ignorant confidence. The limitations of Fisher's policy would shortly be exposed to a very small circle, and they would be appalled. But, once the 1909 scare had died down, the ruling party and the bulk of the nation was content to slip back into familiar illusions. In 1912, despite another perilous international crisis, a Liberal journal, *The Nation*, could proclaim (no doubt in all sincerity):

. . . our sea power and our national security depend on our ability to crush an enemy's fleet. . . . We were never so amply insured— so over-insured—against naval disaster as we are today.[3]

This was entirely untrue; nevertheless, to be fair, at the back of such sentiments there lay a friendliness towards the Navy, a trust in it, which contrasted sharply with attitudes towards the Army.

[1] Marder: *From the Dreadnought to Scapa Flow*, i, pp. 182–183. (My italics.)
[2] Related to the author by Lord Mountbatten in 1966.
[3] *The Nation*, Oct. 26th 1912.

Lord Haldane, in his sphere of reform, had to contend with ignorant hostility. The Army was not a popular Service; it never had been. Sir William Robertson was the only man in the Army's history to complete the long haul from Private to Field-Marshal. In 1877 he was in domestic service—a footman; in that year he joined the 16th Lancers, and when his mother heard of it she wrote to him:

> My very Dear Boy
> ... what cause have you for such a Low Life ... you have as Good Home as anyone else in our Station ... you have kind and Loving Sisters ... you know you are the Great Hope of the Family ... (the Army) is a refuge for all Idle people ... I shall name it to no one for I am ashamed to think of it ... I would rather Bury you than see you in a red coat. ...[1]

Unloved, and ignored as far as possible, by the working class, the Army was positively disliked and frequently attacked by the educated middle class. F. S. Oliver wrote:

> The school of political thought which remained predominant throughout the great industrial epoch (1832–1886) bitterly resented the assumption, made by certain classes, that the profession of arms was more honourable in its nature, than commerce and other peaceful pursuits. The destruction of this supposed fallacy produced a great literature, and even a considerable amount of poetry. It was a frequent theme at the opening of literary institutes and technical colleges, and also at festivals of chambers of commerce and municipalities. Professors of Political Economy expounded the true doctrine with great vehemence and sermons were preached without number upon the well-worn text about the victories of peace.
> This reaction was salutary up to a point. It swept away a vast quantity of superannuated rubbish. ... But this reaction, like most other reactions, swept away too much.[2]

The Army was, in more senses than one, a victim of the English class system. It was also the victim of its own history. It is a fact which is almost universally overlooked that the modern British Army was really a middle-class product. The first modern organisation of a Regular force, and its first peak of high efficiency, were arrived at in the New Model of 1645: a Parliamentary army, fighting against monarchy and aristocracy. One might think that such a

[1] Victor Bonham-Carter: *Soldier True;* Muller, 1963, p. 5.
[2] Oliver: *Ordeal by Battle*, pp. 403–404.

beginning would provide a sure foundation; unfortunately, the Protectorate and the rule of the Major-Generals which followed the Civil War destroyed good-will towards the apparatus created to defend the nation's liberties. By the 19th Century, good-will had almost vanished. F. S. Oliver again:

> Middle-class ideals, middle-class prosperity, middle-class irritation against a military caste which, in spite of its comparative poverty, continued with some success to assert its social superiority, combined against the army in popular discussions. The honest belief that wars were an anachronism, and that the world was now launched upon an interminable era of peace, clothed the nakedness of class prejudice with some kind of philosophic raiment. Soldiers were no longer needed; why then should they continue to claim the lion's share of honourable recognition?[1]

It is amazing that Haldane was able to do as much as he did, given the climate of opinion between 1906 and 1912. In large part his success was due to having the outlines of policy well-prepared before taking office so that he was able to place Bills before the House of Commons early in 1907. As his Military Secretary, Sir Gerald Ellison, later wrote:

> Radical members were waiting impatiently for far-reaching measures of social reform, and pretty disgusted they were to be fobbed off with a military problem in which they took very little interest. The other Departments of State had been too slow in getting off the mark.[2]

There can be little doubt that when war came in 1914 the Expeditionary Force created by Haldane was admirably organised and efficient—it is doubtful whether any country could have fielded such an effective force for its size. But the size was all-important, because the war which broke out in 1914 was a war of mass-armies, as every intelligent expert knew it must be. A first-rate Expeditionary Force of six divisions was not to be despised (its achievement was great) but it was a drop in the ocean in such a war. And it was the belated realisation of this, and the clumsy attempts to overcome this handicap at the twelfth hour, which proved to be one of the greatest of the shocks which the British public had to sustain. All this is clearly attributable to that frame of mind which F. S. Oliver described, and against which Haldane had to struggle.

[1] Ibid., 409–410.
[2] Lieut.-Gen. Sir Gerald Ellison: *Reminiscences* in *The Lancashire Lad*, the Journal of the Loyal N. Lancashire Regt., 1931–1939.

Haldane and his assistants were fully aware of their problems; they knew their enemy. Writing to Ellison in September 1906, in the midst of his preliminary work on the Territorial Army, Haig said:

> Our object in my opinion should be to start a system of finance suited to the 'supposed situation', i.e., *a great war requiring the whole resources of the nation* to bring it to a successful end. Even if the proposed system costs more in peace, it should be inaugurated provided that it is more practical in war. The Swiss system seems to me to be exactly what is wanted 'to root the army in the people'. . . .

Again the italics are mine; the words describe the very situation which most people at the time found too abhorrent to contemplate. Commenting many years later on this passage, Sir Gerald Ellison wrote:

> His allusion to the Swiss system . . . points to the fact that, like most of us at the War Office, he would have welcomed some modified form of compulsion for the Territorial Force, but he readily recognised the political difficulties in the way, and accordingly worked with a will to get the utmost out of the voluntary principle.[1]

Compulsion was the crux of the matter. Compulsion—Conscription—National Service—by any name it was anathema to public and politicians alike in Britain. It is interesting that Sir Gerald Ellison should confess that 'most of us at the War Office' favoured some form of compulsion: the official attitude of the War Office was quite opposite. The whole concept of the Territorial Army arose from the desire to avoid any dealings with this monster. As Ellison also says: 'The mention of compulsory service would have spelt political suicide to any Minister who proposed it'—and Haldane was nothing if not a politician. He knew—and his assistants, like Haig, accepted—that it was of little use to talk of 'rooting the army in the people' if the people flatly refused to have an army rooted in them. Rudyard Kipling, not for the only time, put his finger on the prevalent British hypocrisy:

> Yes, makin' mock o' uniforms that guard you while you sleep
> Is cheaper than them uniforms, an' they're starvation cheap;
> An' hustlin' drunken soldiers when they're goin' large a bit
> Is five times better business than paradin' in full kit.
> Then it's Tommy this, an' Tommy that, an' 'Tommy, 'ow's yer soul?'

[1] Ellison: *Notes on letters from Field-Marshal Earl Haig*, 1928.

But it's 'Thin red line of 'eroes' when the drums begin to roll—
The drums begin to roll, my boys, the drums begin to roll,
O it's 'Thin red line of 'eroes' when the drums begin to roll. . . .[1]

The drums rolled louder and louder after 1906, but could not
penetrate the din of opposition to all forms of military obligation.
In 1911 the German sabre rattled again—once more Morocco provided the arena of dispute. Ever since the Algeçiras Conference,
Germany had watched the growth of French influence in North
Africa with jealousy. In 1911 a French expedition to Fez offered the
opportunity of a minatory gesture: the German gunboat *Panther*
appeared in the Moroccan harbour of Agadir, and an international
crisis immediately blew up. Once more the reality of the *Entente
Cordiale* was put to the test—and this time found an eloquent, if
somewhat unexpected, champion. With the full approval of the
Prime Minister and Sir Edward Grey, the Chancellor of the Exchequer, Mr. Lloyd George, who was due to address the City of
London bankers at the Mansion House, made use of the occasion to
deliver a clear warning:

> I would make great sacrifices to preserve peace. I conceive that
> nothing would justify a disturbance of international goodwill
> except questions of the gravest national moment. But if a situation
> were to be forced upon us in which peace could only be preserved
> . . . by allowing Britain to be treated, where her interests were
> vitally affected, as if she were of no account in the Cabinet of
> Nations, then I say emphatically that peace at that price would
> be a humiliation intolerable for a great country like ours to endure.[2]

The German reaction was immediate, and at first reflected only
anger: four days after Lloyd George's speech the German Ambassador
in London protested to the Foreign Office in such terms that Sir
Edward Grey warned that the Fleet might be attacked at any
moment. Then wiser counsels prevailed, and once more Germany
made a slow climb-down—but the residue of anger remained. In the
Reichstag the Conservative leader won warm applause with his
retort to Lloyd George:

> When we hear a speech that we must consider as a threat, as a
> challenge, as a humiliating challenge, it is not so easy to pass it
> over as after-dinner speechifying. Such incidents like a flash in
> the dark show the German peoples where is the foe. The German

---

[1] *Tommy*, by Rudyard Kipling; Definitive Edition, Hodder & Stoughton
1940.
[2] Lloyd George: Mansion House speech, July 21st 1911.

people now knows, when it seeks foreign expansion and a place in the sun, such as is its right and destiny, where it has to look for permission. We Germans are not accustomed to that and cannot allow it and we shall know how to answer.[1]

A memorable phrase had been given birth; on August 27th it was repeated in an ominous context. At Hamburg the Kaiser spoke of the need 'to strengthen our fleet further so as to make sure that nobody will dispute the place in the sun to which we are entitled'.

The Agadir crisis was an important milestone on the way to war. It *should* have provided the last-minute awakening to political realities needed by both Government and people in Britain. Unfortunately it did not—though the Government now had no excuse left for pretending unawareness. At the height of the crisis it was discovered that despite all the work that had been done at the War Office, and despite all the modernisation carried out in the Navy by Lord Fisher, despite the outcome of the Staff Talks with France, a frightening gap in defence preparations remained: there was no national plan for the contingency of war. Amazed Ministers found that the Navy and the Army had entirely discordant views of what they should be doing if war broke out: the Army had prepared an Expeditionary Force to fight in France beside the French Army; the Navy, in as much as it had a plan at all, was proposing to enter the Baltic and land the Army on the northern shores of Prussia.[2] At the root of this ludicrous (but exceedingly dangerous) state of affairs lay a fact directly attributable to the strange, egoistic character of Lord Fisher: the absence of a Naval Staff—what Repington called 'a serious thinking department at the Admiralty'. It was above all to remedy this terrible omission that Winston Churchill went to the Admiralty as First Lord in October 1911, and initiated, with the help of Prince Louis of Battenberg, a second wave of important naval reforms.

After these revelations no one at the centre of power could plead ignorance of the military probabilities. But from 1911 until the very declaration of war in August 1914 the Liberal statesmen—with the possible exception of Haldane—seem to have entered a shadow land of wilful blindness. Even with the lessons of Agadir fresh in his mind, Asquith (in general, one of the most level-headed of them) either could not or would not recognise the truth which had been revealed. Visiting Balmoral in October 1911, he discussed naval and military affairs with Lord Esher:

[1] Quoted in Balfour: *The Kaiser and His Times*, p. 317.
[2] See Terraine: *The Western Front*, pp. 24–27, for a fuller description of this remarkable episode.

... we talked about the General Staff scheme of landing an army
in France. The Prime Minister is opposed to this plan. He will
not hear of the despatch of more than four divisions. He has told
Haldane so.

But, I reminded him that the mere fact of the War Office plan
having been worked out in detail with the French General Staff
(which is the case) has certainly committed us to fight, whether
the Cabinet likes it or not, and that the combined plan of the two
General Staffs holds the field. It is certainly an extraordinary
thing that our officers should have been permitted to arrange all
the details, trains, landing, concentration, etc., when the Cabinet
have never been consulted.[1]

The subterfuges and evasions of 1906 were still working their mischief. The persistence of this theory of optional obligation up to the
very last moment is remarkable.[2] Its absurdity in the face of political
reality was very soon re-emphasised.

The implications of the Agadir Crisis would appear to have been
more firmly grasped in Germany than in Britain. When it had
simmered down appreciably, the Kaiser suggested, through the
financier Sir Ernest Cassel as intermediary, that there should be a
fresh interchange of views between London and Berlin 'of a personal
and direct kind'.[3] Wisely, the British Government selected as their
emissary Lord Haldane; his knowledge of Germany was greater than
that of any of his colleagues; he had expressed sympathy with the
German point of view with a frankness which would later cost him
dear; yet he understood the dangerous weaknesses of the German
mind.[4] Haldane arrived in Berlin on February 8th 1912, and held
conversations with the new Chancellor, Bethmann-Hollweg, Admiral
Tirpitz (Navy Minister) and the Kaiser himself. The atmosphere was
surprisingly cordial, the exchanges surprisingly unreserved.

Lord Haldane has left detailed accounts of his mission in his book
Before the War; only its main purport need concern us here. He told
Bethmann-Hollweg quite bluntly the circumstances in which British
neutrality could not be counted on: an attack on France, or Belgium
(or Portugal or Japan). He was equally blunt about the fundamental
issue between the two countries: 'we could not sit still if Germany

[1] Esher: Journal, Oct. 4th 1911.
[2] A good short account of the last-minute heartburnings which resulted
may be found in G. M. Thomson, The Twelve Days; Hutchinson 1964,
pp. 168–173.
[3] Haldane: Before the War; Cassell 1920.
[4] 'They are a difficult people because the "abstract mind" predominates
with them.' (Haldane: Autobiography, p. 245.)

elected to develop her fleet to such an extent as to imperil our naval protection'. Bethmann-Hollweg's response was interesting:

> The Chancellor said that he did not take my observations at all in bad part, but I must understand that his admirals and generals were pretty difficult. . . . I left the Chancellor with the sense that I had been talking with an honest man struggling somewhat with adversity.[1]

With Tirpitz it was only necessary to discuss the key question:

> The tone was friendly, but I felt that I was up against the crucial part of my task. The admiral wanted us to enter into some understanding about our own ship-building.[2]

The interview with the Kaiser centred around a surprising act—possibly unpremeditated, probably regretted, certainly damaging to the understanding which he seemed to be seeking:

> . . . the Emperor handed me at this meeting a confidential copy of the draft of the proposed new Fleet Law, with an intimation that he had no objection to my communicating it privately to my colleagues. I was careful to abstain even from looking at it then, for I saw that, from its complexity and bulk, it would require careful study. So I simply put it in my pocket.[3]

The contents of this document proved to contain the demolition-charge of Anglo–German understanding.

What could Haldane report on his return to London? He had not finally lost hope, but he could not conceal uneasiness. The test would be the German Navy Law:

> When we looked closely into the copy of the draft which the Emperor had given to me, we found very large increases contemplated, of which we had no notion earlier, not only in the battleships, about which we did know before, but in small craft and submarines and personnel. As these increases were to proceed further, discussion about the terms of a formula became rather futile, and we had only one course left open to us—to respond by quietly increasing our navy and concentrating its strength in northern seas. This was done with great energy by Mr. Churchill. . . .[4]

[1] *Before the War*, p. 59.
[2] Ibid., p. 61.
[3] Ibid., p. 60.
[4] Ibid., p. 72.

Haldane's final impressions, devoid of comfort for any section of the British Government, were, first

> . . . that the new Fleet Law would be insisted on. The second was the possibility that Tirpitz might be made Chancellor of the Empire in place of Bethmann-Hollweg. This was being talked of as possible when I was in Berlin. The third was the want of continuity in the supreme direction of German policy.[1]

The net result of the mission was thus a confirmation of the danger from Germany, and, as regards the Navy, progress towards meeting it. No clarity ensued about the Army's rôle, and no guidance to the nation, because Haldane's talks were necessarily secret.

The Press and the public cannot react to what they do not know. Later in 1912, however, they did have something to react to, and the response was illuminating. In October, Field-Marshal Lord Roberts of Kandahar, who had reversed the tide of British disasters in South Africa and carried the flag to Bloemfontein and Pretoria, made a speech in Manchester. Since 1905 Lord Roberts had been actively campaigning for National Service, and this speech was part of that campaign. It was delivered in, of all places, that Liberal citadel, the Free Trade Hall, and its significance is that the eighty-year-old Field-Marshal used the occasion to utter publicly what the Government was trying not to admit, but what was, nevertheless, the foundation of all the military policy it had. Lord Roberts said:

> In the year 1912, our German friends, I am well aware, do not—at least in sensible circles—assert dogmatically that a war with Great Britain will take place this year or next; but in their heart of hearts they know, every man of them, that—just as in 1866 and just as in 1870—war will take place the instant the German forces by land and sea are, by their superiority at every point, as certain of victory as anything in human calculation can be made certain. Germany strikes when Germany's hour has struck.

From this unequivocal basis, Lord Roberts repeated his unshakable conviction

> . . . that in some form of National Service is the only salvation of this Nation and this Empire. The Territorial Force is now an acknowledged failure—a failure in discipline, a failure in numbers, a failure in equipment, a failure in energy.[2]

The Conservative (Opposition) Press reported the speech with more or less of approval. Conservative opinion was hardly warmer

---

[1] Ibid., p. 70.
[2] October 22nd 1912.

than Liberal towards the repellent concept of Conscription. The *Evening Standard*, for example, accused Lord Roberts of 'wanton mischief-making'. Parts of the Liberal Press appeared to be so shocked that they could not bring themselves at first to comment, or even report the speech. Others, however, reacted with predictable vigour. The *Manchester Guardian* was disgusted at the 'insinuation that the German Government's views of international policy are less scrupulous and more cynical than those of other Governments'. The paper informed its readers that

> Prussia's character among nations is, in fact, not very different from the character which Lancashire men give to themselves as compared with other Englishmen. It is blunt, straightforward, and unsentimental. . . .

The *Daily News* discovered in the speech the revelation that the whole purpose of the National Service League was 'an attempt to get up, not defence, but an invasion of German territory . . . what the League wants is war'. But the most ferocious counterblast came from the *Nation*, under the heading 'A Diabolical Speech':

> There ought to be some means of bringing to book a soldier, in the receipt of money from the State, who speaks of a friendly Power as Lord Roberts spoke of Germany . . . he interprets the life and interests of this nation and this Empire by the crude lusts and fears which haunt the unimaginative soldier's brain. . . .
>
> Lord Roberts's proposition . . . is merely foolish; it is his way of commending it, which is merely wicked. He speaks of war as certain to take place 'the instant' the German forces are assured of 'superiority at every point', and he discovers that the motto of German foreign policy is that Germany strikes when Germany's hour has struck. Germany does not happen to have struck anybody since 1870, and she struck then to secure national unity, and to put an end to the standing menace of French imperialism. Since then she has remained the most peaceful and the most self-contained, though doubtless not the most sympathetic, member of the European family. . . .
>
> Germany, the target of every cheap dealer in historic slapdash, is in substance the Germany of 1870 with a great industrial dominion superadded by the force of science and commercial enterprise. That is the story across which Lord Roberts scrawls his ignorant libel. . . .[1]

[1] It is wonderful to see how a breed runs true; to compare this denunciation of Lord Roberts for daring to call Germany a potential enemy in 1912 with the following letter to the *Evening Standard* on August 9th 1939:

As Chairman of one of the Ward Committees in Mr. Duff Cooper's

In Parliament a member of the Government, Mr. Runciman, spoke
of the weakness of allowing 'soldiers, armament makers, or scare-
mongers' to direct policy. Sir Edward Grey (with his full knowledge
of the results of Haldane's mission to Berlin that very year) made
reference to 'unwise or provocative speeches'. A Question was asked
about the possibility of revoking Lord Roberts's pension.

Along such paths was Public Opinion guided. Other forms of cant
and humbug were not lacking; the opposition to National Service gave
them ample opportunities of expression. F. S. Oliver wrote in 1915:

> We are all proud of our army; and rightly so. But the opponents
> of universal military service carry their pride much further than
> the soldiers themselves. They contrast our army, to its enormous
> advantage, with the conscript armies of the continent, which they
> regard as consisting of vastly inferior fighting men—of men, in a
> sense, despicable, inasmuch as their meek spirits have submitted
> tamely to conscription.
>
> Colonel Seely,[1] who, when he touches arithmetic soars at once
> into the region of poetry, has pronounced confidently that one of
> our voluntary soldiers is worth ten men whom the law compels to
> serve. Sir John Simon[2] was still of opinion—even after several
> months of war—that one of our volunteers was worth at least three
> conscripts; and he was convinced that the Kaiser himself already
> knew it. What a splendid thing if Colonel Seely were right, or
> even if Sir John Simon were right!
> But is either of them right?[3]

An answer to Oliver's question was supplied by an officer of the

---

constituency, I cannot conceive why you should think it worth while to
publish the vaporous effusions which flow at more or less regular intervals
from his pen. Not content with having resigned from the Government at
a very critical juncture in foreign affairs and having subsequently employed language in Parliament about the head of a foreign State which I
submit is consistent neither with the dignity of the House of Commons nor
with that restrained and responsible attitude which we have a right to
expect from an ex-Cabinet Minister, he apparently thinks he is serving
the best interests of humanity at large by keeping his fellow-countrymen
in a constant state of jittery anticipation, and endlessly fanning the flames
of prejudice and hatred against the wicked Nazis on account of their
supposed acts of aggression. There may be those who think these articles
increase the standing and prestige of your paper. I am not among them.
(Quoted in Duff Cooper: *Old Men Forget;* Hart–Davis 1964.)
[1] Secretary of State for War, 1912–1914.
[2] Attorney-General, 1914; resigned in 1916 in opposition to any form of
conscription.
[3] Oliver: *Ordeal by Battle*, p. 387.

Regular Army who, after a year's experience of battle, read his book
in billets behind the Western Front:

> Is it seriously suggested that one British soldier, a volunteer, is
> equal in battle to six, or even three, conscript soldiers of the
> magnificent German Army? Pure rubbish![1]

At this distance of time the verdict upon Lord Robert's Manchester
speech must be that, in speaking out clearly on the probability of
war, he was doing a patriotic service comparable to Churchill's
during the Thirties. In neither case was the British public con-
spicuously grateful. In his sweeping condemnation of the Territorial
Army, Lord Roberts was wrong. What Haldane (strongly assisted
by Haig) had set out to create was a force of 28 divisions to back the
Regulars: a scale of effort which at least approached the measure of
the task. Economy had forced them to settle for 14 divisions—but
such was the structure of the T.A. that it was capable of reasonably
swift expansion from this base.[2] The tragedy was that when war came
Lord Kitchener, the newly appointed Secretary of State, decided to
relegate the Territorials and raise instead the New Armies. It may
well be that one of the unfortunate influences which guided him
towards this decision was the hostility of his old Chief towards the
Territorials. As regards conscription, by 1912 it was not only out of
the question politically, but also as a matter of practical military
policy. Lord Haldane's evidence is decisive:

> In the year 1912 the then Chief of the General Staff told me that
> he and the General Staff would like to investigate, as a purely
> military problem, the question whether we could or could not
> raise a great army. I thought this a reasonable enquiry and sanc-
> tioned and found money for it. ... The outcome was embodied
> in a report made to me by Lord Nicholson,[3] himself a soldier

[1] *General Jack's Diary 1914–1918.* Edited by John Terraine; Eyre &
Spottiswoode 1964, p. 107.

[2] *N.B. 'reasonably* swift expansion': the attempt to go too fast could be
dangerous. In March 1939 the Secretary of State for War, Mr. Hore-
Belisha, announced that the Territorial Army was to be doubled. Major-
General Sir John Kennedy, then Deputy Director of Military Operations,
wrote:

> The doubling of the Territorial Army sounded a big thing to the public,
> and it may have been a good political move; but it was by no means
> sound from a military point of view, because, although the number of
> our divisions was at once increased on paper, this was not the quickest
> way to get the Army ready for war.

(Kennedy: *The Business of War;* Hutchinson 1957, p. 8.) It is generally
agreed that this paper expansion in fact temporarily wrecked the existing
formations, whose shortage of equipment was already acute.

[3] Field-Marshall Lord Nicholson, Chief of General Staff since 1908.

who had a strong desire for compulsory service and a large army. He reported, as the result of a prolonged and careful investigation, that, alike as regarded officers and as regarded buildings and equipment, the conclusion of the General Staff was that it would be in a high degree unwise to try, during a period of unrest on the Continent, to commence a new military system. It could not be built up excepting after much unavoidable delay. We might at once experience a falling-off in voluntary recruiting, and so become seriously weaker before we had a chance of becoming stronger. And the temptation to a foreign General Staff to make an early end of what it might insist on interpreting as preparation for aggression on our part, would be too strong to be risked. What we should get might prove to be a mob in place of an army. I quite agreed, and not the less because it was highly improbable that the country would have looked at anything of the sort.[1]

It was too late to bring in conscription in 1912. The time to have done it was in 1906, with a new Government, as part and parcel of the great Army reforms (and profiting by the dismay of the German Navy at the launching of H.M.S. *Dreadnought*). The next opportunity was in August 1914, in the flush of public fervour at the outbreak of war. In each case the Liberal conscience of the nation's leaders, and the mental unpreparedness of the people, caused the issue to be fluffed—with eternally sad results. Returning to 1912, the net result was that the country remained wedded to what was generally called the 'Voluntary Principle'. Lord Esher called it the 'Principle of Unequal Sacrifice'; Lord Roberts called it 'Conscription by Hunger'. Abroad (and particularly in Germany) the product was sneered at as a 'mercenary army'. Once again, F. S. Oliver may sum up:

> What they really mean when they say that England is to be despised because she relies upon a mercenary army, is that England is to be despised because, being mercenary, she relies on a professional army. The taunt, when we come to analyse it, is found to be levelled, not against the hired, but against the hirers; and although we may be very indignant, it is not easy to disprove its justice.[2]

The war of the greatest mass-armies so far seen in the world's history was less than two years off; preparedness could only mean preparedness for such a war. By that test, Government and people failed in 1914, as they did again in 1939; the shock of failure was, however, far worse the first time.

[1] Haldane: *Before the War*, pp. 174–175.
[2] *Ordeal by Battle*, p. 390.

D

IV

For Britain's Liberal leaders the birds came home to roost on July 24th 1914. On that day, wearily, once more the Cabinet was revolving the intractabilities of the Irish problem which had already split the Army and brought the country to the point-blank prospect of civil war. One more effort was being made at settlement. One more gloomy scrutiny of the map of Ireland was in progress. The fate of the nation appeared to hang upon parish boundaries in the counties of Fermanagh and Tyrone. And then Sir Edward Grey appeared, and read the text of an ultimatum from Austria to Serbia; it was, said Winston Churchill,

> ... an ultimatum such as had never been penned in modern times. As the reading proceeded it seemed absolutely impossible that any State in the world could accept it, or that any acceptance, however abject, would satisfy the aggressor. The parishes of Fermanagh and Tyrone faded back into the mists and squalls of Ireland, and a strange light began immediately, but by perceptible gradations, to fall and grow upon the map of Europe.[1]

Almost a month had passed since the assassination of the Archduke Francis Ferdinand at Sarajevo. It was not a happy month; civil war is not a happy prospect. But whatever may have been the unpleasantness of the year so far, for the Liberal Government the next ten days would spell agony. Each day posed the same terrible question, but with more force: what *was* the meaning of the *Entente Cordiale*? The same question, needless to say, was very much on men's minds in France; the agonies of the British Cabinet were well matched by those of the French Ambassador, M. Paul Cambon. As the days of July ran out, the certainty of war deepened in French minds. It was M. Cambon's task to hold the British Government to what all France now regarded as a pledge. August 1st was the day on which the Central Powers declared war on France's ally, Russia. Cambon called on Sir Edward Grey, but could extract nothing from him to comfort the French nation, nothing that he even dared to

[1] Churchill: *The World Crisis.*

report back to his Government. He then saw the Opposition leaders; by this time he could no longer master his anguish:

> All our plans are arranged in common. Our General Staffs have consulted. You have seen all our schemes and preparations. Look at our fleet! Our whole fleet is in the Mediterranean in consequence of our arrangements with you and our coasts are wide open to the enemy. You have laid us wide open!

He ended with the searing question:

> Et l'honneur? Est-ce-que l'Angleterre comprend ce que c'est l'honneur?

Sir Edward Grey did understand—at last—what honour meant. In his autobiography[1] he wrote: 'Throughout the whole of this week I had in view the probable contingency that we should not decide at the critical moment to support France. In that event I should have to resign.' But now the pressures upon Grey were intense; the awful consequences of not having carried the Cabinet, the Party and the country along stage by stage with his policy now presented themselves Speaking in the House of Lords in 1928, Grey admitted:

> . . . in the early days of the last week of July 1914, the Government were so deeply divided that the division was apparently irreconcilable. The House of Commons was divided. The country was divided. It is my opinion that if there had been a precipitate attempt to force a decision it would not have helped these divisions of opinion, it would have brought them out and made them irreparable.[2]

From the Press of his Party, the unfortunate Foreign Secretary received very little support or encouragement:

> . . . almost the whole influence and moral weight of the Liberal Press was eloquently against him: C. P. Scott and C. E. Montague in the *Manchester Guardian*, H. W. Massingham and H. N. Brailsford in the *Nation*, A. G. Gardiner in the *Daily News* and F. H. Hirst in the *Economist*. All these powerful voices were raised against intervention. Only in the *Westminster Gazette* could Grey count on steady support, from J. A. Spender.

Day after day the *Manchester Guardian* pounded the government's policy, known, guessed or suspected, in nervous prose sharpened with a Liberal philosophy of unimpeachable orthodoxy. A few hours before Grey's emotional encounter with Cambon the

[1] Grey: *Twenty-five Years;* Hodder & Stoughton 1925.
[2] Quoted in Trevelyan: *Grey of Falloden*, p. 254.

Daily News had hinted ominously that 'pressure on the government from those obscure forces that make for war is heavy and
growing heavier'. The *Nation*, an intellectual weekly with some
influence, found it 'safe to say that there has been no crisis in
which the political opinion of the English people has been so
definitely opposed to war as it is at this moment. A minister
who led this country into war would cease to lead the Liberal
party.'[1]

It was this frame of mind which Grey knew that he had to manage
right up to the very last moment. On August 3rd, Germany declared
war on France, and the violation of Belgian neutrality became an
imminent probability. On that day Grey addressed the House of
Commons and made the speech of his career:

> I ask the House, from the point of view of British interests, to
> consider what is at stake. If France is beaten in a struggle of life
> and death, beaten to her knees, becomes subordinate to the will
> and power of one greater than herself . . . I do not believe, for a
> moment, that at the end of this war, even if we stood aside and
> remained aside, we should be in a position, a material position, to
> use our force decisively to undo what had happened in the course
> of the war, to prevent the whole of Western Europe opposite to
> us—if that had been the result of the war—falling under the
> domination of a single power, and I am quite sure that our moral
> position would be such as to have lost us all respect.[2]

It was not Grey's eloquence, however—the eloquence of his private
pain, seeing the meaning of his work at last—that swayed the issue
of the day. Even in this fateful hour, knowing all that he knew, and
bending all that he had towards the only decision now supportable,
Grey was tethered and inhibited by the fictions in which he had
lived for the last eight years. Even on August 3rd, with France
already at war, Grey found it 'essential to make clear to the House
that its liberty of decision was not hampered by any engagements
entered into previously without its knowledge'.[3] In G. M. Trevelyan's
words:

> To sum up, were we committed to France?—technically not at
> all; whether morally, 'let every man look into his own heart, his
> own feelings and construe the extent of the obligation for himself'.[4]

[1] G. M. Thomson: *The Twelve Days*, pp. 157–158.
[2] Grey: House of Commons, Aug. 3rd 1914.
[3] Grey: *Twenty-five Years.*
[4] Trevelyan: *Grey of Falloden.*

And so decision passed out of the hands of the British Government. The Foreign Secretary might suggest, or powerfully plead; that was the extent of his leadership. Decision itself lay with a dead German general—Count von Schlieffen, who had framed a war-plan which absolutely required an invasion of Belgium. It was this act, and Belgium's defiance of it, which closed the ranks in Britain and carried her into war.

Back in the Foreign Office that evening, *in extremis*, Grey crashed his fists down on his table and cried: 'I hate war! I hate war!' And later that night, standing in the window of his room, watching the lamplighters at work in St. James's Park, he pronounced the obituary of his policy:

The lamps are going out all over Europe; we shall not see them lit again in our life-time.

But neither Grey's sorrows, nor the trepidations of his colleagues, nor the diagnosis of the Liberal Press were in harmony with the real feelings of the ignorant, unmilitary but fiercely patriotic people of Britain. The next day, when Britain's ultimatum to Germany had expired, and the unthinkable war was upon her, the mood of the nation was plainly revealed:

Parliament Street and Whitehall were thronged with people highly excited and rather boisterous. A brilliant sun shone in a cloudless sky. Young men in straw hats were in the majority. Girls in light calico dresses were numerous. All were already touched with the war fever. They regarded their country as a crusader—redressing all wrongs and bringing freedom to oppressed nations. Cries of 'Down with Germany!' were raised. Germany was the aggressor. She must be made to ask humbly for peace. The singing of patriotic songs, such as 'Rule Britannia', 'The Red White and Blue', and also the 'Marseillaise', brought the crowds still closer in national companionship. They saw England radiant through the centuries, valiant and invincible, and felt assured that so she shall appear for ever.[1]

What now followed, hidden from the cheerful, untutored man-in-the-street, and largely also hidden from his rulers, was an extraordinary mixture of efficiency and amateurism. One at least of the Liberal leaders (despite certain fluctuations, depending on what office he might be holding at the time) did not shy away from the thought and implications of war. Winston Churchill, First Lord of

[1] Michael MacDonagh: *In London During the Great War;* Eyre & Spottiswoode 1935, p. 8.

the Admiralty, has recorded how the last nervous moments of crisis touched his office:

> ... there came to us at the Admiralty a strange interlude of calm. All the decisions had been taken. The ultimatum to Germany had gone: it must certainly be rejected. War would be declared at midnight. As far as we had been able to foresee the event, all our preparations were made. Mobilization was complete. Every ship was in its station: every man at his post. All over the world, every British captain and admiral was on guard. It only remained to give the signal.[1]

This somewhat un-British state of affairs was primarily due to the action of one man, the First Sea Lord, Prince Louis of Battenberg, who found in this moment the peak and justification of forty-six years' service in the Royal Navy. It was he, on Sunday July 26th, when no Minister was available for consultation, who had taken on his own responsibility the heavy decision not to stand down the Fleet at the end of the annual manoeuvres. Churchill backed his decision, and on July 28th, a week before war broke out, the Fleet went to its war stations.[2] Characteristically, the *Nation*, catching a hint of what had happened, wrote of Churchill's 'needless, dangerous and ill-advised naval precautions'. Prince Louis, on the other hand, when war broke out, was able to report to the King: 'We had the drawn sword in our hand'.

Two drawn swords—or perhaps one should say, a sword and a dagger. There was also the Army; and here the mixture of readiness and unreadiness was weird indeed. The following episode is indicative of the latter condition. Lord Riddell,[3] on August 2nd, entertained to dinner, among others, Lloyd George and the leader of the Labour Party, Ramsay MacDonald.

> After dinner, Ramsay MacDonald wished to telephone. Just as I was about to ring up the number he required, the telephone bell rang. It was Sir John French, with whom I was on intimate terms. He said, 'Can you tell me, old chap, whether we are going to be in this war? If so, are we going to put an army on the Continent, and, if we are, who is going to command it?' I put my hand over the transmitter and told Ramsay MacDonald who it was and what he had said. R. MacD. smiled and suggested that I should go to the dining-room and ask what answer I should give. I did so, and

[1] *The World Crisis.*
[2] See Terraine: *The Life and Times of Lord Mountbatten;* Hutchinson 1968, pp. 12–13.
[3] Proprietor of the *News of the World.*

as a result told French that I thought we should be in the war, that we should send an army to the Continent, and that he would be in command. I added, 'Lloyd George says: "Be at Downing Street tomorrow at ten o'clock sharp" '. He thanked me and said, 'I shall be there'.

Lord Riddell's information was correct. Field-Marshal Sir John French was indeed appointed to command the British Expeditionary Force.[1] As C.-in-C. he attended the Council of War which took place at No. 10 Downing Street at 4 p.m. on August 5th. This gathering, whose proceedings I have described in detail elsewhere,[2] was astonishing for two reasons: the agenda which it assembled to discuss, and the array of personages, high and low, official and non-official, who were called in. They went as far down the Army scale as Corps commanders (Sir Douglas Haig and Sir James Grierson, both Lieutenant-Generals) and as wide as Field-Marshal Lord Roberts, now eighty-two years old, but full of fire. As I have said before:

> The thought of such a gathering offends against every modern conception of war direction; it is almost impossible to imagine what they could usefully have discussed at this stage, in view of the very different levels of their information and responsibility. What they did discuss was, first, where should the B.E.F. be sent? and, secondly, what should it consist of? Since these were both elementary questions which had been under consideration and had received their answers in the very act of creating the Expeditionary Force years before, the discussion which followed could scarcely fail to be confusing. . . .

In fact, however, the whole occasion reflected the persistence of the Liberal illusion that Britain could retain freedom of decision within an alliance. On August 3rd Grey had insisted in the House of Commons that Britain was not 'hampered by any engagements' to France; untrue—she was. Now, on August 5th, the Prime Minister was acting as though those 'engagements' did not commit her to a particular line of action; again untrue—they did. They had done

[1] In his book *1914* French says: 'On Thursday, July 30th, I was sent for by the Chief of the Imperial General Staff, and was given private intimation that, if an expeditionary force were sent to France, I was to command it.' Presumably his telephone call to a newspaper proprietor three days later was in order to discover whether there was any sign of official weakening on his appointment. It must be remembered that he had been in semi-disgrace for some months over his handling of the Curragh 'mutiny' in March.

[2] See *The Western Front*, pp. 43–53, from which the following extract is taken.

since 1906. Agadir in 1911 had spelt out the truth. But it took until war had actually been declared in August 1914 to bring it home: there *was* a war-plan; there had for years been a war-plan (there was no other plan); and the plan was to convey the British Expeditionary Force to the left wing of the French Army, to take its appointed place in whatever manoeuvre that Army might conduct. Unfortunately, as Sir William Robertson grimly said,[1] because the Government had failed to grasp the point, it had not been possible to examine or discuss the French manoeuvre before the British Army became trapped in it: and now it was too late.

And so the four infantry divisions and the large cavalry division of the B.E.F. went to France. (Asquith had spoken of insisting on only four divisions instead of six in October 1911; but the final decision was taken by Lord Kitchener, the newly-appointed Secretary of State for War. War Office planners, like Sir Henry Wilson, would call this '*criminal* and *sinful*'.) Mobilization, departure and assembly in the concentration areas were carried out with an efficiency never before seen in the functions of a British Army—an efficiency certainly equalling that of the Navy, and a tribute to the long careful work of Haldane and his helpers. It was a fine army—as far as it went; its supply system was excellent; discipline and individual training equally so; its khaki dress was the most modern in Europe; its equipment better than the French, and fully adequate for open warfare; its tactics were more advanced than either French or German. But there were only four divisions; the Germans were deploying the equivalent of seventy-eight on the Western Front.

As the Army departed from its ports of embarkation, it passed behind a veil which would not be lifted for over four years. The war to which it marched was about to provide such a swift succession of novelties as had never been seen before. A vast gap of incomprehension immediately formed between soldiers and civilians, a gap which would become wider and more fatal with every day of the war. In August 1914 it was perhaps more forgivable than at any other time, since the whole experience was new to everyone. In the Army itself there were not many who had any real premonition of what they were about to receive. But there were some who had an inkling; the Officers' Mess of the 1/Cameronians discussed the prospects ahead as the regiment prepared for active service, and Captain Jack noted in his diary:

Regarding our Allies: We hope that the French are again those of Marengo, Ulm, Austerlitz and Jena, with another Napoleon at their head; but the Prussians hammered them in their last big

See pp. 30–31.

campaign (1870). We think that the immense Russian numbers will tell, and trust that their form has improved since the Japanese beat them decisively ten years ago.

Of our Adversaries: The Austrians are gentlemen rather than soldiers. Germany, however, is very highly organised for a European war. Her armies have a tremendous reputation, and have smashed all enemies quite easily during the past fifty years.

A Staff College friend ... told me recently that the German infantry must be considered equal to ours notwithstanding their short service with no war experience compared with our long-service men, many of whom have seen a campaign. (He) added, 'Perhaps we are a little better at musketry'. Our cavalry and artillery, however, which take longer to train than infantry, should prove superior to their two-year men. ....[1]

Concluding his diary entry that day (August 12th) Jack added:

Our quarters, lately so cosy if simple, are dismantled. The corpse-like roll of kit covered with a dust-sheet, which lay on a shelf in Sam Darling's room next to mine, has been packed away. I used to remark to him in jest how real his 'corpse' looked; he replied with his penetrating glance, 'Well, if ever we get into a European war few of us will see the end of it'.

Perhaps these dour Lowlanders were exceptional; the predominant mood of the B.E.F., as it marched away, was gaiety.

The predominant mood of the British public was also gay—a light-heartedness which could be called feckless, had it not been tempered by a resolution which found expression in a remarkable phenomenon. Wedded, for mostly wrong reasons, to their beloved 'Voluntary Principle', the British in 1914 did not shrink from the personal implications of their belief. On August 6th the Prime Minister issued a call for 500,000 men for the Army. Very soon the face and authority of Lord Kitchener were added to this appeal in the famous poster: 'Your King and Country Need You'. The response was astounding. In the first five weeks of the war, some 250,000 men joined up. On September 1st alone 30,000 passed through the recruiting offices. Their motives were various. H. G. Wells, writing in the *Times*, expressed the thought of many: 'Nobody wants to be a non-combatant in a war of this sort'. Such simplicities were, no doubt, the main-spring of the vast majority. An ex-artilleryman, speaking in the B.B.C.'s *Great War* series on Television in 1964, recalled his own gesture:

[1] *General Jack's Diary*, pp. 23-24.

War had been declared and the following Sunday I went with a friend of mine into Shepherd's Bush Empire to see the big show there, and at the end of the show they showed the Fleet sailing the high seas and played 'Britons Never Shall Be Slaves' and 'Hearts Of Oak', and you know one feels that little shiver run up the back and you know you've got to do something. I was just turned seventeen at the time and on the Monday I went up to Whitehall—Old Scotland Yard—and enlisted.

For others, the decision was more complicated. Sir Llewellyn Woodward, an Oxford graduate in August 1914, was oppressed by many doubts:

Could I be satisfied that, behind the appeals to patriotism and duty, the background of the war was not just another squabble over markets? Was not England enmeshed in the same political selfishness as Germany, less crudely and boastfully, but caught up in the same predatory social system? Anyhow why should we interfere in what was primarily an Austro–Russian dispute over areas of political influence in south-eastern Europe? What claim had society upon me to help in getting it out of the political impasse into which it had blundered? Above all, would I be justified in killing Germans? Killing was murder, whatever the recruiting slogans might say about my King and Country needing me.[1]

Sir Llewellyn Woodward joined the Army nevertheless, because, as he says, 'I found no answer to the argument of Socrates'—that, if one has enjoyed the benefit of one's country's laws, one has the obligation to uphold it, even though it may be mistaken at that time. Either inspired by Socrates, or by simpler intuitions, a vast throng accompanied him in his act of enlistment: 1,186,337 by the end of the year, 2,257,521 by September 1915—an unparalleled manifestation.

While all these enthusiastic volunteers were beginning to absorb the first elements of their military training, hampered by lack of every kind of equipment and even of ordinary accommodation, and along lines which many of them were immediately able to recognise as absurdly old-fashioned, the B.E.F. itself was also learning. The truths of total war in the Twentieth Century could not long remain concealed at the point of impact of the armies. It was astonishing how long they would remain concealed from a sheltered public— and from its sheltered leaders. Yet the first shock would not be long delayed, and would be indicative of much confusion to follow.

[1] Woodward: *Great Britain and the War of 1914–1918;* Methuen, 1967, p. xiv.

V

On August 24th 1914, at 7 o'clock in the morning, Winston Churchill was sitting up in bed, working, in his room at the Admiralty. The door opened, and the Secretary of State for War, Field-Marshal Lord Kitchener, appeared:

These were the days before he took to uniform, and my recollection is that he had a bowler hat on his head, which he took off with a hand which also held a slip of paper. He paused in the doorway and I knew in a flash and before ever he spoke that the event had gone wrong. Though his manner was quite calm, his face was different. I had the subconscious feeling that it was distorted and discoloured as if it had been punched with a fist. His eyes rolled more than ever. His voice, too, was hoarse. He looked gigantic. 'Bad news,' he said heavily and laid the slip of paper on my bed. I read the telegram. It was from Sir John French. . . . I forget much of what passed between us. But the apparition of Kitchener *Agonistes* in my doorway will dwell with me as long as I live. It was like seeing old John Bull on the rack![1]

Sir John French's telegram contained the first information to the British Government of the Battle of Mons, which had taken place on the preceding day. 'My troops have been engaged all day with the enemy . . . we held our ground tenaciously. I have just received a message from G.O.C. 5th French Army that his troops have been driven back, that Namur has fallen . . . I have therefore ordered a retirement . . . which is being carried out now. It will prove a difficult operation, if the enemy remains in contact. . . .' The last sentence was electrifying:

I think that immediate attention should be directed to the defence of Havre.

Yet it was the reference to the fall of the Belgian fortress of Namur[2] which produced the first shock in Churchill's mind:

[1] Churchill: *The World Crisis.*
[2] Belgium's other great frontier fortress, Liége, had already gone; the last of its forts surrendered on August 17th.

49

We were evidently in the presence of new facts and of a new standard of values. If strong fortresses were to melt like wisps of vapour in a morning sun, many judgments would have to be revised. The foundations of thought were quaking. . . . 'Fortify Havre,' said Sir John French. One day's general battle and the sanguine advance and hoped-for counterstroke had been converted into 'Fortify Havre'.

The war was now precisely three weeks old. During those three weeks, governments, military leaders and populations had existed in a fog of ignorance and misconception. This was equally true of both sides, but the worst effects were certainly felt by the Allies. Now the fatal defect of the Anglo–French Staff Talks was felt: Britain's army had been committed since 1906 to support French operations; it was now in France for that very purpose; but almost no-one in Britain understood the nature of the operations to which the French had committed themselves. The premises on which the French Plan XVII was based, its strategic validity, had not been examined responsibly in either country—still less between them.

All that was known of war plans in Britain when war broke out was that the famous French Army was going to advance towards the German frontier, and that the British Expeditionary Force was to prolong and strengthen its left wing. (As we have seen, there were not many people who even appreciated that.) Accordingly, advanced parties of the Expeditionary Force had landed at le Havre, Rouen and Boulogne on August 7th. On the same day the French set the first part of their plan in motion. The rest followed, with great outward smoothness. As the armies marched, military reticence and deliberate censorship shrouded their nations in silence, fitfully broken by enigmatic communiqués. In Britain, as in France, there was a natural tendency to view the war as a revenge for the calamities of 1870–1871. It did not, therefore, seem strange or questionable that the French should be marching directly against the frontier across which lay the provinces which Germany had seized in 1871—Lorraine and Alsace. So the Sunday edition of the *Times* (Sunday editions were a regular practice at that time) announced on August 9th:

ALSACE INVADED
FRENCH DASH OVER FRONTIER
Two Towns Entered

The French had indeed invaded Alsace, and had entered the town of Mulhouse, a substantial centre with 95,000 inhabitants. The *Times* featured a proclamation of the French Commander-in-Chief, General Joffre:

Children of Alsace—

After 44 years of sorrowful waiting French soldiers once more tread the soil of your noble country. They are the pioneers in the great work of revenge. For them what emotions it calls forth and what pride!

To complete the work they have made the sacrifice of their lives. The French nation unanimously urges them on and in the folds of their flag are inscribed the magic words 'Right and Liberty'. Long live Alsace! Long live France![1]

On this note the war made its first impact on the French and British people. Subsequent information was in keeping. On August 11th, *Times* readers noted: 'French Mastery of Upper Alsace'. For titillation, they were told of:

WOMEN AGAINST UHLANS
Germans Repulsed by Boiling Water

The next day there were more 'French Frontier Successes'. But this was also the day on which the more discerning could read Repington's article as Military Correspondent, in which he stated the conclusion

> . . . that the bulk of the German Armies about to operate against France is to the northward of Lorraine. . . .

Repington published that day a remarkable (if incomplete) map, showing the concentration of German army corps and divisions against Luxemburg and Belgium—a weighty mass suspended over the left flank of the optimistic French. This was not bad analysis by Repington—a possibility which might profitably have been discussed in the War Office or the Committee of Imperial Defence years before. What he was showing, of course, was precisely the broad intention of the Schlieffen Plan by which German operations were ruled: its whole object was a vast encirclement of the French Armies, a wheel in great strength round their left. Illusory successes in Alsace, or even in Lorraine, could only draw the French away from the decisive point and (short of a miracle) weaken their ability to avoid the net.

All this remained hidden from most men. Those who were willing or able to learn between the lines were few indeed. One of them was Lord Kitchener, working not so much through information (apart from Repington's rough map there was very little of it) as through intuition. On August 12th he discussed the concentration area of the B.E.F. with Sir John French, Sir Archibald Murray (Chief of Staff) and Sir Henry Wilson (Deputy Chief of Staff) with French liaison

[1] The *Times*, Aug. 10th 1914.

officers present. Wilson recorded: '. . . we wrangled with K. for
3 hours. K. wanted to go to Amiens. . . . He still thinks the Germans
are coming north of the Meuse in great force, and will swamp us
before we concentrate'. The combined weight of the Allied staff
officers overbore Kitchener's doubts. The next day, Sir John French
triumphantly announced the concentration area to his two Army
Corps commanders, Haig and Grierson. Haig wrote in his diary:

> We are to de-train in the neighbourhood of Le Cateau and
> Wassigny: some 60 or 70 miles to the East of Amiens! In view
> of the ignorance still existing regarding the enemy's movements,
> the rate of his advance into Belgium, and his intentions, it seems
> to some of us somewhat risky to begin our concentration so close
> to the enemy. A considerable hostile army is probably now
> passing westwards through Liége. . . .[1]

Serving officers could not discuss such doubts publicly. Lord
Kitchener, in his relations with his Government colleagues, made a
cult of silence. (As a staff officer said: 'Lord K. seemed quite incapable of taking his Cabinet colleagues so seriously as people of that
sort take themselves'.[2]) The members of the Government itself, as
F. S. Oliver wrote, 'were content to remain in a kind of dusk with
regard to military operations'—not surprisingly, since we have seen
that they cultivated this 'dusk' from the time of their accession to
power. And Public Opinion, of course, remained in even deeper
obscurity. There were no accredited War Correspondents; all news,
whether from official or non-official sources, was filtered through the
Press Bureau, headed by F. E. Smith (later Lord Birkenhead), an
organisation hastily set up, heavily over-worked, and by no means
clear about its functions.

For nine significant days, optimism was fed upon tit-bits while
disconcerting news was blurred or withheld. Thus the reverses
suffered by the French in Alsace failed to register; Mulhouse was
lost on August 10th to a swift German counterattack, and a new
invasion had to be mounted to sustain morale. This was still struggling
on August 17th, but readers of the *Times* were told:

TWO FRENCH SUCCESSES
Germans Driven from Dinant
A Footing in Lorraine

What, they might have asked, were the Germans doing at Dinant?

---

[1] Robert Blake: *The Private Papers of Douglas Haig;* Eyre & Spottiswoode
1952.
[2] Sir C. E. Callwell: *Experiences of a Dug-out 1914–1918;* Constable 1920.

Was this an omen? But the next day such questions were driven out of mind by the bold headline:

ACROSS THE CHANNEL
British Army in the Field

This gave them something to think about indeed, and the next day General Joffre provided yet another cheerful communiqué:

> During the whole of yesterday, August 17th, we made ceaseless progress in Upper Alsace. The enemy retreated in this neighbourhood in disorder, leaving everywhere his wounded and war materials. . . . In all the actions engaged in during the last days in Lorraine and Alsace the Germans have suffered important losses. Our artillery had a demoralizing and terrible effect on them. . . .

No-one could possibly tell from this that the vast Battles of the Frontiers had opened, still less that they were going seriously against the French. On August 19th the French re-entered Mulhouse, but this was their only success. At Sarrebourg and at Morhange their Armies of the right suffered severe defeat. Portions of these armies were in complete disorder; there were alarming panics in some units. No hint of this was revealed to the public, either in Britain or in France; very little was imparted even to the most senior military officers. On the left, where the fall of the Belgian fortresses had opened the way for the main German movement, there was equal obscurity. Only sharp instinct and strong powers of deduction could unravel these mysteries. Haig wrote in his diary:

> I gather that . . . the Germans are crossing the Meuse in considerable strength . . . and marching with all speed westwards on Brussels and Namur. . . . This looks as if a great effort is to be made to turn the French left (which rests on Namur fortress) by an advance through Belgium. In fact the solution of the problem which was given as the most likely one when I was at Camberley Staff College in 1897! If my surmise is correct . . . the neighbourhood of Waterloo and Charleroi should thus be the scene of another great battle. . . .[1]

Haig's surmise was indeed correct. On August 21st the British public read with astonishment:

THE GERMANS AT BRUSSELS

What they did not read was the full truth that the French armies of

[1] Haig Diary, Aug. 19th; see Terraine: *Douglas Haig: The Educated Soldier;* Hutchinson 1963, pp. 82–83.

the right were now desperately on the defensive; that their armies of
the centre had suffered shattering reverses in the Ardennes; that
their army of the left, the Fifth, was in difficulties along the Sambre
and the Meuse; in short, that all their plans, into which the operations
of the B.E.F. had been so unsuspectingly woven, had gone awry,
while the Schlieffen Plan unfolded inexorably. Haig again (August
21st):

> I and my Staff were rather anxious about our position. We are
> advancing against a difficult position (Charleroi to Mons); a
> boggy valley, many coal-pits and greatly intersected country. . . .
> Briefly a country in which enemy could hold us with a few troops;
> meantime his great masses are marching as fast as possible round
> our left flank, and as far as we know *are unopposed*!

On August 22nd the British approached the little town of Mons,
centre of a heavily industrialised mining area. Already their neigh-
bours on the right, the French Fifth Army, were in retreat from
Charleroi. But with a loyalty to the Alliance which did him credit,
despite the alarming reports of his cavalry and the infant Royal
Flying Corps, Sir John French agreed to stand his ground for
twenty-four hours to relieve pressure on the French. So, on Sunday
August 23rd, within a few miles of the battlefield of Waterloo, the
British Army fought its first action on Western European soil since
the defeat of Napoleon ninety-nine years earlier.

By the later standards of the war, the Battle of Mons was a mere
skirmish.[1] The brunt of the action was sustained by II Corps (now
under General Sir Horace Smith-Dorrien, following the sudden
death of Grierson). All day the Corps held its positions along the
Mons–Condé Canal, against the pressure of three German army
corps. Every German onslaught was 'shot flat' by concentrated and
accurate musketry from invisible British troops. French's G.H.Q.
was even planning a further advance for the 24th when fresh information from Joffre indicated the real strength of the German forces
marching against the British, and confirmed that the French on
their right were still in retreat. So instead of advancing, the B.E.F.
had to withdraw—a delicate operation in the face of a powerful
enemy, but successfully managed. The battle had cost just over
1,600 casualties, a small enough figure out of some 40,000 engaged;
but to some inexperienced participants the noise and confusion and
dispersion of modern war made the action and loss seem much more
serious. Now the Retreat from Mons began.

The British public received its first news of all this on Tuesday,

---

[1] See Terraine: *Mons: The Retreat to Victory;* Batsford 1960.

August 25th. 'British Army's Stern Fight', said the *Times*. A Press Bureau release, dated 2.30 p.m. on the 24th, stated: 'The British forces were engaged all day Sunday and after dark with the enemy in the neighbourhood of Mons, and held their ground. . . .' But a later message (2 a.m. 25th) added:

> The British forces have successfully reached their new position. Fighting has gone on more or less continuously, but the enemy has not effectively harassed our operations. . . . The casualties cannot be estimated exactly but are not heavy. . . .

Soberly the *Times* editorialised: 'Yesterday was a day of bad news, and we fear that more must follow. . . .' Repington stated flatly in his article: '. . . the outlook is not favourable. . . .' With this, the discerning might have prepared themselves for something on the lines of the South African War 'Black Week' in December 1899; and those who made use of coloured pins on large maps would be able to see that the Germans had gained a great strategic advantage. It would have taken very rare discernment, however, to perceive all the potential dangers in the contrast of tone between the sobriety of the *Times* (largely inspired, no doubt, by Repington) and the soporific utterances of the Press Bureau.

On August 26th the first stage of the Retreat from Mons was completed. Smith-Dorrien's II Corps (now reinforced by the newly-arrived 4th Division) was in a state of considerable exhaustion after long marches in great heat. On the unanimous advice of his divisional commanders, Smith-Dorrien decided to stand and give battle at Le Cateau. Gloom and despondency had now replaced the earlier optimism of G.H.Q., which was, in any case, badly out of touch with the fighting troops. Reluctantly and with misgivings, Sir John French agreed to Smith-Dorrien's decision. What followed was one of the most brilliant British actions of the war; once again, II Corps beat off all the attacks against it, and held its ground through the morning until German pressure against its open right flank compelled it to withdraw. Thirty-eight guns had to be abandoned, and over 7,000 casualties were sustained. But the feature of the day was the unhurried, unhindered withdrawal of the three British divisions in broad daylight, under the noses of a greatly superior enemy. This, said French in his Despatch, 'could never have been accomplished unless a commander of rare and unusual coolness, intrepidity, and determination had been present to personally conduct the operation.'[1]

The news of Le Cateau did not at once reach England; when it did,

---

[1] Later, in his book *1914*, he contradicted this, and bitterly blamed Smith-Dorrien.

it set off tremors from which the Public Relations of the war hardly
recovered. On the 26th itself, the Press Bureau was quoting Sir John
French as saying: 'The condition of our troops is in every way
satisfactory'. (His true opinion was almost exactly the contrary, but
he may be forgiven for not making a free gift to the enemy of his
thoughts.) The *Times*, still preoccupied with Mons, was reporting
'Two Thousand Casualties'—which was very close to the real figure
at this stage. The first leader commented: '. . . considering the
numbers engaged the losses are not severe'. (There followed a comparison with the Battle of Inkerman; then the leader continued):
'Our losses will be faced both by the Army and the nation with the
same fortitude which was shown by our troops in encountering the
enemy . . .'. The next day the paper somewhat fretfully announced
'. . . little fresh news . . . the German advance continues . . .'. A
sense of being kept in the dark was growing. On the 28th, the first
stories gleaned from the returning wounded at Mons were printed;
some of them made very colourful reading, with disturbing under-
tones. But on the 29th there was the gratifying news of 'Victory for
the Fleet'—the Admiralty's communiqué on the successful raid in
the Heligoland Bight.

August 30th was a Sunday—just one week from the Battle of
Mons. The *Times* special edition carried on the front page a two-
column dispatch from 'Our Special Correspondent', datelined
'Amiens, Aug. 29'. This was the 'Amiens Dispatch' which was to
put the fat in the fire. The left-hand column of the page was headed:

FIERCEST FIGHT IN HISTORY
Heavy Losses of British Troops

The Amiens Dispatch itself appeared under the headings:

BROKEN BRITISH REGIMENTS
BATTLING AGAINST ODDS
Untarnished Honour of our Troops

With consternation, the readers of the *Times* took in the following:

> I read this afternoon in Amiens this morning's Paris papers. To
> me, knowing some portion of the truth, it seemed incredible that
> a great people should be so kept in ignorance of the situation which
> it has to face. The papers read like children's prattle. . . .
>
> This is not well. I would plead with the English censor to let
> my message pass. I guarantee him that as regards the situation of
> troops I have nothing to say that is not known and noted already
> by the German General Staff. . . . On the other hand, it is important
> that the nation should know and realize certain things. Bitter

truths, but we can face them. We have to cut our losses, to take stock of the situation, to set our teeth.

First let it be said that our honour is bright. Amongst all the straggling units that I have seen, flotsam and jetsam of the fiercest fight in history, I saw fear in no man's face. It was a retreating and a broken army, but it was not an army of hunted men. . . .

Since Monday morning last the German advance has been one of almost incredible rapidity . . . the British Force fought a terrible fight. . . .

Regiments were grieviously injured, and the broken army fought its way desperately with many stands, forced backwards and ever backwards by the sheer unconquerable mass of numbers of an enemy prepared to throw away three or four men for the life of every British soldier. . . . Our losses are very great. I have seen the broken bits of many regiments. . . .

Apparently every division was in action. Some have lost nearly all their officers. The regiments were broken to bits, and good discipline and fine spirit kept the fragments together, though they no longer knew what had become of the other parts with which they had once formed a splendid whole. . . .

To sum up, the first great German effort has succeeded. We have to face the fact that the British Expeditionary Force, which bore the great weight of the blow, has suffered terrible losses and requires immediate and immense reinforcement. The British Expeditionary Force has won indeed imperishable glory, but it needs men, men, and yet more men. . . .

The writer was Arthur Moore, who was on his way to Serbia when the Paris office of the *Times* recalled him and sent him to the B.E.F. sector. He arrived on August 28th in the area of the 4th Division, and found himself on the line of march of scattered portions of that formation. On the same date as his *Times* dispatch, he sent a telegram to the *Daily Mail* (both papers then belonged to the Northcliffe 'stable') which the *Times* printed (with many gaps to indicate censorship, but running to one and a half columns) beside the 'Amiens Dispatch'. This contained reports of interviews with French, British and Belgian soldiers. It began:

This is a pitiful story I have to write. Would to God it did not fall to me to write it. But the time for secrecy is past. Only by realising what has happened can we nerve ourselves for the effort we must make to retrieve it. . . .

Then followed what would now be quickly recognised as a strong 'colour story', conveying a vivid impression of the remorseless

advance of overwhelming German numbers. Towards the end Moore
added:

> I hope I have not been guilty of exaggeration myself in anything
> I have written here. I have aimed at telling a plain tale of mis-
> fortune and defeat. It is a bitter tale to tell of British troops, but
> they were set an impossible task. Let us not try to hush up the
> facts. Let us face them, and let them strengthen our resolve to
> see this war through, whatever happens. . . .

There is no need to doubt the absolute sincerity of Arthur Moore,
or the substantial sincerity of most of the men he spoke to. The
picture he painted would certainly have been endorsed by some at
G.H.Q., whence Joffre's Liaison Officer, Colonel Huguet (who never
really got to know the British Army) was reporting to his chief:
'Battle lost by British Army, which seems to have lost all cohesion. . .'
And later that day (26th) Huguet added:

> The situation is extremely critical. For the moment the British
> Army is beaten and is incapable of any serious effort. The right
> column—1st and 2nd Divisions— . . . still presents some aspects
> of cohesion; the same may be said of the 4th; but the 3rd and 5th
> Divisions . . . are now nothing more than disorganised bands,
> incapable of offering the smallest resistance. . . . Conditions are
> such that for the moment the British Army no longer exists. . . .

This was a travesty. A newly-arrived Correspondent like Moore
may be forgiven for saying 'every division was in action'; Huguet,
at G.H.Q., ought to have known better. The 1st and 2nd Divisions
(I Corps) had hardly been engaged in the whole campaign so far;
their losses were negligible. Not one of the divisions had 'lost nearly
all their officers' (Moore); none was reduced to 'disorganised bands'
(Huguet). The bulk of the 4th Division was in hand and in good shape,
though some portions had become detached from the main body
(including a wing of the Warwicks containing the future Field-
Marshal Montgomery). Neither the 3rd nor the 5th Division, nor
their commanders (least of all Smith-Dorrien) had any consciousness
of defeat, though all were very tired, there were some lapses of nerve
—natural enough—and here again many units were more or less
broken up for the time being. An officer attached to G.H.Q. in the
temporary rôle of a chauffeur found himself constantly meeting
bodies of men in this condition, and has recorded how misleading
such encounters can be:

> 'Who are you?' I would call out, as a dozen tired and footsore men
> approached.
> 'We're the sole survivors of the Blankshire Regiment, sir,' an

old soldier would reply. 'All the rest got done in yesterday. Not a soul except us is left alive.'

'All right. Keep straight on for a couple of miles or more and you will find three or four hundred other sole survivors of your regiment bivouacking in a field.'

This happened not once, but twenty times. On the first occasion or two, one was inclined to place some credence in the statement of the 'sole survivors', but after a while one became so used to the description that it developed into a joke. It is easy, however, to understand that the expression was employed in the utmost good faith.[1]

The skills required by a good War Correspondent were only painfully and slowly learnt between 1914 and 1918—and had to be equally painfully re-learnt between 1939 and 1945. They include a grasp of military affairs and behaviour which must, in part, stem from knowledge of military history; the number of men who (like, notably, the late Chester Wilmot) possess these attributes is small.

By the time Arthur Moore's dispatch reached England, most of the damage which he so graphically described had been repaired, thanks largely to the complete failure of the Germans to pursue and harry II Corps. The British public had no means of knowing this; the impact of the dispatch was consequently of the most violent order. The Press Bureau promptly issued an official statement, associated with the name of Lord Kitchener, saying:

> There has, in effect, been a four days' battle—on the 23rd, 24th, 25th and 26th August. During the whole of this period the British troops, in conformity with the general movement of the French armies, were occupied in resisting and checking the German advance and in withdrawing to the new lines of defence.
> ... The battle of August 26th was of the most severe and desperate character. The troops offered a superb and most stubborn resistance.
> Since the 26th, apart from cavalry fighting, the British army has not been molested.

The Army's total casualties were given as between 5,000 and 6,000 men (a low figure dictated, no doubt, by security considerations) and it was stated that reinforcements of double this number had been sent out. A warning was issued that such reports as Moore's 'Amiens Dispatch' should be received 'with extreme caution'. But the damage had been done. The hue-and-cry was now in full spate. The *Daily Express* said that the *Times* had 'made hearts stand still'.

[1] See *Mons: The Retreat to Victory*, p. 168.

The *Daily Telegraph* spoke of 'highly alarmist stories ... not justified by the facts'. The *Morning Post* wanted a Press Law. London,
it said, had been

> ... tortured last night by a newspaper report of a situation across
> the Channel, published with the dubious prestige of a name once
> illustrious in English journalism. The report begins in the style
> of a hysterical schoolgirl. ...

The *Sketch* also advocated censorship: 'This may not be the official
view, but it is the view of the mothers of our soldiers'.

The *Times* was unrepentant; relying on the reputation which it
had enjoyed 'for five generations' to account for its motives, the
newspaper then passed to the counter-attack upon the Press Bureau
itself as the source of the mischief:

> We welcome a censorship as a valuable support to the Press in
> time of war. No newspaper can conceivably desire to publish news
> which is either inaccurate or calculated to assist the enemy; and
> a Censor with real military knowledge and in close touch with the
> military authorities is a necessary adjunct to the Press. In the case,
> however, of the dispatch under discussion these conditions were
> not fulfilled.

And then came the revelation:

> We not only obtained leave to publish it; we were definitely
> requested, in writing, to do so by the head of the Press Bureau.
> With such a request before us, we should have failed in our public
> duty if we had withheld the dispatch from publication ... our
> hands are clean.[1]

It was, as one might suppose, in Parliament that the storm was
noisiest; all this was strong meat for a generation of politicians which
had steadily averted its eyes from military realities. In the Commons,
Sir Arthur Markham (on the Minsterial benches) provided a preview
of what were to become some main issues as the war developed. He
referred to 'the agony to the people of this country' caused by the
'Amiens Dispatch'. He continued:

> The idea of Lord Kitchener was that all information should be
> held back from the public. He might be a great soldier, but he did
> not understand Parliamentary institutions and that the human
> element was what the public desired. Everybody who had any
> sort of military command seemed to think that the civil power
> must be subordinate to the military power. ...[2]

[1] *Times* first leader, Sept. 1st 1914.
[2] This and following extracts are from the *Times* Parliamentary report,
Sept. 1st 1914.

So, before even one month of war had passed, the jealous conflict between civil and military power—the 'Frocks' and the 'Brasshats'—which later grew to such malevolent force, made its appearance. It is interesting that this début was prompted by Lord Kitchener's autocratic methods as Secretary of State. Sir Arthur Markham warned that British democracy would not 'consent to go to war in the dark'—yet that is precisely what it was going to have to do for a long time.

For the Opposition, Mr. Peto (Wilts. Devizes) took a somewhat different view:

> He was indignant to see in a newspaper like the *Times* the headline in large print 'BROKEN BRITISH REGIMENTS' and then a little smaller 'Untarnished Honour Of Our Troops'. As if anyone required the assurance of the *Times* that the honour of our troops was untarnished. Would it not be wise to take powers during the currency of the war to suppress altogether the publication and sale of any newspaper which printed articles at all comparable to those which created such alarm and distress the previous day?

In contrast with this point of view, Mr. Llewelyn Williams (Carmarthen) asked whether 'the Government would not return to the time-honoured practice of this country and allow Press correspondents to accompany the Army to the front? (Laughter and cries of "No")'. The perspective of years does not make that laughter less inscrutable.

F. E. Smith's statement was awaited with interest. He first explained, at some length and with some opacity, the existing system of censorship. Then, turning to the 'Amiens Dispatch', he said:

> I take the responsibility of having returned it, initialled by me, in the shape in which it appeared in the paper. I think now that if one had known everything that was going to happen, and perhaps had had a little more time to give to every important article which was clamouring for attention, it would have been better if I had written a note to the editor asking him to consider whether . . . it was a wise article to publish . . . I have no doubt, too, that if I had done so he would have suppressed the article altogether.

Asked whether it was true that, so far from asking for suppression, he had actually made an addition to the article himself, F. E. Smith replied:

> I have been asked by Lord Kitchener as far as possible to assist his object, which was, of course, to obtain recruits. In these circumstances I suggested that a reference might be made at the

end of the article to the fact that what was wanted was reinforcements, reinforcements and still more reinforcements; that and that
alone was the nature of the addition made.

Though F. E. Smith fully acquitted the editors of the *Times* and the
Daily Mail of all responsibility, he did not refer to the fact that he
had marked certain passages (cut by the editors on duty) 'Stet', nor
did he make it clear that he had sent a note *asking* for the dispatch
to be published. The *Times* was not satisfied:

> That note is in our possession; we cannot publish it without the
> writer's consent because it is marked 'Private', but Mr. Smith's
> omission to refer to it in his speech is . . . altogether disingenuous.

The chief interest in the whole matter, however, lay elsewhere than
in the curiosities of F. E. Smith's behaviour: it lay in the response of
the Government to an evident breakdown in communications. In
the House of Lords, Lord Haldane spoke for the Government, in
the Commons the Prime Minister. Mr. Asquith considered that the
action of the *Times* had been 'very regrettable (hear, hear) and I
trust it will not recur'. He commended the 'patriotic reticence of the
Press as a whole (cheers)' and dismissed the proposal of sending out
War Correspondents 'under the altered conditions of modern warfare'. But he did make what was taken to be a pledge:

> The Government feel, after the experience of the last two weeks,
> that the public is entitled to prompt and authentic information
> (cheers) of what has happened at the front, and they are making
> arrangements which they hope will be more adequate.

So the immediate crisis of the 'Amiens Dispatch' passed over, lost
to view in the continuing turmoil of the war. It was unfortunate that
the British public's first glimpse of what the war might have in store
had been supplied by a man without sufficient experience of war
situations. In the angry rejection of some of Moore's more sensa-
tional paragraphs there lay a danger—that the public might all-too-
readily relapse into complacency again. Yet there did appear to be
one useful product—the official promise of reform of an evidently
unsatisfactory situation. Nevertheless, a few days later (September
5th, the eve of the Battle of the Marne) we find the *Times* once more
complaining, under a first leader heading, 'The Use of the Press in
War':

> Mr. Asquith's promise—not to the Press, but to the nation—
> remains unfulfilled. . . . In a time of unprecedented crisis the
> Press has a great and patriotic duty to perform. It has to stimulate
> and deepen public interest in a struggle which is bound to last a

very long time, and on which the fate of the Empire depends. It cannot do so if it is kept in the dark. . . . Deeds have been wrought with which the country ought to be ringing. Had properly accredited and experienced war correspondents been with the Army they could by now have been permitted to relate these stirring episodes. They are still cooling their heels in London, and seem likely to remain so, for no other reason than that our Government does not understand how to make a right use of the Press in war. . . .

In the wording of this complaint itself, in the placid assumption that the narration of 'stirring episodes' would solve the problem, one senses some measure of its intractability. And very soon it would be seen that the Government's failure to make the right use of the Press was matched by failure of the Press itself to keep its head.

VI

Sept. 1st

Sir,

Yesterday morning came the news of a serious set-back to our armies. Yesterday afternoon, while Lord Kitchener was telling of the bravery of our wounded and dead, while he was asking for men to take their places, every lawn tennis court in the space near me was crowded by strapping young Englishmen and girls.

Is there no way of shaming these laggards?

The English girl who will not know the man—lover, brother, friend—that cannot show an overwhelming reason for not taking up arms—that girl will do her duty and will give good help to her country.

Your obedient servant,
Henry Arthur Jones

Reform Club,
Pall Mall, S.W.

The correspondence columns of the *Times* were not slow in adding their voice to the impact of the 'Amiens Dispatch'—but, as might be expected, that voice was only rarely sane and helpful. The day on which the above letter appeared (it was written on August 26th) 30,000 men joined the Army.[1] They were obeying a call made in all sincerity, but having obeyed it, they were in for rude shocks. On September 26th the King reviewed three 'divisions' of the New Army at Aldershot. Two of these formations were at least properly clothed in khaki, and had rifles.

The third Division presented a ludicrous spectacle so motley was their array as they marched past the King. Comparatively few were fully equipped as to uniforms and accoutrements. Some were only half made up, wearing the scarlet jackets, the kilts or the trews of the old Army uniforms, mingled with articles of civilian attire, all in glaring contrast. Some again wore a sort of provisional

[1]See p. 71.

uniform of blue serge, suggesting inmates of prisons or hospitals. . . .
But most of the recruits were still in the clothes they wore when
they enlisted. There was to be seen, accordingly, a diversified and
discordant display of straw hats, bowlers and tweed caps. And
many were armed with staves![1]

Appearances were not deceptive. It would be nine months, from the
first recruiting call, before the first New Army division arrived in
France, over a year before any of these troops took part in a major
action—and then with depressing results. Meanwhile the old Regular
Army was bearing the brunt of the war, itself afflicted with every
kind of shortage when its initial equipment issue ran out (through
destruction in battle or wear and tear) and when unforeseen trench
warfare imposed its new demands. It was then that the Army paid
the price of the nation's flat refusal to contemplate the realities of
continental war in the years of preparation.

Between September and December 1914, the war hardened out
into a pattern which was to become permanent until the final battles
of 1918. On the Eastern Front great pendulum-swings of advance
and retreat, as Russia and the Central Powers took their turns of
fortune's favour, while giving occupation to armchair strategists
moving their coloured pins on maps, produced no decisive results.
In the West, grandiose manoeuvres successively cancelled each other
out until by November the continuous trench-line was formed from
Switzerland to the sea. In either case, only the most blurred and
mistaken impressions of the event were received by the British people.

Within days of the publication of the 'Amiens Dispatch' the battle
in France took a significant and hopeful turn. There is no cause for
wonder or scorn that this was not immediately perceived; secrecy
was of the essence of the operations known as the First Battle of the
Marne, and in any case, even the optimistic French High Command
was becoming a little chary of over-bright communiqués. Quite
rightly, the eve of the battle was signalised by a pervading gloom:
'Paris Prepared' announced the *Times* on September 4th, and did its
best to offset this unpleasant suggestion with reports of the Austrian
defeat at Lemberg—'Great Russian Victory' (which was true).
September 6th was the day on which the main French forces passed
to the counter-offensive. The *Times* reported:

GERMAN ADVANCE NEAR PARIS

and a special correspondent wrote:

German forces were little over 20 miles from Paris yesterday

[1] MacDonagh: *In London During the Great War*, p. 31.

evening. If their advance continues as rapidly as it has done within the last few days they might be in the capital tomorrow. Large French forces are, however, preparing to dispute their entry into the city, and an extended action may be expected today. . . .

Subsequent headlines displayed slow appreciation of the decisive victory which was being won (sometimes not very obviously to the participants) on a battlefield 155 miles in length.[1] On September 8th the *Times* announced:

GERMAN CHECK IN FRANCE

and the next day:

TURN OF THE TIDE

On the 11th two column headings were:

BRITISH ARMY IN PURSUIT	GERMANS DRIVEN BACK
	An Exhausted Enemy

(Yet on the previous day General Haig had noted in his diary:

Our Cavalry Division . . . does not seem to have taken advantage of its opportunities today.

Indeed, the whole Allied pursuit was slow, but the B.E.F. slowest of all.) On the 11th, General Joffre telegraphed to the French Minister of War:

'The Battle of the Marne is an incontestable victory for us.'

And the next day the name of the battle made its first appearance in the *Times*:

ALLIES' STEADY ADVANCE	BATTLE OF THE MARNE

The good news continued to flow; September 13th:

160 GERMAN GUNS CAPTURED	THE ALLIES' SWIFT ADVANCE
Over 6,000 Prisoners	German Retreat in Disorder

On the 14th there was jubilation:

VICTORIES IN WEST AND EAST

and the first leader, under the heading 'The Retreat of the New Attila', allowed its imagination to take wing:

[1] See *The Battle of the Marne*, by Henri Isselin; Elek Books 1965, p. 128.

... the long unbroken prestige of German arms has received an irreparable blow. ... The bulk of their forces is hurrying out of Belgium, and the Belgian field army, which has reached Lierre, is marching to retake Brussels. ... From every point comes the same story of triumph. ...

Two days later the headlines struck another note:

THE GERMAN ARMY AT BAY
THE BATTLE OF THE AISNE
Rally of the German Right

and the first leader said:

The retreating German armies are making a courageous stand, and all along their line they are at present holding together. ...

The Germans, in fact, had dug in along the slopes bordering the River Aisne, and the Allies made their first acquaintance with one of the grimmest aspects of the war—the lethal combination of machine guns and barbed wire in defence. It would be a long time before even front-line commanders appreciated what this conjunction could mean in terms of tactical frustration and dreadful casualty lists. It was not to be wondered at, if those at home took even longer to understand. But there was a certain prescience in the *Times* first leader on September 22nd, answering the question 'on all lips': 'Are the Germans giving way?'

We can only say that all along the battle line the signs are hopeful ... but that no decisive movement is yet visible. To discern how the battle is swaying we must look at inches rather than miles. ... Whether the battle can ever be won by frontal pressure alone is another matter. ...

For years the ebb and flow of battle on the Western Front would, indeed, be measured in inches. But for a brief time the war of movement survived, as both sides attempted to break the deadlock on the Aisne by outflanking manoeuvres. Step by step these carried the front back across northern France into Belgium. Place-names which had flickered in and out of the news during the great German advance now became the indelible markers of the battle-line: Amiens, Péronne, Arras, Bethune, Ypres. The quick fall of Antwerp provided another shock, another deceptive demonstration of the powerlessness of seemingly strong fortifications against modern artillery. And this event also provided the first of the tremors which would undermine the position of Churchill among the directors of Britain's war. His impetuous rush of ill-equipped Royal Marine brigades into Antwerp,

his desire to command them himself, regardless of his other duties
as First Lord of the Admiralty, the loss of 931 Marines taken prisoner
and another 1,442 interned in Holland when the defence collapsed,
all contributed to a reputation for unsteadiness which would shortly
prove fatal. In the excitement over Antwerp, and in the lingering
clouds of the optimism reborn on the Marne, it was not at once
perceived that the war had now practically set in its mould. The
withdrawal of the Belgian field army down the coast to positions near
Ypres, and the transfer of the B.E.F. from the Aisne to Flanders,
marked the formation of the continuous front, and the *Times* question
whether battle could 'ever be won by frontal pressure alone' assumed
new significance. What other pressure could there be?

It was while these developments were in train that obscurity once
more descended upon the projection of the war to the British people.
News—hard news—became in very short supply, though rumours
and conjectures abounded. On October 6th the *Times* carried a first
leader with the heading 'The Fog of War'. Profiting (one supposes)
by the distressing experience of the 'Amiens Dispatch', the newspaper now discovered virtues in censorship and the withholding of
information:

> Just now we believe the censors to be exercising a wise and prudent
> discretion, while the inactivity of the Press Bureau in undoubtedly
> fully justified. Not the slightest sinister cause lies at the back of
> the silence which prevails. It simply means that there are moments
> when silence is golden, and this is one of them.

Amid this silence, the veil of unknowing and misconstruction to
which I have referred earlier thickened. Brothers, husbands and
wives, fathers and sons found themselves separated from each other
unbelievably in the act of putting on khaki and obeying its subsequent compulsions. In most illustrations of this there is an inevitable
ludicrous quality which tends to conceal the underlying tragedy. It
should not do so. The tragedy was real, and must not be lost sight of
in digesting what follows here. Sir Osbert Sitwell, an indifferent
militarist, joined the Grenadier Guards shortly after the outbreak of
war. On December 16th 1914 German warships shelled Scarborough
and the Hartlepools, to the great scandal of the island race, and the
Sitwell family home came under fire, to the great scandal of Osbert
Sitwell's father, Sir George Sitwell, who at once wrote to his son:

My Dearest Osbert,
    As I fear a line sent to Chelsea Barracks may not reach you
before you leave tomorrow, I write to you, care of your regiment,
B.E.F., so that you may find a letter waiting for you when you

arrive in the trenches. But I had wanted if possible to give you a word of advice before you left. Though you will not, of course, have to encounter anywhere abroad the same weight of gunfire that your mother and I had to face here—it has been my contention for many years that there are no guns in the world to compare for weight and range with the great German naval guns, and that our own do not come anywhere near them—yet my experience may be useful to you. Directly you hear the first shell, retire, as I did, to the Undercroft, and remain there quietly until all firing has ceased. Even then, a bombardment, especially as one grows older, is a strain upon the nervous system—but the best remedy for that, as always, is to keep warm and have plenty of plain, nourishing food at frequent but regular intervals. And, of course, plenty of rest. I find a nap in the afternoon most helpful, if not unduly prolonged, and I advise you to try it whenever possible.

Ever your loving father,
George R. Sitwell.[1]

This is, of course, a somewhat extreme case of unshared awareness. But it was by no means an isolated case. Possibly the most significant fact about the 1914–1918 war is that it summoned to its bondage classes of the British population which had scarcely been touched directly by war for at least a century. The working-class and the wide spectrum of middle-classes which has been for so long such a distinguishing feature of British society, were all new to it. So was that portion of the upper-class which traditionally found soldiering the occupation of boors.[2] The Voluntary System had kept real involvement with war to a very small proportion of the people. Now, as larger numbers began to find out what the thing was, contact died between that section and those who remained what it had once been. It did not take bombardments to produce breakdowns of communication between men sincerely desiring to communicate. The *Times* on September 29th produced what may remain (despite even Sir George Sitwell) the classic exhibition of misapprehension. On that day it devoted a whole column to

MARCHING SONGS
New Words to Old Tunes

A correspondent, 'A.C.A.', whose initials recall the schooldays of a good many officers in His Majesty's Forces, sends us the following marching songs to old tunes, written, as he says, in the simplest

---

[1] From *Laughter in the Next Room*, by Osbert Sitwell; Macmillan 1949.
[2] See p. 40 et seq.

words possible, and such as a private soldier might think and write
for himself.

'A.C.A.' was Arthur Campbell Ainger, M.A., M.V.O. (b. 1841,
Eton, Trinity College, Cambridge; classics). He was an assistant
master at Eton from 1864 to 1904—hence the reference to 'the
schooldays of a good many officers'—and subsequently became Hon.
Sec. of the Old Etonians' Association. His published works included
school-books, and *Eton Songs* and *Eton: An Anthology of Prose and
Verse*. He had also composed hymns, of which the best-known was
'God is working His purpose out'. What he now offered, for the free
use of the British Army, was a selection of potential hit-numbers,
beginning with (to the tune of 'The Keel Row'):

> He tore the scrap of paper,
> The Belgian scrap of paper,
> He tore the scrap of paper,
> And bade the bullets fly.

> *Chorus:*

> So now we're off to Berlin,
> To Berlin, to Berlin.
> So now we're off to Berlin,
> To ask the reason why.
>   (etc., etc.)

Mr. Ainger appears to have had a Berlin-fixation; to the air, 'Cheer,
Boys, Cheer', he suggested:

> March, boys, march, along the road to Berlin,
> Singing, and cheering, and seeking all the way
> A wild cat whose moustaches went uncurling,
> A man-eating tiger, brought at last to bay. . . . (etc.)

Still preoccupied with European travel, to the air 'John Peel':

> D'ye ken John French, with his khaki suit,
> His belt and gaiters, and stout brown boot,
> Along with his guns, and his horse, and his foot,
> On the road to Berlin in the morning.

> *Chorus:*

> Yes we ken John French, and old Joffre too,
> And all his men to the Tricolor true,
> And Belgians and Russians, a jolly good few,
> On the road to Berlin in the morning. . . . (etc.)

There were others besides,[1] among them what some may consider the *tour-de-force*, to the tune of 'Here's to the Maiden', which, however, provoked a response which the composer had not expected. Before we refer to that response, however, it is worth noting *en passant* an article by the *Times* Music Critic (H. C. Colles) which appeared on October 5th, under the heading 'Music and the War':

> Musical composers and writers of patriotic verse have hastened to lay their offerings at the feet of the Prince of Wales for the benefit of the National Relief Fund. These offerings include recruiting songs, patriotic songs, songs which make a direct appeal for support for the fund, and instrumental marches.
>
> In many cases we may look rather at the motive than the deed. No one will say a word against them; they will bring support to a good cause and do something to stir popular sentiment in the right direction. Still a song can do more than this. When a verse and a tune ring true in themselves and are at the same time the sort of thing which can be taken up by a thousand voices, something follows the stir of sentiment. Such a song may send men to join the colours or to write cheques, but it certainly makes them better and healthier human beings. . . .

Mr. Colles warmly commended a collaboration between Henry Newbolt and Sir Charles Stanford, 'The King's Highway', which was about the Navy; 'Anyone can strum it on the piano; everyone can shout the chorus, but not everyone could have made it up'. He also liked 'Fall In!' by Harold Begbie and Sir Frederic Cowen, but even better Mr. Begbie's 'The Homes They Leave Behind'. There was also Mr. Cyril Scott's 'Britain's War March': 'Popular tunes, such as "Rule, Britannia", "See the Conquering Hero Comes", "La Marseillaise", and "God Save The King", are all worked into the texture of characteristic "Scotian" harmonies. Mr. Scott is showing that even our musical explorers who seek the darkest regions of harmony may feel the thrill of patriotism.'

But already a discordant note had been struck. A correspondent signing himself H. L. (actually a *Daily Mail* reporter called Harold Lake) had written to the *Times* on October 1st:

> Sir,
>   You print this morning a series of marching songs offered for the use of our soldiers. In an editorial you say that 'if our soldiers choose to sing them, they seem to us to be worthy of the honour'. The writer of the words, 'A.C.A.', says that he has written in the

---

[1] Connoisseurs of curiosity will find the full versions in Appendix II.

simplest words possible, such as a private soldier might think and write for himself.

When a writer of eminence and distinction strives so valiantly to lend his powers to the service of common people, it seems ungracious to emphasize the fact of his failure, but this matter of soldiers' songs is really worth considering. When I read the verses of 'A.C.A.' I knew at once that no soldiers would ever sing them, but at first I could not understand why. And then, reading them a second time, I came across the explanation. In the second verse of the last of the songs, your correspondent has written:

'Here's to Lord Kitchener, brown with the sun,
　　Gentle, persuasive, and balmy.'

Whether or not those adjectives describe Lord Kitchener's nature accurately I should not like to say, nor does the accuracy of the description matter very much. The point to be considered is that, in his innocence, 'A.C.A.' has endeavoured to teach the private soldier to insult the Secretary of State for War. 'Balmy' is a word which has no place in the dictionary of Tommy Atkins, but he knows uncommonly well another word of similar sound, which is, I believe, rendered in print as 'barmy', and means imbecile, half-baked, cracked, dotty or lunatic.

Just because 'A.C.A.' did not know or had forgotten the significance of this particular word it was impossible for him to write acceptably for soldiers. You cannot write down to Tommy Atkins. If you do not see life as he sees it and use words as he uses them to express ideas which you share with him you cannot write for him at all.

One could write a column or two on the verses of 'A.C.A.' in particular, and on this subject in general, but it will, perhaps, suffice if I give instead the latest popular marching song from Aldershot. The tune is a wild jumble of half a dozen music-hall airs, and the words are the work of a sergeant of the Gordon Highlanders.

'Send out the Army and the Navy,
Send out the rank and file.
　(Have a banana!)
Send out the brave Territorials,
They easily can run a mile.
　(I don't think!)
Send out the boys of the girls' brigade,
They will keep old England free;
Send out my mother, my sister, and my brother,
But for goodness sake don't send me.'

It is rubbish, of course, but it is Tommy's idea of a marching song—and he sings it.

Yours, &c,
H.L.

This, of course, was exceedingly wounding; but before we pass to the retort of Mr. Ainger, delivered in his own inimitable style on October 3rd, there are one or two considerations worth dwelling upon. First, there is the fact that Harold Lake, although vastly more in touch with reality than Ainger, nevertheless had to read these effusions through twice before he understood what was wrong with them, instead of just laughing himself sick. Secondly, there is the fact that either Lake or the *Times* Correspondence Editor felt impelled to bowdlerise. It has to be admitted that the Army's songs do usually need a certain amount of editorial treatment. A fairly forthright collection of them which appeared in 1931[1] rendered Mr. Lake's specimen as follows:

> Send out the Army and the Navy,
> Send out the rank and file,
> Send out the brave Territorials,
> They'll face the danger with a smile
>   (I don't think!)
> Send out my mother,
> Send out my sister and my brother,
> But for Gawd's sake don't send me!

This is a good deal better, but no doubt there were other versions too. The third point, and this is very much a consideration for our age, is the date at which this song had already become popular—September 1914. With the war less than two months old, there were only three categories of men who could be singing it, and internal evidence seems to rule out one of them. Either it was a product of the Regular Army, which existed for the sole purpose of being 'sent out' anywhere at any time, or it was a product of the Territorials (which I do not believe), or it was a product of the New Army, the most enthusiastic and patriotic mass of volunteers that Britain has ever produced, not one of them possessing any vestige of direct experience of the war they had joined up to fight. It is therefore a superb illuminant of the true meaning of the apparently 'disenchanted' soldiers' songs of the First World War. There is no disenchantment; there cannot be; merely the habitual sardonic humour of the soldier. One wonders whether some of those involved in, say,

---

[1] *Songs and Slang of the British Soldier: 1914–1918*, edited by John Brophy and Eric Partridge; Scholastic Press 1931.

the famous musical entertainment 'Oh What a Lovely War' were
fully aware of this.

With that much said, it is time to turn back to the next act in the
drama of the *Times* correspondence columns—A. C. Ainger's reply
to Harold Lake:

Sir,

It is not for me to criticize my critics, and I quite agree with
'H.L.' that my verses will have the fate they deserve. With regard
to the word he specially finds fault with, may I say that its use
was due not to the 'innocence' of the writer but to the exigencies
of rhyme, and as the whole line in which it occurs is (obviously)
good-humouredly ironical, I thought it might pass!

But the latter part of his letter raises an interesting question.
Naturally the soldier sings the last music-hall songs. As a rule
they have good tunes and amusing words. But 'H.L.' proceeds to
quote a verse from a sergeant in the Gordon Highlanders which
he says is 'Tommy's idea of a marching song'. Is it his only idea of
one? If so—which I do not admit for a moment—then it is clearly
useless for any sane person to try to write marching songs for him:
his only laureate must be the village idiot.

Yours faithfully,
A.C.A.

(This verdict was, of course, subsequently cordially endorsed by the
soldiers of all descriptions:

> What did you join the Army for?
> Why did you join the Army?
> What did you join the Army for?
> You must have been bloodywell barmy.)

The last word in the debate was uttered by a new-comer, 'C.S.',
who introduced a fresh thought on October 8th:

... Your correspondent 'H.L.' ... has unconsciously placed a
weapon in the hands of the German Press.

> 'Send out my mother, my sister and my brother,
> But for goodness sake don't send me!'

Think how this will read, duly translated into German! ... What
will escape observation in Germany is that we have here an
admirable illustration of the difference between a nation which
has a sense of humour and one which has not.

On that happy note we might leave the whole thing, except that
there is a serious element beneath all this pompous idiocy. It has

seemed worth displaying this extraordinary exercise in futility at some length because it would be difficult to find a better illustration of the disintegration of communication which the war caused in Britain. There is, of course, a class factor to be reckoned with. Mr. Ainger, 'C.S.', even Harold Lake, and their *Times* readers would at any time have found communication with the 'lower classes' difficult. But this is not, ultimately, a class question. Men drawn from exactly the Ainger stratum (yes, even Old Etonians) under the pressure of the war quickly found that their affinities were with the songs their comrades (of all ranks) were singing, and not with the uncomprehending people at home. No doubt the following epitome of all the songs (for me, anyway) was sung far more by soldiers than by officers. But let no-one suppose that officers did not sing it, or hum it appreciatively while their men roared it out:

> I don't want to be a soldier,
> I don't want to go to war.
> I'd rather stay at home,
> Around the streets to roam,
> And live on the earnings of a—lady-typist.
> I don't want a bayonet in my belly,
> I don't want my bollocks shot away.
> I'd rather stay in England,
> In merry, merry England,
> And fornicate my bloody life away.

Just as long as we remember that such were the sentiments which carried them 'over the top'. . . .

If, through the fog of war, the British people found it so difficult to understand those who were closest to them, it is not surprising that they found their enemies hard to perceive. Lacking helmeted Germans, with arms in hand, they began to find Germans hidden under extraordinary disguises. As early as August 11th Michael MacDonagh recorded:

That jade Rumour has begun to flap her wings. London is said to be full of German spies. Popular resentment against German tradesmen, principally bakers, provision dealers, watchmakers, waiters and barbers, has developed in some instances into wrecking their shops. It is said that German purveyors of food are putting slow poison in their commodities. As for the barbers, it is said you run the risk of having your throat cut by them instead of your hair.

In reality all I could discover as I walked about the town is that in the windows of German provision shops such *delicatessen* as *Sauerkraut* and liver-sausage are now labelled 'Good English

Viands', and that Union Jacks are being flown over the doors. . . .
But these precautions did not save some of the shops in the East
End from being plundered. . . .[1]

The absence of news and hard reporting of the fighting through
September and into October helped to make their unseen enemies
horribly real to the British public. On October 15th the *Times*
elevated the subject of spies to the dignity of a first leader, criticising
Home Office inaction. This became a running theme, a daily preoccupation. On the 17th there was a centre-page news story about the
arrest of 20 Germans in Willesden. A German printing firm was
discovered with an 'uninterrupted view as far as the Crystal Palace
over a great part of the London area'. What was so particularly
sinister about this establishment was that it possessed floors and
foundations of thick concrete, with a roof of the same material 10 to
12 inches thick, supported by two 3-inch girders. Was this a preparation for gun-emplacements? A letter on the same day said:

> . . . To anyone who, like your correspondent, has spent half a
> life-time in Germany, the claim to have broken up their spy-
> organization reads like a joke. . . .

The almost unbelievable truth was that 'the German espionage
system was broken up by the arrest of all the master-spies within an
hour or two of the outbreak of war'[2]—but naturally the authorities
could hardly say so. As a result, agitation, frequently highly embar-
rassing for the Government, continued to clamour. On October 19th
a *Times* third leader proclaimed:

> Public dissatisfaction with the Home Office in regard to the
> question of enemy aliens is rising to a flood. . . . It is evident that
> neither the Home Office nor the police, who are its advisers, have
> grasped the situation. What they have in mind is the professional
> spy in peace-time. . . .

This, of course, was perfectly true, since only the well-lodged, well-
briefed professional, with established communication-lines, could
constitute a menace. But nothing would assuage the amateur spy-
hunters, and a belated awakening to technology produced a spate of
letters about what was called 'Wireless Spying'. On October 21st
the *Times* reported the discovery of a 'wireless station' at Kirkcaldy,
and a factory at Brixham with the dreaded concrete floors no less
than 6 feet thick. No more was heard about the 'wireless station',

---

[1] *In London During the Great War*, p. 15.
[2] Lord Hankey: *The Supreme Command 1914–1918;* Allen & Unwin 1961,
pp. 166–167.

and it was almost with regret that, a few days later, it had to be admitted that the Brixham floors had proved, on inspection, to be only 6–8 *inches* thick. To those who knew something about the subject, all this could be mildly amusing. Major-General Sir Charles Callwell, then serving at the War Office, wrote later:

> During many months of acute national emergency, while the war was settling into its groove, there was no more zealous, no more persevering, and no more ineffectual subject of the King than the Self-Appointed Spy-Catcher. You never know what ferocity means until you have been approached by a titled lady who has persuaded herself that she is on the track of a German spy. We Britons are given to boasting of our grit in adversity and of our inability to realize when we are beaten. In no class of the community were these national traits more conspicuous in the early days than in the ranks of the amateur spy-catching fraternity and sisterhood— for the amateur spy-catcher never caught a spy. Only after months of disappointment and failure did these self-appointed protectors of their country begin to abandon a task which they had taken up with enthusiastic fervour, and which they had prosecuted with unfaltering resolution. Although it was at the hands of the despised professional that enemy agents were again and again brought to face a firing party in the Tower ditch, the amateurs entertained, and perhaps still entertain, a profound contempt for the official method. One fair member of the body, indeed, so far forgot herself as to write in a fit of exasperation to say that we must—the whole boiling of us—be in league with the enemy, and that we ought to be 'intered'.[1]

Eccentricity, of course, was playing its part in all this—touches of madness, abetted by the busybody instinct which comes so easily to the surface in emergencies. But there was more to it than that; there was also a guilt-complex, which was strongest (or should have been) among those who had most resolutely averted their eyes from the possibility of war with Germany. The *Times* admitted as much editorially on October 23rd:

> We know now that those who believed in the warlike intentions of Germany were right, and that those who did not were suffering from 'peace mania'. So it is with the present question of resident Germans. The mania is on the side of those who think them harmless. . . .

So the new national pastime continued to gain impetus—a product,

---

[1] *Experiences of a Dugout*, pp. 33–34.

as perceptive men like Michael MacDonagh observed, of the shock
of being at war to an unprepared public:

> Their nerves are still jangling, and they are subject to hallucina-
> tions. They seem to be enveloped in a mysterious darkness,
> haunted by goblins in the form of desperate German spies, and
> they can find no light or comfort afforded them by Press or Govern-
> ment. What is it but a bad attack of hysteria—coupled with a
> decline of humour and a rise in the disposition to believe in
> impossibilities under war stress?
>
> The wildest stories are being circulated by these people of
> outrages committed by Germans in our midst. Attempts have been
> made to destroy the permanent ways of railways and wreck trains!
> Signalmen in their boxes, armed sentries at bridges, have been
> overpowered by bands of Germans who arrived speedily on the
> scene and, their foul work done, as speedily vanished! Germans
> have been caught red-handed on the East Coast, signalling with
> lights to German submarines. Carrier pigeons have been found in
> German houses! More damnable still, bombs have been discovered
> in the trunks of German governesses in English county families!
> The fact that these things are not recorded in the newspapers does
> not prove them untrue—at least not to those subject to spy mania.
> What about the Press Censorship? The Government deny that
> there is any foundation whatever for the rumours; but then the
> Government—these people argue—are not going to admit what
> everybody knows them to be—footlers, blind as bats to what is
> going on around them. Why, they have even failed to see that
> tennis courts in country houses occupied by Germans were really
> gun platforms![1]

That was part of MacDonagh's diary entry for October 28th.
The agitation to intern all aliens without further ado was at its
height. MacDonagh noted that it had now reached to naturalised
British subjects of German or Austrian origin—'some of them men
eminent in commerce and the professions. It is argued that as spies
and traitors are not normally scrupulous, naturalisation may be but
a cover for the most nefarious practices'. Injustices and imbecilities
were bound to follow. Lord Hankey records 'the astonishment of
the official world on learning that enemy aliens had been arrested
right and left in London, including one very distinguished financier
of German parentage, who was wholly British in sympathy, and
whose firm it was important to keep in being from a financial point
of view'. Lesser people, no less loyal to the country of their adoption,

---

[1] *In London During the Great War*, pp. 32–33.

but lacking the 'pull' to make the official world take notice of them, suffered indignity, hardship and much grief through the cruelty of the masses under the tutelage of a disgraceful Press. It was evident that tragedy and national disgrace would not be long deferred. They duly transpired on the very next day, October 29th.

In 1914 the sea was Britain's element, the Royal Navy her pride. There was a good deal of sentimentality about the Army (for and against); it was expected to produce its traditional 'thin red line of heroes'—but no-one would be greatly surprised to discover that 'someone had blundered' also. A Balaklava or two might well ensue— was that not also part of the British tradition? (Few suspected that it was a part of the tradition which many of the officers of 1914 wholeheartedly despised. Few took note of Lord Haldane's reference, in his first speech as Secretary of State for War in 1906, to the 'new school of young officers, entitled to the appellation of men of science just as much as engineers or chemists . . .'. Few pondered his further words: 'A new school of officers has arisen since the South African War, a thinking school of officers who desire to see the full efficiency which comes from new organisation and no surplus energy running to waste'.) To a public of amateurs, amateurism in the Army was normal. The Navy was different. The Navy was the 'professional' service, and the proposition that Britannia ruled the waves by right was scarcely questioned.

By October 1914 those who thought in such terms (a very large number) were somewhat at a loss. The Army had taken and held the limelight; such illumination as the Navy had received had been fitful, and occasionally disturbing. At the very beginning of the war, two important German units in the Mediterranean, the *Goeben* and the *Breslau*, had escaped a British squadron into the sanctuary of Constantinople, where they would certainly do much mischief. The German cruiser *Emden* was having an astonishing run of success as a raider in the Bay of Bengal. Worst of all, on September 22nd, a German U-boat sank, one after another, the three old cruisers *Hogue*, *Aboukir* and *Cressy*, off the Dutch coast. What were they doing there, without escort? Many questions were asked about the incident, and about other naval matters. On October 23rd, F. S. Oliver recorded:

In addition to the public, I think the Admiralty had an attack of nerves last week. It is rather difficult to make head or tail of what is happening, but I think one thing is clear—Winston is too self-confident and forgets he is only a civilian. . . .[1]

A week later he had more cause for discontent:

[1] *The Anvil of War*, p. 45.

At least three days ago (I rather think four) one of our biggest
and newest Dreadnoughts, the *Audacious*, was sunk by a mine
off the coast of Ireland. This had not yet been acknowledged, or
even hinted at, in any newspaper and yet thousands of people
have heard as a rumour what I know as a fact.[1]

It was indeed a fact, witnessed by the passengers of a passing liner
on her way to Liverpool; many of them took dramatic photographs
of the sinking—yet the Censorship was justified, because the
Germans only learnt of their success five weeks later. But the net
result of all these events was an uneasiness in the public mind, and
a fear that this might spread to the Navy itself. In conjunction with
the spy scare, and the angry agitation against aliens, the alarm
focussed itself around one man: the First Sea Lord, Prince Louis
of Battenberg, and on October 29th he resigned. Michael MacDonagh
recorded:

> An eminent personage, one within the Royal circle, has fallen a
> victim to the spy mania. . . . The Prince is Austrian,[2] but is
> generally supposed to be of German origin. He became a naturalised
> British subject when he was fourteen, and has had a most dis-
> tinguished career in the Navy.[3] Two years ago he was appointed
> First Sea Lord. . . . It was galling to the spy hunters—all 100 per
> cent Britons—that such a highly important post should be filled
> by an alien in war-time.[4] The *Globe*, a London evening newspaper,
> led the outcry for his resignation or dismissal.
>
> The 'whispering campaign'—an ugly feature of the time—was
> turned against the Prince. The nature of the stories told of him
> may be imagined when I mention it was said and believed he was
> confined in the Tower on a charge of treason. History does repeat
> itself—now and then. During the Crimean War a crowd assembled

[1] Ibid., p. 47.
[2] Incorrect; Prince Louis was the son of Prince Alexander of Hesse, a
professional soldier who rose to high rank, first in the Russian Army, and
later in the Austrian Army. But Hesse is part of Germany.
[3] Prince Louis joined the Royal Navy in 1868.
[4] It is curious how selective prejudice can be. As far as I know, no agitation
was ever levelled against the Master-General of Ordnance (despite manifest
deficiencies in that department) although his name was Sir Stanley von
Donop. Nor did anyone appear to mind the 15th Infantry Brigade of the
B.E.F. being commanded by Brigadier-General A. E. W. Count Gleichen.
As Lord Mountbatten somewhat bitterly recalls, when his father resigned
one newspaper carried a harsh attack on him on one page, and on another
the report of the first death of a member of the Royal Family in action—
his nephew, Prince Maurice of Battenberg, King's Royal Rifle Corps,
killed at Ypres.

on Tower Hill to see the Prince Consort being brought to the Tower manacled and shackled hand and foot as a traitor. Oh, the indignation of the people at being disappointed of the spectacle. They believed they had full justification for demanding his blood!

The virulence of the campaign against Prince Louis of Battenberg may be judged by the following extract from Horatio Bottomley's despicable organ, *John Bull* (October 24th):

Blood is said to be thicker than water; and we doubt whether all the water in the North Sea could obliterate the blood ties between the Battenbergs and the Hohenzollerns when it comes to a question of a life and death struggle between Germany and ourselves.[1]

And so it came about that, with emotions which can be conjectured without too much difficulty, this fine officer was impelled to write to his political master:

October 28, 1914

Dear Mr. Churchill,

I have lately been driven to the painful conclusion that at this juncture my birth and parentage have the effect of impairing in some respects my usefulness on the Board of Admiralty. In these circumstances I feel it to be my duty, as a loyal subject of His Majesty, to resign the office of First Sea Lord, hoping thereby to facilitate the task of the administration of the great Service, to which I have devoted my life, and to ease the burden laid on H.M. Ministers.

I am,
Yours very truly,
Louis Battenberg,
Admiral.

[1] It would be hard to match the fatuity of this comment. The last act in the military career of Prince Louis's father, Prince Alexander of Hesse, was command of an army corps in the war of 1866, between Austria and other South German states against Prussia. Hesse took the Austrian side. The South Germans were beaten in seven weeks by Prussian military efficiency, and part of Hesse was annexed by the victors. Two years later Prince Louis came to England.

John Bull, of course, was in a class by itself. D. H. Lawrence called it a 'bloated ignominy', and added:

No man who has really consciously lived through this (war) can believe again absolutely in democracy. No man who has heard reiterated in thousands of tones from all the common people during the crucial years of the war: 'I believe in *John Bull*. Give me *John Bull*', can ever believe that in any crisis a people can govern itself, or is ever fit to govern itself. During the crucial years of the war, the people chose, and chose Bottomleyism. Bottom enough.

(*Kangaroo*.)

Churchill's own feelings may also be imagined; they were fully shared by the Prime Minister, Mr. Asquith. His daughter, Lady Asquith of Yarnbury (Lady Violet Bonham-Carter) speaking on Television shortly before her death in 1969, recorded:

> My father was appalled; he felt degraded. He felt that it was a stain on his own honour to accept this resignation, and yet he and Winston agreed, regretfully, reluctantly, that it was inevitable.[1]

Replying to Prince Louis's letter on October 29th, Churchill wrote: 'This is no ordinary war but a struggle between nations for life or death. It raises passions between races of the most terrible kind. It effaces the old land-marks and frontiers of our civilization. . . .'[2] This was no less than the truth—a truth which would become more evident as each year of war passed by. The *Times*, in which both letters were published, commented on the resignation in a third leader on October 30th:

> We regret it because (Prince Louis's) action is unquestionably the result of a campaign of suggestions—part of it honest if ill-timed— part of it monstrously unjust—against his remaining head of the Navy in present circumstances. . . . Gossip of this kind is, we suppose, an inevitable concomitant of democratic Government. It exhibits none the less its most contemptible side, and honest men will not care to remember its results in this case. . . .

It was perhaps a little late for such sentiments. In the correspondence which naturally followed, Admiral Hay remarked that the whole episode must be 'German work', and Lord Selborne, a previous First Lord, described it as a 'national humiliation'. This it certainly was, but the remorse awakened did not save the country from another, just as bad.

One great victim was not enough for a democracy which had tasted blood. With uncanny accuracy, the sacrificial knife was throughout directed by the manipulators of public opinion against the one man who had done, if anything, more than Prince Louis of Battenberg to prepare his country for war: Lord Haldane. When war broke out, Haldane was Lord Chancellor. Asquith was combining the responsibilities of Prime Minister and Secretary of State for War—but this

---

[1] *The Life and Times of Lord Mountbatten*, Programme 1, produced by Rediffusion Television, and screened by Thames Television on January 1st 1969.
[2] For full text see Appendix III.

was evidently not a situation which could continue.[1] Those who knew what Haldane had achieved there very naturally wished to see him take back the War Office, now that it faced the test towards which all his preparations had been aimed. Thus, on August 4th, the day war was declared, almost the first thought in the mind of General Haig was a letter to Haldane:

> ... I make so bold as to write and express a hope that you will, even at great personal inconvenience, return to the War Office for as long as war lasts and preparations are necessary. No one knows the details of the problem of organization as you do! ... What I feel is that we have such a mass of undeveloped power which no one knows better than yourself how to organize and control. This will be impossible if the bulk of our highly trained regular officers are at once carted off to France and a Secretary of State is appointed who is new to the existing system. I do hope that you will set to work at once to complete the organization you started in 1906.

It is already too late. It is evident, from the way he wrote, that Haig had an inkling of what was going to happen, and that it offended his wisdom. Partly because of the accident of Lord Kitchener being in the country at that critical moment, a powerful demand had arisen that this great 'organiser' should be installed as a non-party Secretary of State for War. It was only informed men like Haig who could appreciate the danger of leaning on a man who was 'new to the existing system'. And even Lord Kitchener's most intimate associates had yet to learn the truth which one of them, Sir Ian Hamilton, later expressed:

> Although Lord Fisher and a hundred others said, when they sought for some catch-phrase to explain Kitchener's success, that he was an organiser, history has now revealed to us what is the absolute, stark truth; he hated organisations; he smashed organisations. ... He was a Master of Expedients.

But Kitchener's tide was flowing strongly. The *Times*, prompted by

---

[1] It is a quite different matter, and, indeed, in modern conditions indispensable, for the Prime Minister to double up as Minister of Defence in war time. This makes him automatically preside over all crucial discussions of the war effort, enables him to balance the ideas put forward by different Services and Departments, and throw ultimate authority behind decisions taken. To saddle himself with the administration of a particular Office is to throw away these advantages and burden himself with trivia. This, at least, was a lesson learnt for World War II.

its powerful Military Correspondent, Repington, was entirely behind him:

> Lord Kitchener is a capable administrator and a first-rate organiser. He can also improvise new measures and deal faithfully with red tape. . . . The public have confidence in Lord Kitchener, and in a great war opinion counts for a great deal. . . .[1]

Kitchener's own reputation did the rest—much against his own wishes, it must be added. His biographer, Sir Philip Magnus, tells us how, in his attempts to escape back to Egypt, "Kitchener had gone as close as he ever went towards running away, because he was desperately anxious to avoid a summons to join the Government as Secretary for War'. But on August 5th Asquith took the critical decision. Was he to some extent influenced by the *Times* leader that day? It makes curious and unpleasant reading:

> We object to the selection of Lord Haldane for the War Office because, in our belief, and in the belief of the enormous majority of his countrymen, he is not the best man available for the post. . . . There are other objections to the appointment of Lord Haldane which we must state with absolute frankness, though with due qualifications. We do not doubt that England has a faithful patriot in the Lord Chancellor, and that if, like all of us, he contemplates the advent of this mighty conflict with sorrow and reluctance, he nevertheless faces it with calm readiness and resolute determination. But there are manifest difficulties about his translation to the War Office, the chief of which is that such a step might be seriously misconceived by France. Lord Haldane has been long and honourably known for his warm predilections for Germany. He was partially educated in that country, he has frequently spent his leisure there, his mind is coloured by his unremitting study of German literature and philosophy, he cherishes many close German friendships. These tendencies are natural and innocuous enough, but there are other and more important factors which, in our view, render him ineligible. He has been constantly strenuous in his efforts to promote Anglo–German friendship, and in pursuing this course he has unwittingly contributed to cloud British perception of the arrogant dominating aims of German national ambition. He has repeatedly been on confidential missions to Berlin, and we now see how fruitless and illusory these missions were. We in England know that Lord Haldane laboured with the best of motives, but France has watched his well-meant work with a keener understanding of

[1] *Times* third leader, August 4th 1914.

German intentions. France takes a simpler and more elementary view of his activities. To France Lord Haldane has seemed the friend of Germany, and she would regard his appointment to the War Office with dismay. . . .

Sheltering behind the smoke of 'French opinion', one of the most 'respectable' and influential newspapers in the country thus fired the first shots in what was to become a regular fusillade of assassination. Haldane, in the office of Lord Chancellor, was less exposed than Prince Louis as First Sea Lord, and so survived longer. But the hostility to him was as bitter, and ultimately as destructive. In his autobiography he tells us:

> Every kind of ridiculous legend about me was circulated. I had a German wife;[1] I was the illegitimate brother of the Kaiser; I had been in secret correspondence with the German Government; I had been aware that they intended war and had withheld my knowledge of this from my colleagues; I had delayed the mobilisation and despatch of the Expeditionary Force. All these and many other things were circulated. They could only have been effectively disposed of by the publication of documents, and to this the Foreign Office was at that time averse. The result was what might have been expected. The Harmsworth Press systematically attacked me, and other newspapers besides. Anonymous letters poured in. On one day, in response to an appeal in the *Daily Express*, there arrived at the House of Lords no less than 2,600 letters of protest against my supposed disloyalty to the interests of the nation. These letters were sent over to my house in sacks, and I entrusted the opening and disposal of the contents to the kitchenmaid.[2]

A seed well planted may bear prodigious fruit. Fifty years after this display of ignorant malice, in 1964, the *Times* was once again debating, in its correspondence columns, the fate of Haldane, and a later Lord Selborne, explaining why the Conservative Party had been so much against him, wrote that 'It was because Haldane was primarily responsible for having annually pared the Army Estimates to such a point that although he was able to send an Expeditionary Force in 1914, when it got there, it was quite insufficiently provided with guns and ammunition'. This, also, was one of the myths of the time. No-one, reading Lord Selborne's letter, would suppose that each division of the 1914 B.E.F. took to France 76 guns (French division, 36 guns; German division, 72), including 18 field howitzers and 4 heavy guns of types which the French regarded as unnecessary.

[1] Haldane was a life-long bachelor.
[2] Haldane: Autobiography, pp. 282–283.

Nor was there any ammunition shortage until the First Battle of Ypres, when all combatants suffered from it, but the British most of all, as might be expected from the *whole nation's* unmilitary frame of mind before 1914.

To return to that sad year: steadily the attacks on Haldane mounted. The sacrifice of Prince Louis did not appease the hatred-mongers. 'I was threatened with assault in the street, and I was on occasions in some danger of being shot at,' Haldane tells us. In the autumn he offered to resign, but Asquith 'laughed at the idea of this'. He did not laugh for long. The year 1914 ended in frustration; the war, which was to have been 'over by Christmas', had evidently stuck in a groove. Casualties mounted, after the heavy fighting at Ypres, to about 90,000 officers and men by the end of the year. To the British public, although it did not know the exact figures, the sense of loss was acute. The whole of the South African War, which lasted from 1899 to 1902, had cost 119,771 casualties, of which 75,000 were men invalided home through sickness; death in battle in South Africa had accounted for 5,774 officers and men in three years.[1] The cost of just over four months of war in 1914 thus had a terrible look. What the British did not know, what they find it almost impossible to grasp to this day, was that they had, in a sense, got off lightly nevertheless; no-one knows exactly what the war cost France in those few horrible months, for the figures available differ widely.[2] They would seem to have been not less than 600,000. According to the French Official History they reached 206,000 in

[1] Adjutant-General's return, submitted to the Royal Commission, 1903.
[2] M. Paul-Marie de la Gorce, in his book *The French Army* (Weidenfeld & Nicholson 1963) states (p. 103):
'There were 955,000 killed, wounded and captured in 1914. . . .' Marshal Joffre (*Memoirs*, Geoffrey Bles, 1932; vol. i, p. 323) quotes a note drawn up by his Operations Bureau on January 8th 1915. 'In an appendix to the note I gave the following figures: During less than five months of war the irrecoverable losses in our active and reserve armies (killed, prisoners, incurably wounded) amounted to 420,000 men. . . .' (It will be noted that this does not take into account 'recoverable' wounded, so that Joffre's figures may well tally with those of de la Gorce. An incomplete table of my own shows:

Month	Casualties	Source of information
August	206,515	French Official History.
September	213,444	Brig.-Gen. Sir J. E. Edmonds (British Official
October	83,109	Historian), *A Short History of World War I*,
November	77,868	OUP, 1951.

580,936

It will be noted that, even allowing as many losses in December as in November, this total would be well below the two French sources quoted above. But by any standard, France took terrible punishment in 1914, and this fact dominated Allied strategy thereafter.

the month of August alone; since operations did not really begin until August 8th, this ghastly total was reached in only twenty-four days—a rate of loss hardly equalled again by anyone during the war. There was, therefore, a grave disproportion between the losses of the two Allies—a fact which could not fail to affect relations between them for a long time. But as the bulk of the British casualties fell upon the infantry, they have to be compared with the figure of 84,000 infantry in the original B.E.F. to appreciate their impact on the public at the time.

1915 did not bring any good news worth having. The French winter and spring offensives failed with further heavy loss. A premature British offensive at Neuve Chapelle in March fell far short of its objectives, though presenting deceptively hopeful features. In April the Germans launched the Second Battle of Ypres, using poison gas for the first time; in the long-drawn-out struggle which followed their onslaught, the war attained a new grimness, and the British lost 60,000 officers and men merely to hold their ground. In the same month the Dardanelles Expedition (Gallipoli) made its inauspicious beginning at Anzac and Cape Helles; once again, high casualties brought little apparent gain, while a new theatre of war had come into existence with its own inexorable demands for reinforcement. Nor had the Navy, during all this time, immensely distinguished itself. True, in December it had avenged at the Falkland Islands the defeat of Coronel. The cruiser *Emden* had at last been put down by H.M.A.S. *Sydney*, and in January the old German cruiser *Blücher* was sunk at the Dogger Bank—but only at the cost of heavy damage to Admiral Beatty's flagship H.M.S. *Lion*. By May, a sequence of gloomy events was rocking the inner circles of Government. Asquith was forced to accept a Coalition with the Conservatives; their price was the removal of Churchill from the Admiralty, and the absolute exclusion of Haldane. In Churchill's hard words, Asquith did not hesitate to 'throw Haldane to the wolves'.

Sir Edward Grey wrote to Asquith on May 26th: 'It had, as you know, been my intention not to remain in the Government unless Haldane were included in it . . .'. He continued with a lengthy vindication of Haldane which, as his biographer says, was probably written for publication. It was not published, however, and Grey did remain in the Government. To be fair, he had attempted earlier to remonstrate with the Conservative Leader, Bonar Law, but without success; prejudice was too entrenched. Asquith replied to Grey's letter the following day:

May 27, 1915.

My dear Grey,

I have received your letter of yesterday. Like you, I more than

G

doubted whether I could find it possible to sit in a Cabinet in which Haldane was not to be included. He is the oldest personal and political friend that I have in the world, and, with him, you and I have stood together amidst all the turbulent vicissitudes of fortune for the best part of 30 years. Never at any time, or in any conjuncture, have the three of us seriously differed; and our old and well tried comradeship has been cemented during the last 10 years, when we have sat and worked together in the Government.

I agree with everything you say as to the injustice and malignity of the attacks to which, since the war began, he has been exposed. They are a disgraceful monument of the pettiest personal and political spite. . . .

Yet, as a recent writer has said,[1] despite the moving quality of these words (also, perhaps at first intended for publication), 'The tone of Grey's letter suggests that it was a struggle to persuade Asquith of the urgency of fighting to keep Haldane. And, in fact, much as Asquith clearly regretted dropping Haldane, there is no evidence that he fought at all hard with Bonar Law over this condition of the coalition; he hardly seems to have remonstrated about it. His tone in letters of this time was rather one of self-pity. . . .' Haldane himself responded to the event then and afterwards with perfect dignity. He did not reproach Asquith; he was concerned, certainly,

. . . but mostly on his account, for I saw the first signs appearing of the movement to displace him likewise, and I was not sure that he would not have done better if he had displayed more of an iron hand in maintaining his position and that of his colleagues.

That was as far as Haldane was prepared to go. The last word on this sordid passage of British political life may be left to Lord Esher, writing to Haldane on May 26th:

I am just back from G.H.Q. I must write a line to say how disgusted I feel with the base ingratitude of our country towards one who more than any living Englishman prepared for this appalling war.

Everyone who knows the facts acknowledges that without your fine preparative work we should have been powerless on land till now against Germany.

The wretched people at home know not what they say or do. The army knows.

[1] See *History Today*, July 1968: *Haldane and Asquith*, by William Verity.

VII

On May 25th 1915 the Liberal Government, which had been in power since 1906, came to an end: the formation of a Coalition Ministry was announced. A certain rough justice was at work: the Government had failed to give proper reporting facilities to the Press; it had failed to give a lead, and it had failed in control, despite censorship. Now the Liberals owed their demise, in substantial part, to yet another mishandled Press campaign. The 'trigger' of the event was a different subject; but the 'ammunition' was just precisely that— Ammunition.

On May 15th Lord Fisher, who had returned from retirement to replace Prince Louis of Battenberg as First Sea Lord in October 1914, resigned on a fundamental disagreement with Churchill about the Gallipoli Campaign. Always an eccentric, Fisher carried out the deed in his own incalculable manner. He not merely sent Churchill a note conveying his resignation, but when the latter went to find him,

> ... I found that he had entirely disappeared. He was not in the (Admiralty) building; he was not in his house. None of his people knew where he was except that he was going to Scotland at once. . . . I went over to the Prime Minister and reported the facts. Mr. Asquith immediately sent his Secretary with a written order commanding Lord Fisher in the name of the King to return to his duty. It was some hours before the First Sea Lord was discovered. He refused point-blank to re-enter the Admiralty or to discharge any function. . . .[1]

Nothing could shift Fisher from his determination, and of course it was impossible to conceal the resignation of the professional Head of the Navy on a vital question of war direction. Rumours reached the Opposition immediately, and on May 17th (as so often in British affairs, the sanctity of the weekend played its part: May 17th was a Monday) Bonar Law asked Lloyd George whether the rumours were true.

[1] Churchill: *The World Crisis.*

On being told by me that his information was correct Mr. Bonar
Law emphasised the grave nature of the political question raised,
*especially as he was convinced that the Government were misinformed
about the shell situation.*[1] His party had supported the Government
consistently throughout the months of the War, without seeking
party advantage, but there was a growing discontent amongst
Conservatives at this attitude of unqualified support, especially
over *the treatment of alien enemies,*[1] the deficiency of shells, and
the failure of the Dardanelles expedition. Matters indeed, had
come to such a pitch that it would be impossible for him to
restrain his followers, and yet it was essential to avoid any division
in the nation in face of the enemy. He was specially emphatic as
to the impossibility of allowing Mr. Churchill to remain at the
Admiralty if Lord Fisher persisted in his resignation. On this
point he made it clear that the Opposition meant at all hazards to
force a Parliamentary challenge. . . .[2]

So that was it: Coalition had to be accepted as by far the lesser
evil. Churchill had to go—and, as we have seen, Haldane went out
with him. It is the background of all this which now concerns us:
Bonar Law's reference to 'the shell situation', 'the deficiency of
shells'—for certainly it was this factor which put the Opposition
into the intractable mood reported by Bonar Law to Lloyd George.
On that very day there was a House of Commons debate on munitions,
in which the word 'shells' would engrave itself on the hearts of
Members as the word 'Calais' was engraved on the heart of Bloody
Mary. The same word was by then also engraved on the hearts of
soldiers and officers of the B.E.F., for, on the day Fisher resigned
(May 15th) the British First Army (Haig) had resumed its attempt
to give effective support to the French in their Second Artois
offensive. This battle has gone down in history as 'Festubert'—a
name of ill omen. In dismal, water-logged conditions, the British
lost, in the ten days of battle, over 16,000 casualties for a miserable
gain of ground. Added to the heavy losses of the Second Battle of
Ypres, which was in its final stages, this loss, though small, had a
depressing effect—depressing, and frustrating. The Official History
says:

> The German infantry, with its wonderful array of heavy howitzers,
> its numerous trench mortars and machine guns, and its most
> effective 'stick-grenades', was certainly admirable in the defence,
> but the British infantry, with far inferior means, had in 1914

[1] My italics.
[2] Lloyd George: *War Memoirs*, ch. viii.

obtained equally good results. The British commanders not un-
naturally felt that, given anything like the same artillery support
and the same equipment for close fighting that the enemy battalions
possessed, their infantry, even with its hastily trained subordinate
leaders, could be relied on in the attack to do better than the foe.
Unfortunately sufficient numbers of heavy guns, of high explosive
shell and of implements of trench warfare, were all lacking owing
to British unpreparedness for war. . . .[1]

The disappointment of Festubert, and the dismay engendered,
were merely the sequel to a transaction already begun. The French
Artois offensive, under General Foch, had started on May 9th (by
the time it ended, in mid-June, it cost the French over 100,000
casualties, beside which figure the British experience, though grim,
begins to pale). The British attempted to support their allies with
an attack on the Aubers Ridge (First Army); this was broken off
after twelve hours, during which almost no progress at all was made
at a cost of over 10,000 casualties. Colonel Repington, the *Times*
Military Correspondent, was visiting the B.E.F., and wrote:

Whereas . . . the French on our right in Artois, on May 9, used
240 rounds of H.E.[2] shell per field gun per day, and prepared
their attack by a violent and continuous bombardment lasting for
four hours, we could only afford forty minutes' similar bombardment; and while the German trenches in front of the French were
knocked to bits, those in front of us were not similarly treated.
Much barbed wire remained uncut, the German defences remained
but little injured, and the very numerous machine guns of the
enemy were not placed out of action. I witnessed the attack. We
obtained insignificant results at the cost of heavy loss. . . . I was
enraged by this loss which was attributed by the troops solely to
the failure of the guns, due in its turn to want of shells.

I therefore determined to expose the truth to the public, no
matter at what cost. I sent off to the *Times*, on May 12, without
consulting any one, a telegram which became famous, and stated,
amongst other things, 'that the want of an unlimited supply of
high explosive shells was a fatal bar to our success'. These words
were my own, and were not suggested by Sir John French . . .
away the fateful telegram went, dreadfully bowdlerised (by
Censorship), it is true, but still containing, in the one little phrase,
enough high explosive to blow the strongest Government of
modern times into the air.[3]

[1] *Military Operations, France and Flanders*, 1915, vol. ii, p. 79.
[2] High Explosive.
[3] Repington: *The First World War*, p. 36.

Repington exaggerates. It was not his telegram alone, as we have seen, that caused the fall of the Liberal Government. His exaggeration is not so bad as that of an American writer, who became excited enough to say: 'Never before perhaps in the history of the world, certainly of war, have sixteen words in a newspaper produced such epoch-making results'.[1] Nevertheless, on two counts, Repington does exaggerate: it is not merely that Fisher's resignation brought Conservative feeling to the boil, it is also a fact that his telegram to the *Times* was backed up by considerable behind-the-scenes activity. Interesting contrasts in methods are here revealed. This was a period of the war when intrigue of one kind or another was much in vogue, and accusations on that score have been bandied about ever since. The proceedings of May 1915 are worth a brief inspection from that point of view alone.

One of those most persistently accused of intrigue during the year was Haig, who supplanted Sir John French as C.-in-C. at the end of it. On May 9th, no doubt with perfectly straightforward intentions —it *was* the First Army's battle, after all—Repington came to see Haig, and learn his views. Haig disliked Repington, who had been forced to leave the Army some years before the war, on account of a scandal concerning the wife of a brother officer. The Army in those days was somewhat narrow-minded about such matters (even in World War II it clung to the belief that they tend to undermine mutual confidence). It was no pleasure to Haig to learn that Repington had arrived at his headquarters:

> In reply to a request to see me I said that neither I nor my staff had authority to see any newspaper correspondent and that all information for the Press must be obtained from G.H.Q.[2]

Sir John French had no such inhibitions. He not only showed Repington his full correspondence with the War Office on the subject of ammunition, but also sent his private secretary, Colonel Brinsley Fitzgerald, and his A.D.C., Captain Guest, to London to show the papers to Opposition leaders, as well as to Mr. Lloyd George. While they were about their work, the *Times* printed Repington's despatch; this was the opening salvo, and couched in relatively mild terms:

NEED FOR SHELLS
BRITISH ATTACKS CHECKED
LIMITED SUPPLY THE CAUSE

That was on May 14th; two days later, Repington himself returned to London, and saw Lloyd George, who was by now displaying what

[1] Ibid.
[2] Blake: *Private Papers of Douglas Haig*, p. 93.

he calls a 'special interest' in the subject of Munitions. Yet, according to Repington,

> ... he seemed to know nothing of what was happening. I gave to Lloyd George a hastily-drafted paper exposing all our deficiencies in munitions and guns of all types, and giving the history of the shortage. I had no need to make a further disclosure to the public, for I found a first-class political crisis in full blast. Having posted up Lloyd George with the facts, and having his promise that he would go straight to the Prime Minister, I saw Lord Curzon, Mr. Bonar Law, Sir Edward Carson, Sir F. E. Smith, and other Unionist leaders; and at dinner at Bonar Law's house, when Carson was present and F. E. came in later, I told them all I knew, and neither minced my words nor concealed my feelings. My exposure was fully sustained by the report which Sir John sent over. The Unionist Party informed the Prime Minister that there would have to be a debate, and the Prime Minister, realising that he had been inaccurately informed, that he would be beaten, and that he had no defence, ran for shelter under the Opposition umbrella and decided to accept the Coalition Ministry which a week before he had rejected with contumely.[1]

Repington's position in all this is understandable, and may be forgiven. He did not hold an official position; he was working for a newspaper; he was deeply concerned with the efficient prosecution of the war, and remained so. There *was* a deficiency of munitions; it *was* affecting the Army seriously. This is not the place to examine that subject in detail; it must be said, however, that Repington might have done better to have enquired more carefully into the War Office side of the question—though it must be added that Lord Kitchener was not a man to welcome such enquiries. Sir John French's position, however, was different. Kitchener wrote to him on May 14th:

> A good many remarks are being made about the *Times* correspondent who is apparently staying with you and writing to his paper. At the War Council today I heard for the first time that this was a fact. Until war correspondents are allowed by the Government, I do not think it is right for you to allow Repington to be out with the Army.[2]

French replied next day:

> Repington is an old friend of mine and has constantly stayed with

---

[1] Repington, p. 39.
[2] Quoted in **Magnus**: *Kitchener*.

me for the last 10 or 12 years. He was here for a day or two in
an entirely private capacity. I really have no time to attend to
these matters. . . .[1]

Sir Philip Magnus comments: 'Kitchener kept his temper with
difficulty; and the Press attacks continued for some weeks'. They
did indeed. On May 21st the *Daily Mail* carried the headlines:

THE SHELLS SCANDAL
LORD KITCHENER'S TRAGIC BLUNDER

It was by now the set policy of the Northcliffe Press, not content
with the heads of Prince Louis of Battenberg and Haldane, to pull
down Kitchener too. Lord Beaverbrook records how, one afternoon
in the Ritz Hotel, Northcliffe told him that it was his intention 'to
go on attacking Lord Kitchener day in, day out, until he had driven
him from office'. But the Press baron over-reached himself; all that
he achieved on this occasion was to have the *Daily Mail* burnt
publicly outside the London Stock Exchange, and an appreciable
drop in the circulation of the Northcliffe newspapers. Kitchener's
reputation with the nation at large was still impregnable. Haig,
hearing of these attacks, called them in his diary 'a most disgraceful
state of affairs' and wrote to Kitchener's personal military secretary
that 'in any well-governed country the editor of the *Times* would have
been placed against a wall and shot'.[2] The only satisfactory outcome
of the whole business was the creation of a Ministry of Munitions,
which was a necessity of modern war. Under the direction of Lloyd
George, and later of Winston Churchill, that Ministry ultimately
(but not suddenly) did invaluable work; yet, as Sir Charles Callwell
remarks,

> . . . it is a pity that unwarrantable claims should have been put
> forward on behalf of the department in not irresponsible quarters
> at a time when they could not be denied, claims which have
> tended to bring the department as a whole into undeserved
> disrepute amongst those who know the facts.[3]

So ended, in May 1915, the last important product of ill-thought-out,
irregular methods of projecting the war to the nation waging it. It
has to be stated that the tight-lipped personality of Lord Kitchener
himself had much to do with the disorders we have described. It is
ironical that in this very month a better system had been agreed;
it, too, as we shall see, had manifest defects, but at least it put an
end to a situation in which a well-known newspaper figure could

---

[1] Quoted in Magnus: *Kitchener*.
[2] Magnus.
[3] *Experiences of a Dug-out*, p. 207.

send explosive reports from the battlefront with the Commander-in-Chief's blessing in 'an entirely private capacity'.

It was in early May 1915, as a result of unremitting pressure by editors and newspaper proprietors, and with some Parliamentary backing, that the Government reversed its policy and agreed to permit accredited war-correspondents in the battle zones. Until then an absurd situation had persisted—an absurdity well illustrated by Repington's irregularities. The 'Amiens Dispatch' undoubtedly had much to do with it: at the time of the great alarm caused by that effusion, France was swarming with correspondents for the British newspapers, moving about with perfect freedom, and welcomed by Britain's allies, France and Belgium, even if regarded by the British Army with some suspicion. After the 'Amiens Dispatch' all that changed. One by one the correspondents were hounded out of the zone of operations. Some of them showed great resource in managing to hang on precariously for a time (living an almost outlaw existence, with several *pieds-à-terre*, and an elaborate courier system to get their reports back to England); but by January 1915 only two were still functioning regularly, and when these two were detected and expelled, then there were none. After that the only reporting by professional correspondents was on the rare occasions when a party of them was permitted to make a quick motor-tour, guided by a staff officer. One of the last two correspondents to survive, Mr. Basil Clarke, comments with some bitterness:

> There is little doubt that the British Government, advised by the then Controller of the Army, Lord Kitchener, who had singular views (views shared by none of his successors) with regard to the Press, was at the bottom of this joint allied arrangement for excluding newspaper representatives from all work in the zone of the armies. The earlier attitude of both France and Belgium showed clearly that no such policy had been contemplated by them at the outset. The persistence of the British Government in putting difficulties in the way of newspaper correspondents, while other allied countries were but luke-warm in the matter, tends to confirm the view that the British were the leaders in this crusade.[1]

Even Lord Kitchener, however, naturally secretive and unaccustomed to the workings of a democracy at war though he was, could not avoid making some gesture towards informing the public. The expedient which he adopted was characteristic: he tried to put the dissemination of news on a military footing. It was to be supplied

[1] Basil Clarke: *How the Progress of the War was Chronicled by Pen and Camera;* Amalgamated Press.

by an official 'Eyewitness', who would be attached to the Staff of the
Commander-in-Chief, would approach his task as a military duty,
and send his reports (after censorship at G.H.Q.) direct to the War
Office for Kitchener's personal approval before they were released
to the Press. 'One way and another, what finally passed ought to
have been fairly innocuous,' wrote the officer concerned. He did not
overstate the case.

The officer in question was Colonel (later Major-General) Sir
Ernest Swinton; he was a Royal Engineer, who had been Assistant
Secretary to the Committee of Imperial Defence until the outbreak
of war, when he received the appointment of Deputy Director of
Railways in the B.E.F. This post he only occupied until September
7th 1914, when Kitchener sent for him to tell him what his new
duties would be. The manner in which Swinton was selected was
also characteristic. He had written two books before the war under
the pseudonym, 'Ole Luk-Oie', and another, *The Defence of Duffer's
Drift* (on tactics, after the Boer War), under the pseudonym 'Back-
sight–Forethought', which had won a certain amount of attention.
There was a meeting to discuss who the official 'Eyewitness' should
be:

> ... Mr. Churchill suggested me as a suitable man for this post.
> My name conveyed nothing to Lord Kitchener, though I had
> served under him in South Africa and he had dealt with me directly
> on more than one occasion. When Mr. Churchill explained that I
> was the author of *The Defence of Duffer's Drift*, the Secretary of
> State gave instructions that I should be sent for at once to under-
> take this duty. This is the explanation of how a well-meaning
> officer of Engineers was suddenly snatched off a railway bridge to
> write articles about the British Army.[1]

Swinton continued until July 1915 to supply a regular flow of reports,
about twice a week, on what was happening at the Front. But his
status and his brief were both calculated to reduce the value of his
output. As he candidly informs us:

> The principle which guided me in my work was above all to avoid
> helping the enemy. This appeared to me even more important
> than the purveyance of news to our own people. For the Germans,
> therefore, I endeavoured to dispense doses of lowering medicine
> with a few drops of poison added where possible. For home
> consumption—that is for those who were carrying the burden and
> footing the bill—I essayed to tell as much of the truth as was
> compatible with safety, to guard against depression and pessimism,

[1] Swinton: *Eyewitness;* Hodder & Stoughton 1932, pp. 51–52.

and to check unjustified optimism which might lead to a relaxation of effort.[1]

General Swinton was a good writer, with a dry, humourous style—when he wrote for pleasure. His war reports, shackled by the principles with which he bound himself, do him little justice. Since they were the only steady, authoritative fodder by which the British public could nourish itself for many months, some examples are worth giving. First (September 18th 1914), Swinton's description of the beginnings of trench warfare on the Aisne:

> In order to convey some idea of the nature of the fighting it may be said that along the greater part of our front the Germans have been driven back from the forward slopes on the north of the river. Their infantry are holding strong lines of trenches amongst and along the edges of the numerous woods which crown these slopes. These trenches are elaborately constructed and cleverly concealed. In many places there are wire entanglements and lengths of rabbit fencing both in the woods and in the open, carefully aligned so that they can be swept by rifle fire and machine guns, which are invisible from our side of the valley. The ground in front of the infantry trenches is also as a rule under cross-fire from field artillery placed on neighbouring features and under high-angle fire from pieces placed well back behind woods on top of the plateau.
>
> . . . Where our men are holding the forward edges of the high ground on the north side they are now strongly entrenched. They are well fed, and in spite of the wet weather of the past week are cheerful and confident. The bombardment by both sides has been heavy, and on Sunday, Monday, and Tuesday was practically continuous. . . .[2]

Possibly Lord Kitchener and others in the War Office were able to make something of this. How the general public, untutored in military phraseology, would interpret this description of an unfamiliar mode of war which was jolting the Army itself, can only be conjectured. Captain Jack of the Cameronians was writing at the same time:

> The public at Home can never realise the repeated high trials sustained by regimental officers and men, nor the terrible conditions under which they carry out most of their duties here. . . .[3]

---

[1] Ibid., p. 53.
[2] *Eye-witness's Narrative of the War;* Edward Arnold 1915, pp. 13–14.
[3] *General Jack's Diary*, p. 55.

Certainly 'Eyewitness' would do little to help them. Here is the
gripping opening of his account of the supreme crisis of the First
Battle of Ypres, on November 11th:

> The diminution in force of what may by a paraphrase be described
> as the German *Drang nach Westen* in this quarter has not lasted
> long. The section of front to the north of us was the first to meet
> the recrudescence of violence in the shape of an attack by the
> enemy in the neighbourhood of Dixmude and Bixschoote. Our
> turn came next, and after eight days of a comparative relaxation
> of pressure—from Tuesday, the 3rd, to Tuesday, the 10th—the
> 11th saw a repetition of the great attempt to break through our
> line to the French coast.
>
> What was realized might happen has happened. In spite of the
> immense losses suffered by the enemy during the five days' attack
> against Ypres which lasted from October 29 to the 2nd of this
> month, the cessation of their more violent efforts on the latter day
> was not an abandonment of the whole project, but a temporary
> relinquishment of the main offensive until fresh troops should
> be massed to carry on what was proving to be a somewhat costly
> and difficult operation. . . .[1]

These are the battles which, a few weeks later, Haig was trying to
describe to the King:

> I told him of the crowds of fugitives who came back down the
> Menin Road from time to time during the Ypres Battle having
> thrown everything they could, including their rifles and packs, in
> order to escape, with a look of absolute terror on their faces, such
> as I have never before seen on any human being's face.[2]

With one last glimpse of his incomparable opacity, we shall have to
leave 'Eyewitness': the Battle of Neuve Chapelle on March 10th
1915 produced in him something almost bordering on a state of
excitement:

> At 7.30 a.m. on the 10th the battle began with a bombardment by
> a large number of guns and howitzers. Our men in the trenches
> describe this fire as being the most tremendous both in point of
> noise and in actual effect they have ever seen or heard. The
> shrieking of the shells in the air, their explosions and the con-
> tinuous thunder of the batteries all merged into one great volume
> of sound. The discharges of the guns were so rapid that they
> sounded like the fire of a gigantic machine gun. During the 35

[1] *Eye-witness's Narrative of the War*, p. 100.
[2] Haig's Diary, Dec. 4th 1914.

minutes it continued our men could show themselves freely and even walk about in perfect safety.

Then the signal for the attack was given, and in less than half an hour almost the whole of the elaborate series of German trenches in and about Neuve Chapelle were in our hands. Except at one point there was hardly any resistance, for the trenches, which in places were literally blotted out, were filled with dead and dying partially buried in earth and *débris*, and the majority of the survivors were in no mood for further fighting. . . .[1]

All in all, it was a strange war that 'Eyewitness' presented to the British people, via their newspapers. Well might one editor call his dispatches 'charmingly futile descriptions which used to tantalise the British public more than absolute silence would have done—always literary, always elegant, and always—magnificently uninformative'.[2]

In fairness to Sir Ernest Swinton, it must be added here that his mind was preoccupied with other matters than reporting. As a professional soldier, he was well aware (more than most) of the realities of war which he so successfully disguised from his newspaper readers. 'I shall not forget my first night at the Front,' he later wrote. The Battle of the Marne was three days old; Swinton joined G.H.Q. at Coulommiers, and very soon met an old friend—Brigadier-General J. E. B. Seely.[3] Seely told him about the crossing of the Marne by the British 11th Brigade, and the casualties sustained by the East Lacashire Regiment which Swinton knew well. 'But the feature of his narrative,' says Swinton, 'which struck a chord of greater compass than any that a sense of personal loss could produce, was the part played by the enemy machine guns cunningly placed and concealed. . . .' During the Battle of the Aisne, and the Race to the Sea which followed, this feature recurred again and again; the German machine gun was already an outstanding 'villain' of the war:

Our efforts to advance were in most cases frustrated by machine guns, frequently in combination with an obstacle hastily made from rabbit wire or fencing. The tale I had heard on my first night at Coulommiers daily received fresh confirmation. If our resourceful, industrious, and well-equipped opponents were able to accomplish so much in haste and with improvised means, what might they not do, given time, even with field defences? During the first week in October my mind continually returned to this. And, vaguely, I pictured to myself some form of armoured vehicle immune against bullets, which should be capable of destroying

[1] *Eye-witness's Narrative*, p. 278.
[2] Quoted by Basil Clarke.
[3] Ex-Secretary of State for War; later Lord Mottistone.

machine guns and of ploughing a way through wire. This picture, though not yet in focus and ill-defined, was the germ of the future Tank.[1]

It was the conjunction of Swinton's ideas and pressure with those of Churchill which gave Britain the Tank before any other nation—so he may perhaps be forgiven for some bad war-reports. But all this is a digression.

It was, as we have said, in early May 1915 that the system changed, and the Public Relations of the war were at last placed on a rational footing. Permanent Press correspondents were attached to the British armies to supply 'a regular service of war news'. Basil Clarke, of Amalgamated Press, was one of them, and has given a very clear picture of what sort of men they were, and how they worked. The Press Correspondents' Mess moved about according to the shifts of the Army's Advanced Headquarters. When Clarke joined it, it was in a château in the main street of St. Omer:

> In the château worked not only the correspondents, but also the Press officer and his assistant officers, a major, captains and lieutenants, and a staff of typists, orderlies, servants, and others. The correspondents had a room apiece upstairs, and shared writing-room, dining-room, and 'salon' downstairs. Most of them preferred to do their writing in the quiet of their own room, and at the close of a busy day on the front the polished wooden corridors of the château echoed to the merry patter of industrious typewriters.

Always, for each one of them on the Western Front, there was the inescapable reminder of why they were there, what the job was really about, and what made it different from any other assignment that they had ever known: 'the never-ceasing rumble of the distant guns'.

> ... they never ceased, day or night. Sometimes they rose to a banging tempest—you knew then that a 'strafe' was in progress. At other times, especially when the wind was contrary, they sank to a low murmur—constant, regular, and almost soothing, like the rumble of distant trains heard in a quiet countryside on a silent night.

The days of war could never exactly resemble each other, for men concerned with depicting every aspect of the face of war. In any case, 1914–1918 was a period unusually packed with novelties—shocks, excitements, disappointments, fear in a thousand shapes. Yet there was a rough pattern of life for the Press-men:

[1] *Eyewitness*, p. 64.

The correspondents' normal daily programme was to meet together after breakfast in a sort of conference, at which the Press officer, their colonel, presided. First, he announced to them in rough outline any development, changes in position, or actions that had taken place during the night. The correspondents themselves on this information decided their respective programmes for the day. The colonel's information usually made it clear in what districts of the front interesting developments had occurred, and they agreed mutually which of them should visit these districts and obtain full details of what had happened.

Their motor-cars and drivers were by this time waiting at the château gate, and soon they were radiating from the city of —— to different quarters of the front. Each car contained, besides one or more correspondents, an assistant Press officer, who served in a curious dual capacity as friend and monitor to the correspondents whom he accompanied. It might fall to this officer to shepherd a correspondent at the risk of his life over a shell-swept waste, or to chaperone him into the august presence of a British general, so that he might glean first-hand details of events that had happened in that general's area of command. Or it might fall to him to pass a quiet veto if the correspondent's innocence or enthusiasm led him to contemplate doing anything that 'should not be done'. So far as the writer observed them, they exercised this more unpleasant part of their function sparingly and kindly. In fact, they were excellent fellows. . . . Most of them were officers who through wounds had been invalided and put on 'light duty'—a euphemism under which might lurk many onerous and hazardous Army tasks. . . .

With good fortune a correspondent might arrive home in time for a cup of tea at 4.30 with his fellow-correspondents; and over the tea-cups the news gleanings of the day would be exchanged. . . . After tea each man went to his room to 'write up', putting the day's events in such perspective as seemed fitting to him. The news he had himself collected might be the most important of the day, or it might be overshadowed and dwarfed by facts which a colleague had collected.

. . . for the most part despatches were finished by dinner-time, for there was an additional goad to quickness of writing besides that of mere hunger. The despatches were either telegraphed to England—in which case they had to be brief—or they were carried by a King's Messenger who had to leave, of course, in time to catch the boat. The censoring of the despatches was done by the Press officers in the château itself, and they fixed each day a time at which all the despatches had to be in their hands. . . . Your

despatch, good or bad, complete or incomplete, had to be finished
by this time, unless, for some special reason affecting all correspondents alike, an extension of time had first been obtained. . . .[1]

Everything has to have a beginning; war-correspondents of later
times will recognise here the routines with which they themselves
became familiar. They will recognise also the human stresses which
their predecessors of 1915–1918 faced day in, day out:

> Time was short while the world waited for our tales of tragedy or
> victory . . . and tempers were frayed, and nerves on edge, among
> five men who hated each other, sometimes, with a murderous
> hatred (though, otherwise, good comrades) and desired each other's
> death by slow torture or poison-gas when they fumbled over
> notes, written in a jolting car, or on a battle-field walk, and went
> into past history in order to explain present happenings, or became
> tangled in the numbers of battalions and divisions. . . .[2]

So Philip Gibbs recalls a recurring scene—and Basil Clarke recalls
Philip Gibbs:

> Few men there are who can idle so unsatisfactorily as he. . . . A
> man of great sympathy is Gibbs; a man in whom the soul-wound
> caused by war and war's horror and war's suffering is ever fresh
> and raw. Such a war as this weighs heavy on a mind like that.

Philip Gibbs reported for the *Daily Chronicle*. Outstanding among
his colleagues was Perry Robinson of the *Times*, the oldest man of
the group of permanent correspondents—'a face strongly characteristic, a profile finely chiselled, grey hair and moustache of military cut,
strikingly contradicted by bushy eyebrows of jet black. When sentries
and guards on the road see that face in a passing motor-car they
automatically give a "general's salute".'[3] Perry Robinson, according
to Gibbs,

> liked detail, minute, accurate, geographical detail. He insisted
> upon it. He prepared the ground-work for incidents of battle, and
> went into the past history of divisions, and referred to ancient
> notes. When time was hurling by, and minutes became more
> precious than diamonds—the despatch-riders were waiting and
> the censors were sulking—he entered into strategical considera-
> tions or tried to discover a gap between two divisions, with grim
> and quiet persistence.

---

[1] Clarke: op. cit.
[2] Gibbs: *Realities of War;* Heinemann 1920, pp. 19–20.
[3] Clarke.

My impatience at such times became a real torture. I was more interested in the things I had seen than in map references and divisional boundaries. That typewriter of mine wanted a new ribbon. It would waste ten minutes more. Ten minutes, while the world waited for a narrative of astounding and dreadful things. . . .[1]

It is the true nature of a correspondent to suppose that the world waited for his next word; it would be a long war; there would be many words, sometimes monotonously familiar. Another colleague who succeeded in getting on Gibb's nerves without losing his affection was Beach Thomas of the *Daily Mail*. 'A love of letters and the classics,' wrote Basil Clarke, 'shares almost an equal place with his love of Nature, outdoor life and pastimes.' Sir William Orpen, who met them all in his capacity as a war-artist, wrote:

In my mind now I can look clearly from my room across the court-yard and can see Beach Thomas by his open window, in his shirt-sleeves, writing like fury at some terrific tale for the *Daily Mail*. It seemed strange his writing this stuff, this mild-eyed, country-loving dreamer; but he knew his job.[2]

'Dear old Beach Thomas,' adds Gibbs,

gazing behind his gold-rimmed glasses, like the God Pan watching a distant wood-nymph, why did he tap out a silly rhythm with his long brown fingers on a bony knee? Why did he let his green arm-band[3] slip down to his wrist? . . . (The trivial points of personal characteristics were very trying to the nerves at such times.) And how they all hated me—me with my intolerable look of tragedy, me with my unconcealed impatience and anguish. . . .[4]

'Despondent, gloomy, nervy' was how Orpen described Gibbs; but they did not hate him. They saw what Orpen saw—the 'intense sadness in his very kind eyes'. Then there was Percival Phillips of the *Daily Express*, one of the first to arrive in May 1915, and a war-correspondent from the age of twenty, when, says Basil Clarke, 'with pack on shoulder, so to speak, he set off on his own account from his home in America to the Greek War, where he wrote war despatches and sent them "on approval" to editors, American and British, who were forced by their very excellence to use them'. He was, says Orpen, a 'deep thinker on war, who probably knew more about it than all the rest of the correspondents put together'. And Gibbs

[1] *Realities of War*, p. 20.
[2] Orpen: *An Onlooker in France;* Williams & Norgate 1921, p. 32.
[3] Green brassards were the correspondents' distinguishing mark.
[4] *Realities of War*, p. 20.

leaves us a sharply-drawn miniature of Phillips, fighting to meet his deadline, turning pink and white under the strain: 'A little pulse throbbed in his forehead. His lips were tightly pressed. His oaths and his anguish were in his soul, but unuttered.'

There were, of course, many more. Sir Max Aitken (Lord Beaverbrook) was the Official 'Eyewitness' with the Canadian Forces. C. E. W. Bean would later become Australia's brilliant Official Historian of the War. Ward Price reported for the *Daily Mail* from the Balkans. John Masefield, post-war Poet Laureate, wrote on the Gallipoli landings—a book of lasting repute. Rudyard Kipling went out. Muirhead Bone, with an Army commission, was an official artist—one of a distinguished band which included the Nashes, Nevinson, Brangwyn, Kennington. And there were the photographers —too few of them, but heroic, unflagging and steadily improving in their technique. By all of these means, as the years went slowly by, the British public was presented with better information about its war; yet somehow the picture never really clarified.

There were good reasons for this. Better organisation from the start, more sensible procedures could—almost certainly would— have mitigated some of the subsequent misunderstandings of the war. In turn, this would almost certainly have mitigated some of the 'disenchantment' which followed it. Nevertheless, it is evident that a high degree of unclarity was inevitable, because of the nature of the event itself. It cannot be too often said that novelty was of the essence of the First World War—more novelty than any similar span of time has ever produced. Those who had to conduct the war, and those who had to report it, faced circumstances which might, in each particular case, have been predicted, but as a totality created an unimaginable combination. The very elements within which the action took place were doubled: war at sea was multiplied by war under the sea; war on land was multiplied by war over land. The addition of the new dimension, the Air (which would produce a new Service, the Royal Air Force) had incalculable effects. What could be reasonably foreseen in terms of the airships and aeroplanes of 1914 was not within even approximate relationship to the advanced capabilities of the aircraft of 1918. (Indeed, nearly twenty years would pass after the war before the appearance of first-line air forces significantly changed; the brave, sad exploits of Gladiators and Swordfish biplanes well into World War II underline the point.) Air combat (and air tactics), air bombing (and air strategy), air co-operation (observation, photography, drop-supply, direct attack) were all entirely new factors, transforming hitherto familiar modes of war.

The internal combustion engine was the chief agent of air power;

it also went far towards transforming war on land. The horse (or mule) would remain throughout the chief motive power of transportation: on November 30th 1918 the Army (in all theatres) contained 735,409 horses and mules, and over half a million had come and gone in the war's wastage. All the same, mechanisation was a steadily mounting process, until by the date of the Armistice the Army had in use 85,138 four-wheeled motor vehicles and 34,711 motor cycles, with a total personnel of 173,570.[1] On the field of battle, the internal combustion engine made possible the Tank, the only means (despite the drawbacks of all the early models) of breaking the front of an undefeated enemy; by 1918, 2,818 Tanks of all marks had been produced.[1] The growth of mechanisation can be estimated best, perhaps, by petrol requirements: 250,000 gallons a month in 1914, 10,500,000 gallons a month in the autumn of 1918.

Communications were also transformed. The field telephone was not a novelty; the scale of its use undoubtedly was. The millions of miles of barbed wire which protected trenches on both sides of the front were matched by millions of miles of telephone wire which became the basic tool of command at all immediate operational levels. The protection of this wire against bombardment became a major effort; by 1916, this meant, for real safety, a six-foot 'bury'. In three months of that year, the Canadian Corps alone laid 420 miles of cable six feet deep in the Kemmel area. The same unit, in the same sector in 1918, illustrates the significant development of a quite different method of communication: Wireless Telegraphy. Navy and Army alike were quick to discover the potential of this new achievement of technology. Introduced into aircraft in the later stages of the war, it gave a degree of precision to air operations without which the Air arm could not have expanded as it did. By 1918 W/T was a fully-fledged weapon of war. In July of that year, when the Canadian Corps was ordered down to Amiens to take part in the British counter-offensive there, its departure from Flanders was 'covered' by a flow of dummy wireless signals designed to persuade the enemy that the Canadians were still in strength in their old sector; the fruition of such techniques of wireless deception was seen in 1944, when the Germans were convinced that the Allies would re-invade Europe via the Pas-de-Calais, instead of Normandy. But the beginning was during the First World War.

The innovations of the war are too many and too various to list: the foregoing is only meant to illustrate the entirely new dimensions and contexts of combat and command. Yet one more element must

---

[1] All statistics on this page are from *The Military Effort of the British Empire*, H.M.S.O. 1922.

be mentioned, because it provided a dominant characteristic of the war: its quality of sheer violence and outrage. The war of 1914–1918 was, above all, an artillery war; the majority of battle casualties were inflicted by gun-fire; the stench, the noise, the constant fear and attrition of the nerves were more due to guns than to anything else; the most horrible wounds and some of the most disgusting forms of death were their work.

> We wander on and our luck remains out, for, at the junction of Elgin Avenue and the fire trench we meet a man with a human arm in his hand. 'Whose is that?' I ask. 'Rifíleman Broderick's, Sir,' is the reply. 'Where's Broderick?' is my next question. 'Up there, Sir,' says my informant, pointing to a tree top above our heads. There sure enough is the torn trunk of a man fixed securely in the branches of a shell-stripped oak. A high explosive shell has recently shot him up to the sky and landed him in mid air above and out of the reach of his comrades.[1]

> We are the guns, and your masters! Saw ye our flashes?
> Heard ye the scream of our shells in the night, and the shuddering crashes?
> Saw ye our work at the roadside, the shrouded things lying,
> Moaning to God that He made them—the maimed and the dying?
>   Husbands or sons,
> Fathers or lovers, we break them. We are the guns![2]

Some of the statistics of an artillery war are, providing one has a head for dizzy heights, quite interesting. In Britain, during the war, 25,031 new guns were made. By mid-1918 there were, with the B.E.F. in France alone, 6,709 guns and howitzers. Their total ammunition expenditure during the war was 170,385,295 rounds. The preliminary bombardment for the Third Battle of Ypres ('Passchendaele') lasted from July 17th to July 30th 1917; during that time 4,283,550 rounds were fired, at a cost of £22,211,389 14s. 4d. Attacking the Hindenburg Line in 1918, in twenty-four hours from noon September 28th to noon September 29th, the Army reached its maximum expenditure of ammunition in one day: 943,847 rounds—at a cost of £3,871,000. As the enemy's response was frequently on an even more lavish scale, it is not to be wondered at that a lot of people were killed. It was that sort of war. It is not to be wondered at, either, that commanders were frequently baffled by its problems, to which no text-book could yet supply them with an answer. And it is not to be wondered at if War Correspondents often blurred the edges of their descriptions of it all.

[1] F. P. Crozier: *A Brass Hat in No Man's Land;* Cape 1930, p. 94.
[2] Gilbert Frankau: *The City of Fear;* Chatto & Windus 1917.

What could they say?

In digging new trenches and new dug-outs, bodies and bits of bodies were unearthed, and put into sandbags with the soil that was sent back down a line of men concealing their work from German eyes waiting for any new activity in our ditches.

'Bit of Bill,' said the leading man, putting in a leg. 'Another bit of Bill,' he said, unearthing a hand. 'Bill's ugly mug,' he said at a later stage in the operations, when a head was found.

As told afterwards, that little episode in the trenches seemed immensely comic. Generals chuckled over it. Chaplains treasured it.[1]

It was all right for Philip Gibbs to write that afterwards with angry passion, in 1920. At the time it would not have gone down well—except, perhaps, among 'Bill's' surviving mates, who were glad of the difference between him and them. But it was not at all the thing to give to the British public in 1915, when the long dream of Liberal, progressive peace had not yet vanished.

What, then, *could* a correspondent say? What did they say? What did Gibbs, the hyper-sensitive, war-hating Gibbs say, on that First of July, 1916, the worst day in the British Army's history, when its casualties totalled 57,470 officers and men—*in one day?*

With the British Armies in the Field, July 1, 1916. The attack which was launched today against the German lines on a 20-mile front began well. It is not yet a victory, for victory comes at the end of a battle, and this is only a beginning. But our troops, fighting with very splendid valour, have swept across the enemy's front trenches along a great part of the line of attack, and have captured villages and strongholds which the Germans have long held against us. They are fighting their way forward not easily but doggedly. Many hundreds of the enemy are prisoners in our hands. His dead lie thick in the track of our regiments.

And so, after the first day of battle, we may say: It is, on balance, a good day for England and France. It is a day of promise in this war, in which the blood of brave men is poured out upon the sodden fields of Europe. . . .[2]

Gibbs was not lying. Nor was he taking the easy way of merely accepting a hand-out from the Staff.

Some people imagine, and some critics have written, that the war correspondents with the armies in France have been 'spoon-fed'

---

[1] *Realities of War*, p. 109.
[2] Gibbs: *The Battles of the Somme;* Heinemann 1917, p. 21.

with documents and facts given to them by General Headquarters, from which they write up their dispatches. They recognize the same incident, told in different styles by different correspondents, and say, 'Ah, that is how it is done!' They are wrong. All that we get from the General Staff are the brief bulletins of the various army corps, a line or two of hard news about the capture or loss of this or that trench such as appears afterwards in the official communiqués. For all the details of an action we have to rely upon our own efforts in the actual theatre of operations day by day. . . . (My dispatches) tell the truth. There is not one word, I vow, of conscious falsehood in them. But they do not tell all the truth. I have had to spare the feelings of men and women who have sons and husbands still fighting in France. I have not told all there is to tell about the agonies of this war, nor given in full realism the horrors that are inevitable in such fighting. It is perhaps better not to do so, here and now, although it is a moral cowardice which makes many people shut their eyes to the shambles, comforting their souls with fine phrases about the beauty of sacrifice.[1]

So there were many factors at work. As Gibbs himself wrote later, 'in those days, as war correspondents, we were not so expert in balancing the profit and loss as afterwards we became'. But it was not only the war correspondents: the High Command, and the Army itself had everything to learn about this style of war which technology had created. Yet all three were learning, day by day, through first-hand experience; at second-hand, through the newspapers, a public with no experience and little to guide its imagination fruitfully, would evidently remain much longer in the dark. There was a price to be paid for this at the time; but the full price would be paid later. The British people, between 1914 and 1918, displayed great fortitude; enough to make one feel that a little more truth, a little more reality (even at the cost of giving some small comfort to the enemy at times) would not have been beyond their power to bear, and could have saved them the worst of the penalty they later incurred, the dire sickness of Disillusion.

[1] Ibid., pp. 16–17.

PART II

BATTLE FRONT

VIII

It would be pleasant to record great changes and improvements in the relations between the British public, its Government and its Army by 1918—at the very least an acuter awareness of the real nature of the War. It would be difficult to go very far with such an argument. Certainly, the passing years had underlined the fact that the War was no picnic. Casualties, conscription, mobilization of women, food and other shortages, aerial bombardment, had produced an impact of war on the people of Britain unlike anything they had experienced at any time before. The effect, however, would seem in retrospect to have been, not better understanding, but deeper bewilderment. This was probably largely inevitable; there was much to be bewildered at. Yet it is hard for a military historian not to feel that a little more military education among the nation's governors, imparted in some measure to the governed, might have helped. 'Why, my dear Hankey,' wrote Lord Esher to Lord (then Lieutenant-Colonel) Hankey in March 1915,

> do we worry about history? Julian Corbett writes one of the best books in our language upon political and military strategy.[1] All sorts of lessons, some of inestimable value, may be gleaned from it. No one, except perhaps Winston, who matters just now, has ever read it. . . . Obviously history is written for schoolmasters and arm-chair strategists. Statesmen and warriors pick their way through the dusk.

Military education was lacking then, and in important respects remains lacking to this day on the subject of the First World War. Thus it was possible, as late as 1965, for an industrious American to compile a book sustained by a vast bibliography entitled *British Strategy and Politics 1914 to 1918*[2] which only once glimpsed and then hastily retreated from the fundamental truth that there *was* no British strategy (and therefore could hardly be effective British

---

[1]*Some Principles of Maritime Strategy*, 1911.
By Paul Guinn; Oxford.

politics) during that War. The author's glimpse of truth is contained
in the half-sentence: '. . . it was German successes that really dictated
British strategy during the remainder of 1915'. What he should have
said was that the only choice which had ever existed in determining
British strategy was between a maritime and a continental strategy—
and that choice was made in 1906, as we have seen in Part I of this
book. Once the choice had been made, the British military effort was
inevitably (thanks to the Voluntary Principle) dominated by France;
and the French military effort was dominated by Germany's seizure
of the initiative in August 1914. Thereafter, until July 1918, France
and Britain and all their allies danced to the German tune. Even the
closing campaign of the War (which began in July 1918) was con-
ditioned by the errors of the German High Command which preceded
it. If it was still possible, with all the advantages of hindsight and
fuller information, for this mistake to be made in 1965, it is perhaps
not surprising that such unpalatable truth should have been shunned
during the War itself.

Just how difficult it was, even for intelligent members of that
generation, fifty years after the event, to grasp the fact that there was
foreign participation in the war, is displayed in Professor Sir Llewellyn
Woodward's book *Great Britain and the War of 1914–1918* which
came out in 1967.[1] Looking back at his own experience and memory,
he recalls that 'I never lost confidence that, even with the generals
we had to accept because we had no better ones, we should not lose
the war. We were, however trying to win it in the crudest possible
way at least as far as our land forces were concerned.' As a result,
continues the Professor, 'the victorious generals nearly destroyed
European civilisation by the methods which they employed to save
it'. But who were the 'victorious generals'? To Professor Woodward,
in 1967 as strongly as fifty years earlier, the victorious generals who
'nearly destroyed European civilisation' were the British generals—
a large claim indeed, but reflecting accurately the entrenched mis-
conceptions of his time. He goes on:

> English society had taken no trouble to ensure that its armed
> defence would be directed by men as able as those who managed
> its civil affairs. The intellectual requirements for entrance into
> the army were far below those laid down for entrance into the
> higher branches of the civil service. One of my Oxford colleagues
> said to me in 1919, when I was complaining of the low mental
> level of our military leadership, that the army was 'run by pass
> men'. The English people had been willing to allow this dangerous
> state of things. They could not complain of the consequences

[1] See p. 48.

when they had left the fate of a generation in the hands of a custom-bound clique which would never have been permitted to take over the management of any other important department of state or of a great business.[1]

The death-knell of this eloquent argument is, however, uttered by the Professor himself:

Fortunately for the Allies the enemy generals were equally obtuse.

We are thus left with the proposition that *all* generals were obtuse. But how we can then proceed to blame the obtuseness of the German General Staff, the Imperial Russian High Command, Grand Quartier Général and the products of West Point on the faults of English society is not explained. This mental confusion is very revealing: it is the direct product of the failure of Government to realise and communicate the true rôle of Great Britain in what was, from first to last, a Coalition war. Moreover, it was a Coalition war whose decisive front lay on the home territory of the senior partner, France —a further consideration of great weight.

The national experience of past limited wars, conducted with a large Navy and small armies, offered little guidance in a situation which, by November 1918, had caused some $8\frac{1}{2}$ million men to pass through the ranks of the armies of the British Empire. It was this overwhelming novelty which, more than anything else, provoked the misunderstandings between Army and Government, Government and people, which by 1918 had bedevilled the conduct of the War, and remain alive in the embitterment of Professor Woodward and others. Closer analysis of recruiting figures for the War in the United Kingdom offers further clues to the outrage of sentiment. Out of the $8\frac{1}{2}$ million referred to above, the British Isles contributed 5,704,416. Subtracting existing forces at the outbreak of war (Regular Army, Army Reserve, Territorial Army) we have a recruitment figure for the War itself of 4,970,902—an astonishing total. This represented 22·11% of the estimated male population. More significantly, it represented 24·02% of the male population of England and 21·52% of the male population of Wales. Neither of these countries had been accustomed to large-scale participation in military activities. In the old Regular Army there had for centuries been a disproportionate percentage of Irishmen and Scotsmen; even regiments with fine old English county names had filled up the gaps in their ranks from over the Border or across the Irish Sea where the spur of poverty was usually sharper than in the English shires. The Scottish response to the War (23·71% of the male population) may be

[1] Woodward, pp. xix–xx.

regarded as 'normal'; the Irish was certainly not—134,202 recruits, compared with England's 4,006,158, or 6·14% of the male population. The War was therefore touching very closely not only classes but nations unprepared by previous experience for such a shock.

Not only were the numbers themselves staggering, but the methods used to arrive at such numbers also represented a break with all that had gone before. Including the 'half-way house' of the Derby Scheme, voluntary recruitment in one form or another supplied the Army with 3,621,045 men, a total at which one may still marvel. But even the now almost unimaginable patriotic enthusiasm of that period was bound to run dry sooner or later in the face of the demands of such a war. It remained for Conscription—the solution so long ago advocated by Lord Roberts, so much abhorred and reviled by politicians of all parties (but no more than by the nation itself)—to supply the remaining 1,349,854 men who put on khaki. In the last year of the War, the fate of this category of men (in 1918 232,444 of them were boys under 19 years old) was much in the minds of their fellow-countrymen and the nation's leaders. Compulsory Service for Home Defence had been introduced in Australia and New Zealand in 1909—much the British public cared about that—but in 1916 a referendum in Australia (influenced by the suppression of the Easter Rebellion in Ireland) had declared against conscription for service overseas. It was precisely at this time that the public of the United Kingdom was introduced to the new and always disliked system: there seemed to be something particularly wrong about the spectacle of boy-conscripts leaving for the blood-baths of the Western Front. In the case of those who were killed, in horrible circumstances, or of those who were maimed early in life, this sentiment was well-directed; in other cases there was a residual benefit, not easily discernible at the time. One who, having volunteered in 1914 and served through the Somme and 'Passchendaele', had the task of training the young conscripts in 1918 has written:

> The skinny, sallow, shambling, frightened victims of our industrial system, suffering from the effect of wartime shortages, who were given into our hands, were unrecognisable after six months of good food, fresh air, and physical training. They looked twice the size and, as we weighed and measured them, I am able to say that they put on an average of one inch in height and one stone in weight during their time with us. One boy's mother wrote to me complaining that her Johnny was half-starved in the Army and what was I going to do about it. I was able to convince her that Johnny had put on two stone of weight and two inches of height, and had never had so good an appetite before. Beyond statistical

measurement was their change in character, to ruddy, handsome, clear-eyed young men with square shoulders who stood up straight and were afraid of no one, not even the sergeant-major. 'The effect on me,' I wrote in a letter, 'is to make me a violent socialist when I see how underdeveloped industrialism has kept them, and a Prussian militarist when I see what soldiering makes of them.' Then I added, rather inconsequently, in a phrase that dates: 'I shall never think of the lower classes again in the same way after the war'. An odd forecast but true; I never have.[1]

Casualty totals for the First World War vary endlessly. Thus, *Statistics of the Military Effort of the British Empire, 1914–1920*, published by H.M.S.O. in 1922, gives a total, for the whole Empire in all theatres of war, of 2,998,583 officers and men killed and wounded. C. R. M. F. Cruttwell, in his *History of the Great War* (Oxford, 1934) quotes Hansard for May 5th 1921 in support of a figure of 3,260,581. Brigadier-General Sir J. E. Edmonds, the Official Historian of the War, in his *Short History of World War I* (Oxford, 1951) gives figures which add up to 3,286,090. It will be seen that all three of these statements remain within the approximate area of three millions. For the United Kingdom, the accounts vary between 2,300,000 and 2,400,000, of whom 704–740,000 dead. For the purposes of what follows later, it is only necessary to remark that the bulk of these losses had already occurred, and made their mark on the national consciousness, when the year 1918 began, although the scale of losses in that year was (for the British) the highest of all.

What did not reach the national consciousness, either then or at any later time, was the relationship between British totals and those of her enemies and allies. The contrast with France is the most important and the most striking. France called, from beginning to end, no less than 7,800,000 men to the colours—compared with 8½ millions for the British Empire. This represented about one fifth of the total population, as compared with 10·73% for the British Isles. French casualties (including the French Empire) amounted to some five million. To give only one direct yearly comparison (but important because it created the context for all that followed), in the five months of fighting of 1914 the British lost 96,000 officers and men on the Western Front; the French may well have lost 955,000.[2] Because the French figures were not known at the time, there was a failure at home to grasp the necessities under which strategy laboured —above all the necessity to take off some of the crushing burden of

[1] Charles Carrington: *Soldier from the Wars Returning;* Hutchinson 1965, p. 230.
[2] De La Gorce: *The French Army*, p. 103; but see note on p. 86.

loss from the French Army, even at the price of heavy British casualties among troops who should have had longer training. Even at the front itself, the full story was not known, and many ex-soldiers to this day find it difficult to believe, or to see how their own hardships were the direct result of greater hardships suffered by their allies. British insularity is no doubt a large cause of this, coupled with a widespread belief among the many who had never seen the French in action that French troops usually 'ran away'. One who did not share this blindness was Sir Douglas Haig, who wrote to his wife shortly after becoming Commander-in-Chief:

> It is sad to read of the selfishness of many people at home over the Universal Service Bill. The French have shed their blood lavishly, all married men have been fighting for their country since the very beginning and have suffered very heavily. For instance General d'Urbal has organised as his Guard a Company or more of men who have 5 children or more!—and now in England only the unmarried are to be sent out to fight! How very different the British Public would feel if they had the Germans on their soil, and how anxious they would be to leave nothing undone to secure that the Enemy is driven out![1]

Never fully comprehending the implications of partnership, still less of junior partnership, some members of the British Government had become well-nigh hysterical about casualties by 1918; one might almost have supposed that every dead soldier in France wore a British uniform. It was particularly unfortunate that the Prime Minister, Mr. Lloyd George, was among those who were most susceptible to these impressions. As early as 1916, as Secretary of State for War, he had begun to speak of the 'military Moloch'; by 1918 he had come to loathe this beast, and despise the soldiers whom he regarded as its impersonations—General Sir William Robertson, Chief of the Imperial General Staff, and Field-Marshal Sir Douglas Haig, Commander-in-Chief of the British Expeditionary Force in France and Flanders. The prospects for the New Year, under their ministrations, seemed to him (with the grim memory of 'Passchendaele' and the bitter disappointment of Cambrai all too fresh in mind) poor indeed. 'Every nation,' he later wrote,

> was profligate of its man-power in the early stages of the war and conducted its war activities as if there were no limit to the number of young men of military age who were fit to be thrown into the furnace to feed the flames of war. The Allies, who had an enormous superiority in the number of fit young men available, nearly

[1] Haig to Lady Haig; Jan. 13th 1916.

threw away their advantage by the reckless prodigality of their military leaders. . . . The idea of a war of attrition was the refuge of stupidity and it was stupidly operated, with the consequence that the overwhelming superiority in man-power which the Allies enjoyed at the beginning of the War had by the fourth year been melted down to the dimensions of a dubious equality.[1]

We shall shortly see how this frame of mind affected the crisis of the War which was about to occur. But it is necessary to recall that Lloyd George spoke with two voices; towards the military leaders he put on a distrustful growl as each demand for men was presented to him; towards the country at large, and towards organised Labour in particular, he adopted more winning tones, in case nothing should be forthcoming at all. 'The desire for peace,' he tells us[2] 'was spreading amongst men and women who, although they were convinced of the righteousness of the War, felt that the time had come for putting an end to its horrors in the name of humanity, if it could be done on any terms that were honourable and safe. . . . Amongst the workmen there was an unrest that was disturbing and might at any moment become dangerous. The efforts we were making to comb out more men for the Army were meeting with resistance amongst the Trade Unions, whose loyalty and patriotism had throughout been above reproach. I attached great importance to retaining their continued support in the prosecution of the War.' Accordingly, on January 5th, the Prime Minister addressed a crowded Trade Union Conference in the Caxton Hall; his subject was 'War Aims', and he told his audience:

When men by the million are being called upon to suffer and face death and vast populations are being subjected to the sufferings and privations of war on a scale unprecedented in the history of the world, they are entitled to know for what cause or causes they are making the sacrifice.

Lloyd George proceeded to take the Trade Union delegates carefully through the Government's intentions, beginning with the categorical statement: 'We are not fighting a war of aggression against the German people'. One by one he enumerated the Government's attitudes,[3] concluding with this general answer to the question he had put:

---

[1] Lloyd George: *War Memoirs*, Chap. LXXII.
[2] Ibid., Chap. LXX.
[3] The full text of the speech is given in Appendix II to Chapter LXX of his *War Memoirs*.

We are fighting for a just and lasting peace, and we believe that before permanent peace can be hoped for three conditions must be fulfilled.

First, the sanctity of treaties must be re-established; secondly, a territorial settlement must be secured based on the right of self-determination or the consent of the governed; and, lastly, we must seek by the creation of some international organisation to limit the burden of armaments and diminish the probability of war. In these conditions the British Empire would welcome peace, to secure those conditions its peoples are prepared to make even greater sacrifices than those they have yet endured.

Lloyd George had taken steps to ensure a solid political consensus behind him before he made his speech. It was well received by the Trade Union delegates, and rapturously acclaimed in the *Times* next day:

There has been nothing in the long history of British politics comparable with the demonstration of national unity which the Prime Minister made in his war aims speech to the trade union delegates. . . . It was instantly recognised as the most important State document which has appeared since the outbreak of the war. . . .[1]

And next day the *Times*, under the heading 'The Allies and the Speech' was commenting: 'Rarely since the war began has British opinion been so unanimous as in its approbation of the Prime Minister's speech. Not a single discordant note has been heard in any responsible quarter.'[2]

Nine days later, in the course of a conference between Government and Trade Unions, Sir Auckland Geddes, Director-General of National Service, offered to the House of Commons 'the most interesting and comprehensive survey of the man-power problem to which it has listened during the war'. Thus the *Times* Parliamentary reporter, who continued:

He announced that it was necessary to raise immediately in this country 420,000–450,000 men from among those now in civil life, and that the Government had decided to make available for military service a very large number of the young men now employed in essential industries. He warned the nation that the alternatives to the continued immunity of these men were:
    to drag out their fathers,

[1] *The Times*, Jan. 7th 1918.
[2] Ibid., Jan. 8th.

> to send those who had been wounded again and again to the
> trenches, and
> to stop the leave of the men at the front. . . .

This admonition was also well received by the *Times* in its editorial
capacity, but with a rider which was indicative of Government
thinking at the time:

> Sir Auckland Geddes prefaced his explanation of his plan . . . by
> a reference to the importance of husbanding our strength. He
> declared that the Government were 'determined that carelessness
> with regard to human life, and thoughtlessness with regard to
> casualties, shall be stamped out wherever it appears'. The state-
> ment had no application to individuals, but it emphasized *a
> principle which must govern our future strategy*,[1] in view of the fact
> that our remaining resources are not unlimited. . . .[2]

The astonishing reference of a member of the Government to the
need to 'stamp out' 'carelessness with regard to human life' must
detain us for a moment. Despite the disclaimer that this 'had no
application to individuals', it is impossible not to connect it with the
whispering campaign then in progress against Haig. His 1917
Despatch had just been published, with its account not only of the
long-drawn-out Third Battle of Ypres ('Passchendaele') but also of
Cambrai. This battle, which had begun with the brilliant success of
the Tanks against the Hindenburg Line on November 20th, had
been the occasion of great national rejoicing, including the ringing of
church bells. Then, only ten days later, the Germans had struck back,
and inflicted on the British almost as much damage as they had
sustained themselves. The chagrin was acute, and rankled in the
minds of Lloyd George and his colleagues. They would have liked
a scapegoat—perhaps General Sir Julian Byng, Commander of the
Third Army, perhaps one of his Corps or Divisional commanders;
but Haig's Despatch gave them no openings—he quietly took to
himself full responsibility for all that had happened. On January
15th Mr. Bonar Law, Leader of the House of Commons, had to tell
the House that a public discussion of Cambrai would be 'highly
detrimental'. This did not go down well, and the matter continued
to simmer. While it did so, discontent with the High Command
built up in Government circles, and Auckland Geddes was for the
moment its spokesman. Lord Esher, writing from Paris, commented
sarcastically to Sir William Robertson:

---

[1] My italics.
[2] The *Times*, January 15th 1918.

I

Do you know what the natural deduction is from Sir Auckland Geddes's speech? It strikes the average outsider thus:

'The English Government believes that the Allied Armies can sit down for one year or two years or three years, until such time as owing to the growth of the American forces they have acquired a numerical superiority and that then, after a blast of the Wilsonian trumpet, the walls of Jericho will fall down.'

Furthermore: 'Meanwhile the tenderfooted British Government will "stamp out" all "thoughtless" waste of life, which means that if the Boche attacks there will be no counter-attacks or any such antiquated follies, but retirement "according to plan", and that under no circumstances will initiative ever be countenanced.'

This is the new gospel of warfare in the fourth, fifth and sixth years of the war, according to the evangel of the high Councils of War among the Allies, who are opposed to that old fogey Hindenburg. So let us set aside the old leaders and expounders of antiquated Clausewitzian doctrine—send them to meditate in the blessed islands of Alderney, Jersey and Sark over the Napoleonic legends, the wasteful battles of the Somme, Arras, Messines and Passchendaele, where 'human life' was 'thoughtlessly' and 'carelessly' sacrificed, and where they can contemplate in the veracious daily press the miraculous results of masterly inactivity in war coupled with a maximum of rhetorical display on the platform.

These are the methods of democracy, and the principles of democratic warfare. They are the surest way of accomplishing victory and achieving the millenium. What German in his senses would not readily exchange them for the Kaiser and Hindenburg and Ludendorff?[1]

Lord Esher was palpably disturbed out of his usually meticulous prose style; but there was cause for disturbance enough. The notion that 'future strategy' should be 'governed' by the consideration that the Army might be run by homicidal lunatics was disturbing indeed. The notion that the country might be run by men who thought such a thing—and permitted it to continue—was no less so. Yet the latter alternative would appear to have been the case, if Mr. Lloyd George's later writings are to be believed. His dilemma was evidently acute: the collapse of Russia had released large German forces from the Eastern Front, and all the evidence was that they were being brought across to the West for a major offensive; the military authorities were complaining loudly that the Army in France was seriously under strength; the condition of Britain's allies, especially France

---

[1] Esher to Robertson, Jan. 17th 1918, *Journals*, iv, p. 174.

(under a new Prime Minister, and in the toils of treason trials and other public scandals) was far from brilliant; the combination of these factors could well spell outright defeat. On the other hand, there was a marked restlessness in the British public, much harassed by food shortages and (Londoners at any rate) by the resumption of German air raids, and becoming less and less enthusiastic about soldiering in a war whose measure it was beginning to take; added to this was the Prime Minister's by now almost pathological aversion to his own military chiefs. It has to be stated, to Lloyd George's credit, that although he was now unable to repair the damage of earlier false policies or lack of policies, his immediate reaction to the dilemma was to give the country, at last, a strong lead which might bear fruit in the future—if a future was permitted. On January 18th he again addressed Trade Union leaders at the re-convened general assembly of the man-power conference. 'Do not,' he urged them, 'let us harbour any delusions. . . .

> You might as well stop fighting unless you are going to do it well. If you are not going to do it with all your might, it is real murder of gallant fellows who have been in the trenches for three years [Hear, hear]. . . . If there are men who say that they will not go into the trenches, then the men in the trenches have a right to say, 'Neither will we remain here!' Supposing they did, would that bring the War to an end? Yes, it would. But what sort of an end?

It was not difficult, even in January, to answer that question; daily the newspapers carried accounts of the pathetic writhings of the Russian Bolshevik delegates attempting to wring reasonable peace terms from the triumphant Germans. 'If we stopped now,' Lloyd George told his Trade Union audience, 'we should leave Britain as well as France at the mercy of the most relentless military autocracy the world had ever seen. We could not turn Hindenburg out of Belgium with trade union resolutions, but we could with trade union guns and trade unionists behind them.' He concluded with a dire warning:

> We must take the world as it is, and the story of democracy is this: no democracy has ever long survived the failure of its adherents to be ready to die for it. . . . If one profession, one trade, one section, or one class in a community claims to be immune from obligations which are imposed upon the rest, that is a fundamental travesty of the principles of democracy. . . . Democracy must mean that the people of all classes . . . must merge their privileges

and their rights in the common stock. . . . My own conviction is this, the people must either go on or go under.[1]

It was a remarkable speech, an example of the great strength which Lloyd George brought to the rallying of the nation in difficult times—a faculty which few have challenged, but which he himself too often stultified.

Good as his speech on January 18th was, it was Lloyd George's stultifying activities at the same time which were most effective. The most important of these were the implementation of the findings of a Cabinet Man-power Committee, to which we shall return later, and his persistent, undercover attempts to dislodge Robertson and Haig without raising a public storm. Underlying all his brave words about fighting 'with all your might' were the stark realities of Sir Auckland Geddes's actual policies, the fruits of his conference with the Trade Unions. On these Repington commented:

> We are only to get 430,000 men from youths in essential trades, such as munitions—but these are for Army, Navy, and Aircraft; and the Army—though Geddes concealed this fact—only gets 100,000 'A' men, as I expected. Moreover, as men twice severely wounded are to be kept at home, the net increase probably will vanish. Geddes stated that 1,600,000 enemies may reinforce the Western front! A nice reply! Is all the British world mad? The *Times* writes a pathetically silly leader about it.[2]

Repington had come to the parting of the ways. The next day (Jan. 16th) the *Times* again carried an editorial on the Geddes plan, describing it as an 'imperative necessity':

> The Germans are bluntly telling the Bolshevists at Brest-Litovsk that they propose to deal with them as victors deal with the vanquished. Unless the Western Allies are prepared to back up their declared purposes by fighting for them, we shall run the risk of ending in a similar situation. We have now had the plainest of warnings that to hold the fighting front large and prompt reinforcements are required and every man of common sense in the land sees that they must be provided. . . . [The *Times* went on to refer to opposition to recruitment 'smouldering' in munitions factories and elsewhere.] . . . We trust that the fear of hostile action is exaggerated, but we are equally certain that if there is any failure to support the troops at the front, the bulk of the nation will expect the Government to act with promptitude and firmness.

[1] From *War Memoirs*, chap. LXXII.
[2] *The First World War*, ii, pp. 186–187.

The people of this country have made great sacrifices, and they will not tolerate any hesitation when the final struggle is at hand.[1]

It would be difficult to judge from this that there already *was* a most serious 'failure to support the troops at the front'—and the Government itself was the guilty party. Repington was disgusted:

This was too much for me. I should deserve to be hanged as a Boche agent if I remained with these imbeciles any longer. In the late afternoon I went to the *Times* and had a stormy interview with Dawson, the editor. He kept me waiting a long time before he saw me, and this made me in no better humour than before. I told him that I could not go on with him; that his leader this morning was mendacious; that his subservience to the War Cabinet during this year was, in my opinion, largely the cause of the dangerous position of our Army; that he had paid no attention to my constant exposure of the War Cabinet's failure to provide men, and that I considered he had been misleading the country. I further said that his constant deletion of whole paragraphs of my articles was . . . dishonest to the public, since it prevented the country from knowing the truth, and unfair to me. . . . The discussion became heated, and I told him that neither the interests of the country nor those of the Army were safe in his hands, and that I proposed to write a letter to the manager resigning my position.[2]

This Repington duly did that evening, with another to Lord Northcliffe, congratulating himself on 'a good day's work'. He shortly afterwards joined the *Morning Post* to continue his struggle against the Government there. But the truth was that it was all now too late; neither Repington's efforts in the Press to awaken public opinion to a deeper sense of reality, nor Sir William Robertson's efforts to hold a wavering Government on course, nor Lloyd George's efforts to rally the nation without offending it, nor the resentments of sections of the Labour movement, nor the delusions of the nation at large mattered any more. For in these early weeks of 1918 the War itself underwent a fundamental change— a reversion to the circumstances of its opening weeks in 1914. Once more the German High Command seized an initiative, and gripped it firmly; once more the deliberations and anticipations of the Allies became irrelevant. The German Army would call the tune, and very shortly the world would face a crisis exceeding that which preceeded the First Battle of the Marne. And, as in 1914, that crisis would

[1] The *Times*, Jan. 16th 1918.
[2] *The First World War*, ii, pp. 187–188.

have to be dealt with by the commanders and soldiers at the Front—
with this difference, that whereas in 1914 it was above all the French
Army which had met and held the enemy, under the leadership of
General Joffre, now it would be the British, under Field-Marshal
Sir Douglas Haig.

IX

On November 26th 1917 the new Bolshevik Government of Russia sued for an armistice as a preliminary to 'concluding a democratic peace without annexations and indemnities'.[1] Firing ceased along the Eastern Front two days later, and on December 2nd armistice negotiations began in the citadel of the gutted town of Brest-Litovsk. The terms were hammered out and agreed by December 15th; on December 20th the peace negotiations proper began. They were to last ten weeks—ten weeks during which illusion after illusion was swept away, and the ancient truth grimly reasserted, that Might is Right. Given the prevailing mood of Germany, there was never any question, except in the minds of doctrinaire pacifists and revolutionaries, that this would be so. The Eastern Front had long been Germany's nightmare; its liquidation was her opportunity.

An instructive exercise was carried out during January 1918 by the newspaper *Berlin Lokalanzeiger*; it put to its readers the question, 'What do you expect from Brest-Litovsk?' The published replies had an impressive unanimity in one respect. Thus Professor von Wilamovitz, of the University of Berlin, a famous classical scholar:

> My expectations are of such a kind that my anxiety about the future of the Fatherland rudely disturbs my sleep at nights; this is the experience of many whose Fatherland is still Germany and not a Utopian Europe, or even a Utopian world. What the real men of this Germany demand is, above all, *a peace with Russia which will leave our hands entirely free against our other enemies. Any abandonment of this point of view I regard as a crime.*[2] The needs of our allies will be easily satisfied, but our needs must be satisfied also. . . . We are victors and conquerors. . . .[3]

More succinctly, a Conservative leader, Herr von Heydebrand replied:

[1] *Brest-Litovsk: The Forgotten Peace*, by Sir John Wheeler-Bennett; Macmillan 1938.
[2] My italics.
[3] Quoted in The *Times*, Jan. 18th 1918.

What I expect from Brest-Litovsk is a serviceable peace with Russia, *while we tie our helmets on all the tighter against our other enemies*[1].[2]

At five o'clock in the afternoon of March 3rd, the Treaty of Brest-Litovsk was signed. The contracting parties were, on the one hand, the Empires of Germany, Austria–Hungary and Turkey; on the other, the Russian Bolshevik Government. This Government had come to power in October 1917 on the slogan: 'Down with the war!' Now it had fulfilled its pledge to the Russian people (ignoring any obligation to Russia's allies) and brought its war to an end. By the terms of the treaty which her delegation signed, 'Russia lost 34% of her population, 32% of her agricultural land, 85% of her beet-sugar land, 54% of her industrial undertakings, and 89% of her coal mines'.[3] This was a German peace. Exasperation at Bolshevik tactics and propaganda had killed any disposition towards leniency which might have existed in Germany. In any case, such concepts were liable to a somewhat different interpretation there from that of some other countries. The newspaper *Norddeutsche Allgemeine Zeitung*, for example, wrote on the following day:

> The significance of the treaty with Russia lies in the fact that the German Government has worked only for a peace of understanding and conciliation.

The Bolshevik delegate G. I. Sokolnikov, Member of the Central Executive Committee of Councillors to the Deputies of the Working-men, Soldiers and Peasants, on the other hand, called it 'a peace which Russia, grinding its teeth, is forced to accept'. One thing, at least, was beyond doubt: Brest-Litovsk was a clear indication of what Germany's other enemies might expect, if she won another victory. It was what the War was about.

Brest-Litovsk, furthermore, supplied Germany with the means of obtaining such another victory. When the Russians had first sued for their Armistice, Ludendorff had asked Major-General Max Hoffmann, the German Chief of Staff in the East:

'Is it possible to negotiate with these people?' Hoffmann replied:

> Yes, it is possible. Your Excellency needs troops, and this is the easiest way to get them.

Evidently, the full mass of German forces in Russia could not be brought to the West all at once (and in the event, the rigours of the

---

[1] My italics.
[2] Quoted in The *Times*, Jan. 18th 1918.
[3] Wheeler-Bennett.

German peace terms defeated their own ends, provoking resistance which forced her to keep a million men in the East); but all through the winter a steady build-up took place on the Western Front. On December 8th British G.H.Q. Intelligence made a very accurate forecast of the likely increase of German strength on that Front up to August 1918:

1919 Class	400,000
New divisions from Russia	300,000
Drafts from divisions on Russian front	150,000
Returned prisoners-of-war (from Russia)	40,000
	890,000[1]

So this was Germany's opportunity: it would be now or never. Her allies, certainly, would be able to do little to help her; they were at the end of their tether, only upheld by the power of Germany herself. The Empires of Austria–Hungary and Turkey were in the worst plight. 'We had to take into consideration,' wrote General Ludendorff, 'that Austria–Hungary might actually arrive at the end of her military power. . . . Turkey was faithful to the alliance, but at the end of her strength. . . .' The Bulgarian Chief of Staff informed him that Bulgaria was 'secure'—but active operations had practically ceased on the Bulgarian front. 'That he could, of course, never ask for enough German stores and German troops was inherent in his office. With every word he expressed the hope of a German victory in the West.'[2]

Against these sombre realisations had to be set the condition of Germany herself. For the Home front, peace with Russia came opportunely. In material terms, it held out a promise of better food supplies from the 'granary' of the Ukraine and by forcible requisition (though these expectations remained largely unfulfilled); psychologically, it went a long way towards counteracting an unquestionable war-weariness. Even so, as the year opened, there were dangerous manifestations. A sailor in the idle, discontented High Seas Fleet (which so very rarely saw the high seas) wrote in January:

> The lower classes are seething with discontent. If there were only someone who could channel that discontent, a great eruption would become virtually inevitable. But as it stands right now, the pressure from below noisily erupts here and there and soon dissipates itself. . . .[3]

[1] Haig Papers.
[2] Ludendorff: *My War Memories;* Hutchinson 1919.
[3] *The Private War of Seaman Stumpf;* Leslie Frewin 1969.

One such eruption, of menacing portent, was the strike of 180,000 munitions and metal workers in Berlin on January 28th, which spread to Hamburg, Leipsig, Cologne, Breslau and Munich, until it involved over a million workers. Food was an important factor in this demonstration, but Socialist agitation undoubtedly helped to foment it, and profited by it. Even the stolid patience of the German people was by now shaken—as well it might be, by a war which had brought them wholly unexpected suffering and unbelievable loss of life.

More serious was the state of the German Army itself. This organism had throughout supplied the 'motor' of the War—its driving force; it had also borne the weight of the War from its outbreak in August 1914; and now it was a declining force. 'As our best men became casualties,' wrote Ludendorff, 'our infantry approximated more nearly in character to a militia, and discipline declined.'[1] Deserters were numerous—tens of thousands of them had fled to Holland. 'They and the skrimshankers at the front, of whom there were thousands more, reduced the battle strength of the fighting troops . . . to a vital degree.'[1] In other words, the Allied strategy of attrition, the strategy to which Mr. Lloyd George and his colleagues were so much opposed, and which drew forth the full venom of the Prime Minister's scorn in later years, was, according to Germany's leading soldier, bearing fruit. He continues:

> Against the weight of the enemy's material, the troops no longer displayed their old stubbornness; *they thought with horror of fresh defensive battles*[2] and longed for a war of movement. . . . In the West the Army pined for the offensive, and after Russia's collapse expected it with the most intense relief. . . . The condition of our allies and our Army all called for an offensive that would bring about an early decision. This was only possible on the Western Front. All that had gone before was merely a means to the one end of creating a situation that would make it a feasible operation. . . . All that mattered was to get together enough troops for an attack in the West.[1]

Another serious consideration was present in Ludendorff's mind. The United States of America had entered the war against Germany in April 1917. In theory, this implied an accession of strength to the Allied cause which could easily outweight the collapse of Russia (already visibly impending since the first outbreak of revolution on March 12th). In practice, however, in view of her military un-

[1] Ludendorff: *War Memories*, vol. ii.
[2] My italics.

preparedness, and her deep existing commitments to supplying the Allies with war-material,[1] America found it strangely difficult to mobilize her full power. By December 1917 there were only four American divisions in France,[2] and only one actually in the line. Nor was there any immediate prospect of a change in this situation. Yet it was clear that it would not last for ever; one day practice would coincide with theory; one day the Americans would be there. Ludendorff wrote:

> The American danger rendered it desirable to strike in the West as early as possible; the state of training of the Army for attack enabled us to contemplate doing so about the middle of March. . . . If all went smoothly at Brest-Litovsk, if our people there worked with real energy, we could expect to have our forces ready for a successful attack in the West by the time mentioned. No delay could be justified. It will be obvious with what interest we watched the peace negotiations.[3]

In view of Russia's impotence, it is not likely that O.H.L.[4] would

---

[1] Repington's Diary for Jan. 4th 1918 reveals some of the difficulties under which the Americans laboured:

> America was coming on very slowly. The 4th Division was only now arriving in France where the numbers were not over 140,000. Most Americans believed that they had over half a million men in France, and would be very disgusted when they learnt the truth. The U.S. Parliamentary Committees were beginning to examine things, and all the faults would come out. The Americans were not using their merchant ships sufficiently, and were leaving too many at their normal commercial work. Also, the American decision not to use our plant in America for turning out our rifles, 8-inch and 9·2-inch guns, etc., had proved disastrous, and America had not yet turned out a single heavy gun as she had neither the tools nor the workmen. She had been bluffed by M. Thomas into accepting French guns and so had not accepted our field guns and had also chosen the French calibre of 9·5-inch instead of our 9·2-inch, and so all new plant for it had to be made in America and was not yet ready. We only expect six divisions to be in France by the middle of February, but hope that arrivals will soon be speeded up.

[2] Four divisions was the strength of the original B.E.F. of August 1914; it was extraordinary that after 8 months of war the Americans had no more in the field. By comparison, the British build-up in six months had been:

Sept. 15th 1914	163,897
Nov. 15th	224,647
Dec. 26th	245,197
Jan. 31st 1915	347,384

Some 100,000 casualties have to be taken also into account, as well as forces in other theatres of war.

[3] Ludendorff: *War Memories*, ii, p. 544.

[4] Oberste Heeresleitung—German Supreme Command.

have found any need to depart from the date selected for the great
attack—March 21st; but the knowledge that the enemy in the East
had been definitely eliminated must have been a comfort. As we
have noted, the transfer of material and troops from the Eastern
Front to the West had been in progress all through the winter
(beginning in November 1917). In all, including some from Italy,
42 extra divisions were made available for the Western attack.
German divisions in the West increased from 150 at the beginning
of November to 160 at the beginning of December and 171 at the
end of that month. British G.H.Q. Intelligence plotted their further
arrivals within a surprisingly short time of each completion:

February 6th	174
February 21st	179
February 25th	180
March 3rd	182
March 10th	184
March 11th	185
March 18th	187[1]

By March 21st there were 192, 190 of which were identified by
G.H.Q. Intelligence on March 22nd. The number finally rose to a
peak of 208.

Mass is important, but it is not everything in war. This vast array
required intensive training for the task it had to perform. The
divisions coming from the East were in many cases unfamiliar with
Western Front conditions, where they were bound, no matter how
successful, to face a technological resistance never remotely matched
on the Russian front. The divisions already located in the West had
to eradicate the habits formed in three years of defensive fighting
and learn the new tactics of offensive warfare which had been
evolved. The essence of the training laid down was 'to adopt loose
formations and work out infantry group tactics clearly. We must not
copy the enemy's mass tactics, which offer advantages only in the
case of untrained troops.'[2] Penetration, envelopment, and swift
reinforcement of success were the thoughts inculcated into all ranks
of the Germany Army—the concept propagandised in the phrase
'Storm Troops'. But the Storm Troops were only a part of the
Army; the quality of the whole mass was too uneven for the universal
application of the new elixirs. This was gloomily recognised by
O.H.L., which allotted training and equipment priorities to 'attack
divisions' as opposed to 'trench divisions'. 'General Headquarters

[1] Haig's Diary.
[2] Ludendorff, ii, p. 574.

regretted that the distinction ... became established in the Army. We tried to eradicate it, without being able to alter the situation which gave rise to it.'[1]

The German attack, when it came, was to prove, after all, a conventional attack. The patient, obedient, adept German soldiery, led by a remarkably intelligent and professional body of officers and N.C.O.s (though by now severely depleted) proved able to do many things better than most of their opponents had yet been able to do; but they did little that their opponents had not attempted, and were in some cases soon to surpass. And the mainspring of their battle would be what it had been all through the war: artillery. By 1918, however, this meant artillery in a quantity never before dreamed of, and used with all possible sophistication. Out of their 13,832 pieces of artillery on the Western Front, the Germans assembled 6,473 on the sector of attack—a concentration beyond any previous comparison, and 'orchestrated' at the key point by the outstanding artillerist of the War, Lieut.-Colonel Bruchmüller.

'We had no tanks ... our attacks succeeded without them.'[2] Tanks, says Ludendorff, 'did not impress me. ... Not until our infantry lost its discipline and fighting capacity did the employment of massed tanks, combined with artificial smoke, produce a fatal effect on the course of events.' Ludendorff is not exact in saying that the Germans deployed no Tanks on March 21st; in fact, they used nine—four of their own A7Vs and five captured British Mark IVs.[3] But in essence he is correct, since few would dispute his verdict that 'tanks are only effective in masses'. This was official doctrine in the Royal Tank Corps, warmly supported by the Commander-in-Chief, provided only that 'masses' were actually available, which was only the case on the British front on two days during the entire war. But the Germans never at any time employed more than thirteen on a single occasion. Ludendorff's doubts about the new arm are less interesting than a broader situation reflected by them. Not only did the Germans not produce Tanks for their March offensive; armoured cars were equally missing, and, to the best of my knowledge, so were motorised machine guns (carried in motor-cycle side-cars) which the British Army certainly possessed.

Not only were mechanical aids absent: so also was the traditional mobile arm—cavalry. The effectiveness of cavalry on the Western Front after the opening combats of the war of movement in 1914

[1] Ibid., ii, p. 583.
[2] Ludendorff, ii, p. 575.
[3] *Tanks in Battle*, by Col. H. C. B. Rogers; Seeley Service & Co. 1965, pp. 64–65.

was always limited. Yet it was the only arm which retained any true cross-country mobility—provided it could move at all, which depended largely on the enemy's machine guns. Armoured cars and motor-cycles were essentially road-bound; the maximum speed of a Mark IV tank (1917) was 3·7 m.p.h., of a Mark V (1918) 4·6 m.p.h., and of a 'Whippet' (Medium Mark A, 1918) 8·3 m.p.h.—but these were all road speeds; over rough ground they rarely averaged better than 1 or 1·5 m.p.h. Thus the mechanical element can hardly be regarded as a weapon of pursuit, while, in certain conditions, cavalry might be. A British artillery officer, describing the scenes which met his eyes on the fourth day of the German onslaught wrote:

> The roads were fairly full, and this time while it would be wrong to say there was a panic the retreat resembled more of a rout than had previously been the case. Everyone seemed anxious to get away as quickly as possible and regardless of anyone else. . . . A few military policemen dashed up and down on horseback trying to enforce some kind of order, but no one took much notice; had the Germans been able to break through with cavalry or armoured cars the war would have ended for most of us.[1]

Describing a similar scene in May, an infantry officer wrote:

> It was a crowning mercy that (the Germans) had no cavalry. How many times during the retreat did we thank heaven for this! The sight of a few mounted men in the distance would at once start a ripple of anxiety, the word 'Cavalry!' being whispered and passed from mouth to mouth down the firing-line. Men looked apprehensively over their shoulders, fearful lest horsemen might be already behind them. Cavalry was the one factor which would have smashed the morale of the defence in a twinkling.[2]

But Germany's cavalry divisions were in the Ukraine, supporting grandiose and senseless dreams of power. And so it came about that the German Great General Staff launched what it fully intended to be the decisive battle of the War, in an area which, Ludendorff admits, 'seemed to lack any definite limit', with no mobile arm for exploitation at all. It hardly seems credible, yet it was so. This attack would go as far as the German infantryman's legs could carry him; no further. As Sir John Wheeler-Bennett has said, it was Ludendorff the Politician who defeated Ludendorff the Soldier.[3]

Long discussion took place about the area to be attacked. Another

[1] Arthur Behrend: *As From Kemmel Hill;* Eyre & Spottiswoode 1963.
[2] Sidney Rogerson: *The Last of the Ebb;* Arthur Barker 1937, p. 112.
[3] *Brest-Litovsk*, p. 327.

assault on the French Army at Verdun was contemplated, but rejected. An assault on the British in Flanders seemed the most promising possibility, but March was too early for operations in that wet low-lying region. So the final choice fell 'on the area between Arras and Péronne, towards the coast. If this blow succeeded the strategic result might indeed be enormous, as we should separate the bulk of the English Army from the French and crowd it up with its back to the sea.'[1] It was recognised by the German Command that there were drawbacks here: the 'lack of any definite limit' mentioned above, and the wilderness of the 1916 Somme battlefields not far behind the British front, through which the momentum of advance would have to be maintained. Preparations were therefore continued for the Flanders attack, aimed at the vital Channel Ports, which the British could not possibly afford to lose. If the first attack succeeded, the Flanders blow would clinch the matter; if the first attack should, by any chance, fall short of its purpose, this might yet fulfil Germany's hopes.

So the stage was set for the 'Kaiserschlacht'—the 'Emperor Battle'—which would be fought for the ultimate stakes. Three Armies, *Eighteenth*, *Second* and *Seventeenth*, would deliver the attack: 71 divisions, of which 32 would be in the first line of assault. Forty-three of these divisions faced the front of the British Fifth Army, commanded by General Sir Hubert Gough. He was a man of robust spirit; but for the ordeals ahead of him he would have needed to be superhuman.

---

[1] Ludendorff, ii, p. 590.

X

Germany's intentions were clearly formulated; her preparations were vast and meticulous; her progress towards her appointed goal deliberate and seemingly inexorable. On the other side of the line the exact opposite was the case. The disarray of the Allies at the beginning of 1918 was lamentable, and this, it has to be stated, was largely the fault of the British Government.

We have seen how slowly the forces of America were coming into action. Russia was out. Italy was making a slow recovery from the disaster of Caporetto in October 1917; six French and five British divisions were sent to bolster her army in the event of another Austro–German offensive. All this meant that the control of the War, on the Allied side, remained effectively with Britain and France. But France herself, in 1917, had been brought nearly to breaking-point. The mutiny of an important part of her army on the Western Front in May and June of that year had cast a blight over her entire effort from that time forward. It created a haunting dread which undermined her military capacity. Not even the new men to whom she turned in her extremity could ignore this fearful, all-too-recent fact of history. Not even her new Prime Minister, Georges Clemenceau, 'The Tiger', could dismiss it from his mind; he was always aware of two enemies threatening the nation's security:

> No more pacifist campaigns, no treachery, no semi-treachery: only war, nothing but war. Our armies are not going to be caught between two fires. Justice shall be established. The country shall know that it is being defended.[1]

In these words Clemenceau proclaimed that he meant to guard the Army's rear; 'the moment the Tiger went into action, democracy temporarily died in France. And died unmourned'.[2] At the head of the Army now stood General Pétain, the man who had stopped the mutiny. He possessed the confidence of the French soldiers in a rare

---

[1] Speech to the Chamber of Deputies, Nov. 20th 1917.
[2] R. M. Watt: *Dare Call it Treason;* Chatto & Windus 1964, p. 237.

degree, but he would never be able to forget that hour of France's extreme weakness. The Army itself had made a great recovery since those black days of early summer in 1917; two short, sharp, clever victories later that year had improved morale. But reserves were few, divisional establishments had to be reduced, and three divisions were actually broken up. The French Army, as 1918 came in, remained an unknown quantity.

This was the moment when, by right and by default, the lead among the Allies should have passed to Britain. By default, because of the sundry failings of the Allied powers which we have noted. By right, because of Britain's own record. Slow to develop her strength, she could now point to a large achievement. She had asserted and retained throughout her supremacy at sea; the most serious threat to this supremacy, the U-boat campaign, was now in process of being defeated. Thanks to her sea-power, she had been able to mobilize her Empire on the side of the Allies; by November 1918, that meant an accretion of 2,881,786 men.[1] In January 1918 Jerusalem had been taken, and the Turkish Empire seemed to be reaching collapse, almost entirely due to the efforts of British Empire forces. Britain's Air Force was in process of becoming (for a very short time) the most powerful in the world; in December 1917 it numbered 115 Service Squadrons with 15,522 officers and 93,738 other ranks. Her war industry was by now a pillar of the Allied war effort. But above all towered the facts that, for a year and a half, she had borne the main burden of fighting in the decisive theatre, the Western Front, and that it was upon her that the great German blow was about to fall in that theatre. For all these powerful reasons, it might be supposed that Britain's voice would be strong, clear and dominant; yet the sad fact is that both her authority in negotiation and her actual military force were dissipated. The reason for this was the now embittered conflict between her civil and military leaders at which we have briefly looked already.

It is time now to look again at the statement (p. 123) that the British Government was guilty of a most serious failure to support the Army at the Front. It is a proposition which is, naturally, hotly contested by Lloyd George. And it is, unfortunately, a subject which can only be discussed in terms of statistics—yet one in which

[1]Canada	628,964
Australia	412,953
New Zealand	128,525
South Africa	136,070
India	1,440,437
Other Colonies	134,837

These are the totals recruited, not forces sent overseas.

K

statistics can be at their most misleading. As a foundation of his
argument, Mr. Lloyd George adopts the method most beloved by
politicians (Sir Winston Churchill proved adept at it in World War
II): counting heads. 'According to the General Staff's amended
tables,' he wrote,

> the position in the West in December 1917 was that the Allies
> had 169½ divisions on the French Front against 151 German
> divisions; and a combatant strength of 3,420,000 (exclusive of
> 11,800 Indian troops) compared with 2,536,000 Germans—i.e.,
> an Allied superiority of 18½ divisions, and of 884,000 combatant
> troops.[1]

This, he goes on to point out, would give the Germans only a slight
superiority in men when their reinforcements were all duly assembled,
but an overall inferiority in artillery and mechanical equipment. And
for good measure he adds that the Allies had had, for the previous
three years, a much larger numerical advantage, without ever being
able to break the German front.

These are the arguments of the incorrigible amateur. In the case
of a British politician of the Liberal Party (though the Liberal Party
had little enough cause to be proud of Lloyd George in 1918) they
seem to be a natural product of a lifetime's opposition to military
preparation. They ignore fundamental factors, far more important
in the waging of war than mere numbers. They ignore the unity of
command and immediacy of decisions which the Germans always
enjoyed on the Western Front. (In due course we shall see how
powerfully this factor operated.) They ignore homogeneity. We have
already seen that the German High Command lamented the differen-
tiation of its army into 'attack divisions' and 'trench divisions'—yet
they were all *German* divisions. On the Allied side there were also
differences of quality to be reckoned with—but in addition there
were the problems of five nationalities present: the Allied array was
made up of 99 French divisions (including their colonials), 58
British, 6 Belgian, 4 American and 2 Portuguese. The amateur will
never grasp the loss of efficiency in such a polyglot force. Finally,
and this also he finds anathema, there was the German *system*: the
long-standing, well-tried method of recruiting, training and leading
German soldiers, evolved and applied long before the War, and
invaluable throughout it.

Only once did Germany depart from this system, and the result
was disastrous. To meet the demands of the War's early crises in
1914, with thoughts of quick, decisive victory still much in mind,

[1] *War Memoirs*, chap. LXXII.

the Germans raised a number of volunteer Reserve Corps, very much on the lines of Lord Kitchener's New Armies (though better equipped from Germany's then ample stores). The fate of these formations, flung into the First Battle of Ypres, was later described as the 'Slaughter of the Innocents'. Writing about it in 1918, General von Freytag-Loringhoven, the Deputy Chief of the General Staff, said:

> The first new formations did not stand the test. It was impossible to avoid the employment in the field as early as October, 1914— and that in particularly difficult circumstances—of the new Reserve Corps, the formation of which had been ordered in the middle of August. Hardly ever have troops, as a whole, consisted of material so splendid in spirit and will as these new regiments. Three-quarters of them were volunteers, and, apart from a number of older men, they were drawn from the youth of all classes, and included many university graduates. Nevertheless, it was found that enthusiasm and self-sacrifice cannot be a substitute for thorough training in soldiering. . . .[1]

The Germans never repeated this error. They reverted at once to their normal, well-thought-out system, whereby, year by year, class by class, the conscripts were turned into a reliable, adept soldiery. Heavy losses, above all losses in the invaluable corpus of N.C.O.s, inevitably reduced the quality as time went by—hence Ludendorff's reference to a 'militia'. But, compared with the Allies, the German advantage was immense. The only Allied army with a system at all comparable was the French—and they were by now a doubtful quantity for reasons which we have noted. The Belgians had scarcely fought at all since 1914, and showed no particular disposition to do so. The Americans had everything to learn, and time would show that the lesson was as hard for them as it had been for everyone else. There remained the British—and the hard truth is that the British Army had been, every since 1915, what Ludendorff feared that the German Army was becoming in 1918: a militia. For the Germans this spelt a decline, while the British were undoubtedly improving, so there was an equalising factor; but it would take some bitter battles, and blood-letting on an unbelievable scale, before the balance of advantage finally swung over to the British side. The folly of counting heads (or divisions) lies in the fact that, when the German blow came, it would be the 58 divisions of the British Army which would have to bear it. It is the state of those divisions, then, that really matters.

[1] von Freytag-Loringhoven: *Trained National Army or Militia?;* sub-title: 'War Teachings From the Past and the Present'.

With the turn of the year, the British man-power problem resolved
itself into two issues: the number of men to be raised for the Army
in 1918 (long-term), and the distribution of the forces already in
arms (immediate). To resolve the first question, a Cabinet Committee on Man-power was set up in December 1917; it consisted of
Lord Curzon, Mr. G. N. Barnes (a Trade Union leader), Sir Edward
Carson, General Smuts and Mr. Lloyd George in the chair. The
Official History remarks that not a single soldier was invited to sit
on it. Lloyd George retorts 'That General Smuts should be classed
as "no soldier" is surely a consummate example of the workings of
the professional military mind'. The remark is certainly a consummate example of the workings of Lloyd George's mind. General
Smuts had first achieved distinction as a leader of Boer commandos
in the South African War; in 1914 he had assisted General Botha in
the swift over-running of German South-west Africa; in 1916 he
had commanded the British forces in East Africa, returning to
London in January 1917 to become a member of the Imperial War
Cabinet. In London he stated: 'The campaign (in East Africa) may
be said to be over'. Yet his German opponent, General von Lettow-
Vorbeck, remained in the field undefeated until November 23rd
1918, the last German commander to surrender, twelve days after
the Armistice. Of European armies Smuts knew nothing; of European warfare his experience was nil. Fortunately, he was saved from
the worst consequences of this ignorance by a lively mind.

The Cabinet Committee's task was to determine priorities, and its
conclusion was that the Navy, the Air Force, ship-building, munitions, food-production, timber-felling and the provision of cold-
storage accommodation should all have priority over the Army.
'The Army had no special knowledge of these problems,' wrote Lloyd
George, 'and could claim no more right than the Navy, the Ministry
of Munitions, the Treasury, the Board of Trade, the Ministries of
Labour and Agriculture, the Shipping, Coal or Food Controllers to
a representative on the Committee.' In a total war, of course, every
part of the nation is involved in the struggle for survival; every one
of the departments mentioned had a vital part to play; but none of
them was designated as the target of the vast preparations of the
German High Command. That honour was reserved for the Army
alone—which somewhat weakens the force of Lloyd George's argument. It had, however, an even more serious weakness than that.

The Army authorities, on the basis of past experience and future
expectation, were asking for 615,000 men. The Cabinet Committee
decided to allot 50,000 Category 'A' men to the Navy, 100,000 to
the Army, with 100,000 men of lower medical grades. The Committee took leave to doubt the figures on which the Army based its

demands: 'The British Army had of course been fighting hard on the offensive all through 1917; but as it was to stand on the defensive for the early part of 1918, the Committee considered that the military estimate was likely to prove unduly large'.[1] The belief that the defensive was less costly than the offensive was deeply entrenched; Lloyd George was certain of it; Winston Churchill, in *The World Crisis*, made it a powerful argument against the theory of attrition; it persists strongly to this day. In due course we shall see how it worked out on the field of battle. At this stage we need only consider two contrary points of view: we may ask ourselves again why Ludendorff should say that the whole German Army 'thought with horror of fresh defensive battles'; and we may note Sir William Robertson's comment on the theory of the 'cheaper' defensive:

> This argument was so utterly fallacious as to be almost incredible, for the losses sustained would depend, as always, upon the intensity of the fighting, and, as was pointed out, this in its turn would depend not so much upon the policy of the *Entente* as upon that of the enemy.[2]

The Cabinet Committee did not, however, rest on this. To justify (or seek to conceal?) the paucity of reinforcements for the Army, it further proposed a drastic reorganisation of the B.E.F. 'Since there was not the man-power avilable . . .' says Lloyd George, 'it became a question of either cutting down the number of divisional formations, or of reducing the establishment of infantry in each division. The second course was that recommended and already adopted by all the other leading belligerent armies.' And so the decision was taken to reduce every British division from twelve infantry battalions to nine, every brigade from four to three. This was a very large decision for five political gentlemen to take in Whitehall—against the advice of the Army Council and the Commander-in-Chief. Here, at least, one might have thought that they would feel the need for a serving soldier to take part in their deliberations. On the contrary, they brushed aside all objections from their responsible advisers:

> They were accustomed to 12-battalion divisions, and they could not understand that methods of warfare had been revolutionised since the days of the Expeditionary Force of 1914 when we depended on the firing efficiency of our riflemen and their skill at bayonet practice, and when our artillery was almost entirely light; when we had few aeroplanes, still fewer heavy guns, not many machine-guns and no tanks.[1]

[1] Lloyd George.
[2] *Soldiers and Statesmen*, i, pp. 317–318.

It is scarcely to be believed that, only on the previous page, Lloyd George had referred to the Army's demand for 165,300 men 'for expanding the flying corps and artillery, and creating new units in such growing services as machine-gun corps, tanks, etc'. Lloyd George's suggestion that the Army was demanding so many men because it had no use for modern weapons is mere dishonest rhetoric.

Worse still, however, was the Cabinet Committee's suggestion that the units withdrawn from the British divisions should then be constituted into new divisions to form a reserve. This was merely adding insult to injury. 'Even the Committee,' says Robertson,

> though composed for the most part of civilian ministers, should have remembered that about half the personnel of a division consisted of artillery and other non-infantry units, and that shortage of men in these units was fast becoming as great as it was in the infantry.[1]

A further reason why, even had it been possible, such a step would have been undesirable, had already been supplied by Haig: 'any reduction in the present establishment would be extravagant in so far as staffs are concerned, and the question of finding commanders and staffs is becoming increasingly difficult'.[2] But the subject was in any case irrelevant; the saving effected by reducing the divisions only covered the existing deficit of infantry in the Expeditionary Force, as Smuts himself reported to his Cabinet colleagues in January.[3] But neither Robertson nor Haig nor Smuts could prevail upon them in any way.

The Army Council lodged the most vehement formal protest against the Cabinet Committee's proposals:

> . . . the Council would regard the acceptance of the recommendations in the draft report, without further effort to provide the men they consider necessary for the maintenance of the forces in the field during 1918, as taking an unreasonably grave risk of losing the

---

[1] *Soldiers and Statesmen*, i, p. 319.
[2] Haig to the War Office, November 24th, 1917.
[3] '. . . it must be borne in mind that the infantry are 100,000 men below strength *until the new organisation has been completed.*' Smuts: Memorandum to the War Cabinet, January 1918. The italics are mine: they are the proof that the Government was playing with 'paper soldiers'. The infantry would remain below strength as regards their practical needs; the new organisation did not alter, it merely camouflaged the fact. This is where all comparison with French or German methods breaks down: their reorganisations were, indeed, undertaken to increase the number of divisions (and thus the ratio of artillery to infantry, etc.); the British was not.

War and sacrificing to no purpose the British Army on the Western Front.[1]

Nothing availed. On January 10th 1918 the War Office was compelled to order a reorganisation on the lines indicated. Thus, as German preparations for the greatest battle of the war remorselessly proceeded, the British Commander-in-Chief found himself forced to disband two out of his five cavalry divisions (another Cabinet Committee proposal), and was given a list of 145 infantry battalions out of which he was permitted to select the four which might survive and the 141 which must go. In one of his more grotesque passages, Lloyd George seeks to rebut the Official History's comment that this was not the time for such a change, no matter how 'eminently desirable':

It would be interesting to know what better time than January and February—a quiet time at the front—could have been chosen for an 'eminently desirable' change. The diary of the War shows that there was a complete cessation of all serious military operations on the Western Front from the end of December, 1917, to the middle of March, 1918. It was the longest quiet spell we had known for two years.

It is staggering that a Prime Minister, seventeen years after the event, could write such rubbish—more staggering still that anyone could believe him. The truth is that, during this all-too-brief lull before the most devastating storm of war, the Army was training, as best it could, for a defensive which it had not practised for over three years. It was also working with all its might on defensive works which in some sectors were almost entirely lacking, and on all sectors were weak because they had not been needed for three years. Upon these weary and over-burdened men the Prime Minister and his Committee now laid their new load. For what happened in the event was this: 115 battalions were disbanded out of hand, to provide the reinforcement required to make up the infantry's existing deficit; thirty-eight were amalgamated to produce nineteen; seven were converted from infantry to pioneers (of whom the Army was always chronically short). The result was twofold: first, all existing tactical schemes, whether for division or brigade, had to be scrapped, and new ones devised. If there had been time, it would, of course, have been helpful to train the troops on the new system. But there was no time. Secondly, there was the matter of dislocation.

In France, Germany and other continental countries, divisions,

---

[1] Official History, 1918, vol. i, pp. 51–53.

at the outbreak of war, consisted of two infantry brigades; each
brigade consisted of two regiments; each regiment of three battalions.
To reduce a division from twelve to nine battalions was a simple
matter; one merely took away one regiment (and one brigadier). The
British army was organised differently: a division consisted of three
brigades, and a brigade of four battalions. Only rarely were two or
more of these battalions regimentally linked. Thus, in 1914, we
find the 4th (Guards) Brigade consisting of:

> 2nd Bn. Grenadier Guards
> 2nd Bn. Coldstream Guards
> 3rd Bn. Coldstream Guards
> 1st Bn. Irish Guards.

The presence of the two Coldstream battalions was unusual; the
5th Infantry Brigade, for example consisted of:

2nd Bn. The Worcestershire Regiment
2nd Bn. The Oxfordshire and Buckinghamshire Light Infantry
2nd Bn. The Highland Light Infantry
2nd Bn. The Connaught Rangers.

By 1916, with the entry into battle of New Army and Territorial
Army divisions, this pattern had changed to some extent. Thus, in
the 34th (New Army) Division we find both the 102nd and 103rd
Brigades consisting entirely of battalions of the Northumberland
Fusiliers. Even so, they were not absolutely interchangeable: the
102nd was Tyneside Scottish, while the 103rd was Tyneside Irish.
Perversity was sometimes carried to extreme lengths: in the 36th
(Ulster) Division the whole of the 107th Brigade consisted of Royal
Irish Rifles. The 108th Brigade had three battalions of Royal Irish
Rifles and one of Royal Irish Fusiliers. What had happened? Had
the Royal Irish Rifles run out of battalions? By no means: the 109th
Brigade had three of Royal Iniskilling Fusiliers—and one of Royal
Irish Rifles! But all these were exceptional: the basic composition of
brigades remained assorted. This, coupled with seniority, made
reorganisation a very complicated matter. One example, for the 19th
(Western) New Army Division will suffice; this division received its
orders to reorganise on January 24th:

> . . . all four battalions of the 56th Brigade[1] were to be disbanded
> and the brigade reconstituted as follows: 8/North Staffords from
> the 57th Brigade, 9/Cheshires from the 58th Brigade, and
> 1/4/King's Shropshire Light Infantry from the 63rd Division.

---

[1] 7/King's Own, 7/E. Lancs., 7/S. Lancs., 7/Loyal N. Lancs.

The date from which the reorganisation was to take effect . . . was
the 4th of February. It is impossible to express adequately the
heart-burnings which these changes created. . . .[1]

Needless to say, this astonishing and demoralising exercise took
time—time during which the roads of France were filled with
British units seeking their new 'homes', and during which an
esprit-de-corps built up in years of common experience was thrown
away. In the First Army, the process was completed by February
19th; in the Fifth Army, by February 25th; in the Third Army, by
February 27th; and in the Fourth Army, not until March 4th—
only 17 days before the German attack. For a final complication, it
must be added that the Governments of Australia, Canada and New
Zealand declined to adopt similar measures, with the result that the
ten Dominion divisions on the Western Front retained their twelve
battalions each.

It is upon this amazing scene that the gravamen of the charge
against Mr. Lloyd George and his Government rests—this spectacle
of the British Army, facing the most formidable offensive of the War,
actually disbanding units, and disorganised by the ensuing arrangements. Lloyd George, of course, by every device of pleading, has
sought to shuffle off responsibility for putting his country in such
deadly danger. 'In March 1918,' he wrote,

> the total strength of the British Army, Regular and Territorial,
> raised in this country—excluding all Dominion, Colonial, Indian
> and native troops—was 3,889,990. This was the colossal giant
> which the War Cabinet are accused of having reduced to a skeleton
> army. *It was the highest total strength which the British Army ever
> reached. At no time in the whole course of the War were there so
> many men from this country in the ranks of the Army at home and
> overseas as at the date of the German offensive in March, 1918.*[2]

He adds, with similar emphasis, that at the same time the Expeditionary Forces in all theatres also reached their high-water mark for
the War. He does everything that a man can do with figures, except
explain those 141 battalions which vanished from the Order of Battle
in France.

There remains the question of the distribution of the very large
number of men who were certainly in uniform at the beginning of
1918. On January 5th the B.E.F. in France numbered 1,949,100.

---

[1] *The History of the 19th Division 1914–1918*, by Everard Wyrall; Edward
Arnold, p. 129. It will be noted that the disbandment of this one brigade
affected 3 others—one in another division altogether.
[2] *War Memoirs,* chap. LXXII. (Lloyd George's italics.)

At home, in the United Kingdom, there were no less than 74,403 officers and 1,486,459 other ranks.[1] This is a total which requires some explanation. A large number of the men concerned were in hospital or convalescing from wounds; others were in training formations; others constituted the Home Forces, under Field-Marshal Lord French. These were the nation's 'second shield' (behind the Navy) against invasion, which was still talked of as a possibility.[2] Over 90,000 men (62,000 infantry) were in Ireland, a country still simmering after the 1916 Rising. Nevertheless, there were over 600,000 trained Category 'A' men in the country, of whom the Cabinet Committee considered 449,000 as 'available' for drafts. In the subsidiary theatres of war there were, in addition, 36,695 officers and 852,620 other ranks. A large proportion of these were, of course, Indian or Colonial contingents, who would not have been considered as potential reinforcements for the Western Front; yet, when the moment of truth arrived, it was found possible to bring approximately 100,000 British soldiers from these theatres to France —rather late in the day.

It remains to look at the distribution of force within the B.E.F itself. A great many words and oceans of ink have been expended on the argument whether the B.E.F. was stronger at the beginning of 1918 than at the beginning of 1917. Most of the disputation has been pointless. A G.H.Q. paper of May 1918 shows quite clearly what was happening: large increases in ration strength were accompanied by a decrease in fighting strength—a phenomenon less surprising to later generations than it was then. The figures are:

---

[1] Excluding Overseas contingents.

[2] Repington wrote on January 5th:

Went down to dine quietly at Coombe with Sir A. Paget (General Sir Arthur Paget, commanding the 'Southern Army') and to talk Home Defence. I told him the figures I had been given, and he told me that in his opinion they were valueless unless it were understood that the men lining the beaches were cripples, all B and C men, and that the mobile reserve behind were largely boys of 18 and 19, very keen good boys, but impressionable and partially trained, with bad officers. He had been told that Lord French could not bring up his reserve till the third day, and Sir A. thought that if a convoy with 30,000 men could reach the coast of Kent they could land under cover of smoke-screens and their ship's fire in boats with steel shields which would be proof against machine gun and rifle fire: 30,000 Boches would be in Maidstone by the third day, and he had no confidence that he could stop them. Many of his men on the beach had long fronts to defend and held them very thinly. His cyclists, on which he relied as first reinforcements, were being taken away for Ireland, and three out of his four divisions behind were to be scrapped to make up the horrible deficits of the Army in France.

Ration strength, Dec. 31st 1916   1,630,511
Ration strength, Jan. 5th 1918   1,949,100
Increase   318,589.

The outstanding contributions to this were an increase of 37,000 in Transportation, and 271,100 in labour units (white and coloured).[1] To offset these increases, there was a decline of 93,550 fighting troops, chiefly accounted for by a decrease of 126,100 in the infantry. (The Royal Flying Corps, Royal Artillery, Machine Gun Corps and Tank Corps had all increased.)

This was an unsatisfactory state of affairs in itself, but made far worse by the decision taken in October 1917, against the rooted opposition of the C.I.G.S. and the C.-in-C., to extend the British front by 25 miles. It was a constant demand of the French that the British should take over more front; they pointed repeatedly to the disproportionate lengths held by the two armies, and insisted that only by decreasing their front could they build up a reserve.[2] The British Government had accepted these arguments, with the result that in 1918 the already weakened Expeditionary Force was even further stretched. Apart from the inevitable disorder of taking up new positions, there was the disagreeable discovery that the defences in the area taken over had been badly neglected by the French. This now became part of the front of General Gough's Fifth Army, and the work which had to be done was beyond the capacity of his labour force. Once again the infantry, who should have been resting and training, had to exhaust themselves in the rôle of navvies.[3]

It was against this background that the C.-in-C., Sir Douglas Haig, had to assess his problem. His front fell into three sectors, each with its special characteristics: in the north, in Flanders, and particularly in front of the vital rail centre of Hazebrouck, the British positions lay much too close to the sea for comfort[4]—retreat here could easily be fatal; in the centre, not only was there more space, but after the capture of the Vimy Ridge in April 1917 there was a strong natural position to defend. On February 23rd, visiting the First Army, and climbing the Ridge, Haig wrote: 'I look upon this part of our front as the backbone and centre of our defensive system (it) must be held firmly at all costs'. To the south of Arras, extending down in front of Amiens, came the sectors of the Third and Fifth

[1] In 1918 some 97,000 Chinese were brought to France to swell the labour force; in principle it was agreed that they should not be expected to work in the battle zones.
[2] In February 1918, after the extension, 99 French and 1 American division held 324 miles of front; 58 British and 2 Portuguese divisions held 126 miles.
[3] See Appendix IV.
[4] Hazebrouck to Dunkirk = 20 miles.

Armies; here the British had space to sell, here there was room for manoeuvre—'elastic defence'. Haig's dispositions were made accordingly:

ARMY	SECTOR	DIVISIONS		
		(Line)	(Army Reserve)	(G.H.Q.)
Second (Plumer)	Ypres Salient (23 miles)	9	3	2
First (Horne)	Armentières–Arras (33 miles)	12	2	2
Third (Byng)	Arras–Manancourt (28 miles)	10	4	2
Fifth (Gough)	Manancourt–R. Oise (42 miles)	11	1+3 Cav.	2
		42	10+3 Cav.	8

There are certain points to be noticed: first (obviously) the great weakness of the Fifth Army in relation to the length of its front, despite the presence of the entire Cavalry Corps in its sector; secondly, the paucity of the reserves under the hand of G.H.Q.; thirdly the apparent even distribution of these G.H.Q. reserves. On closer inspection, however, it will be seen that this distribution was even more heavily biassed in favour of the northern sectors than at first appears: in the north there were 4 G.H.Q. divisions to 56 miles (with another not too far away), as compared with 4 to 70 miles in the south. Evidently it was the northern front with which Haig was preoccupied, and elsewhere he was taking a calculated risk. He has been accused of taking a heedless risk, through misjudgment of the enemy's intentions. This was not so; the risk was entirely calculated, on the basis of agreement with the French Commander-in-Chief, General Pétain. His very acceptance of the extension of his front had, from the first, been linked with the understanding that this would enable the French to build up a large reserve which, while five British divisions remained in Italy, would be the effective reserve of the Western Front. Pétain had carried out his intentions: thirty-nine of his ninety-nine French divisions, and three American divisions besides, now stood in reserve. But it had also been part of Haig's agreement that a part of this reserve (General Humbert's Third Army) should be stationed behind the point of junction of the Allies, ready to intervene on Gough's front. Belief in the validity of this agreement is the full extent of his misjudgment: his relations with Pétain were normally very good—'businesslike' was the word Haig often applied to him—and he supposed that he could rely on the French general's word.

Nevertheless, whatever happened, as the February and March days ticked by, it was clear that the British Army was in for a bad time. An officer at G.H.Q. summed it all up:

So . . . we are confronted with:

1. A longer front to hold.
2. Reduced establishment to hold it.
3. No hope of reinforcements.
4. A German attack in greater strength than anything we have yet experienced.

Not a cheerful prospect.[1]

The imminence of dire events lay heavily upon the whole Army; it was just a matter of waiting, doing what one could to make ready, and hoping for the best.

---

[1] Brig.-Gen. J. Charteris: *At G.H.Q.;* Cassell 1931. Charteris was Haig's Head of Intelligence until January 1918.

XI

At 10 minutes past 5 I was awakened by the roar of a bombardment, which . . . was so sustained and steady that it at once gave me the impression of some crushing, smashing power. I jumped out of bed and walked across the passage to the telephone in my office and called up the General Staff. On what part of our front was the bombardment falling? The answer came back almost immediately: 'All four corps[1] report heavy bombardment along their front. . . .'[2]

So, on the morning of March 21st 1918, General Sir Hubert Gough learned that the long-awaited German blow had fallen upon his Fifth Army. It was yet another curiosity of the German plan that the command of the greatest single effort of the War to date should be divided: on Gough's front was deployed the whole of the *Eighteenth Army* (von Hutier, twenty-five divisions) belonging to the Army Group of the German Crown Prince. Gough also had to contend with the bulk of the *Second Army* (von der Marwitz, twenty-one divisions). The remainder of this Army, plus the *Seventeenth* (von Below, twenty-five divisions), both belonging to the Army Group of Crown Prince Rupprecht of Bavaria, extended the attack northwards into the sector of the British Third Army, commanded by General Sir Julian Byng. It was, in fact, these two northernmost Armies which were intended to deliver the main attack, with von Hutier in a very freely interpreted 'covering' rôle. Nevertheless, the divided command remains a mystery, and proved to be a weakness; the British Official History explains it with the suggestions that O.H.L. hoped thereby to exercise more direct control, or that dynastic reasons prevailed against concentration under Crown Prince Rupprecht. It was fortunate for the Allies that Germany, too, had her problems and discords.

---

[1] From right to left: III (Butler), XVIII (Maxse), XIX (Watts), VII (Congreve).
[2] Gen. Sir Hubert Gough: *The Fifth Army;* Hodder & Stoughton 1931, p. 260.

The bombardment was a signal to General Gough to alert his scanty reserves; but there was very little that he—or anyone else—could do.

> All the necessary steps to meet the storm had been taken: the German infantry would not attack for several hours. I looked out of my window, and in the morning light I could see that there was a thick fog, such as we had not yet experienced during the whole of the winter. We were getting into spring, and it was extraordinary to have so dense a fog at this date. Very dimly I could see the branches of a tree in the garden about forty feet from my window. The stars in their courses seemed to be fighting for the Germans. . . .[1]

In the memories of those who came through the 'March Offensive', two recollections of this terrible first day stand out: the pulverising weight of the German bombardment, delivered by 6,473 guns and howitzers and 3,532 trench mortars of all calibres, firing at maximum intensity for five hours—and the fog. There has, it is true, been some discussion as to whether the British or the Germans were most hampered by the fog on March 21st; the question would seem to be largely unreal. In the words of the British Official History:

> The fog enhanced the value of superior numbers by restricting the fire of the infantry defence to very close range, thus minimizing German losses, although it did not prevent the artillery from firing on predetermined areas. Like the obscurity of night, it rendered nearly useless the machine-gun, that weapon which, given opportunity, can in a few moments destroy any balance of numbers with which an attack may start, as we had experienced on the Somme in 1916. Moreover the system of defence adopted was particularly dependent on the machine gun. Mist, or the semi-darkness of early dawn, on the whole favours the attackers, enabling them to approach unseen, and escape not only the machine guns and rifles of the trench garrison, but also the artillery barrages which would be called for, if their approach had been observed, and communications, either cable or visual, were intact.[2]

As far as time and available labour permitted, the British defences were constructed in depth and based on mutually supporting machine gun and Lewis gun posts, rather than on lines of trenches. The combination of a shattering bombardment with fog on such a system was overwhelming. When the German infantry came forward

---

[1] Gough: p. 261.
[2] 1918, i, p. 255.

through the murk, 'the Forward Zone as a whole was overrun at the first rush, the machine guns still in action hardly firing a shot'.[1]

The fate of individual British units in the Forward and Battle Zones was frequently obscure, and generally harrowing. The 7/Rifle Brigade was in the Battle Zone of the 14th Division; the bombardment fell upon it at about 4.40 a.m. 'From that moment nothing was heard of, or from, the Seventh Battalion.'[2] In the 24th Division, the headquarters of the 2/8/Lancashire Fusiliers were 'captured in a dug-out before becoming aware that the infantry attack had begun'.[3] In the 16th Division, of two companies of the 7/Royal Irish in the Forward Zone, 'not a man succeeded in escaping'.[3] The Second Battalion of the same regiment had even worse luck: 'after a desperate fight, most of the battalion was killed or captured'.[3] These were all Fifth Army formations—and such episodes could be multiplied all the way along that Army's 42-mile front. In the Third Army, holding a much shorter line with stronger forces, there were nevertheless similar experiences. In the sector of the 153rd Brigade, 51st (Highland) Division, for example, 'the troops occupying the Forward Zone had been mostly killed, buried by the bombardment, or taken prisoner; the few survivors were not capable of much resistance, and none returned to tell the tale'.[3]

In short, a disaster of the first magnitude had struck the British Army. The Germans had achieved the cherished aim of so many attacks during that war—they had reached the gun-line. On March 21st, the Fifth Army lost 382 guns; by midnight on the 22nd the Third Army reported a loss of 150. This spelt a clear breach in the British line, and on the second day of battle the Germans poured through. It was no longer a question of assault: it was pursuit.

> Along the road a slow stream of traffic was moving towards Bapaume and beyond, first waves of the tide which rolled westwards for days and days. Here and there a battery in column of route, walking wounded in twos and threes, an odd lorry or two, a staff car carrying with undignified speed the dignified sign of a Corps Headquarters, a column of horse transport, and a biggish batch of German prisoners captured by the 51st Division . . . it was with something approaching a shock that I realized everything was in retreat . . . I stood watching the unforgettable scene for ten minutes; it was too sad for words.[4]

---

[1] Official History, 1918, vol. i, p. 166.
[2] W. W. Seymour: *The History of the Rifle Brigade in the War of 1914–1918*, vol. ii, p. 232.
[3] Official History, 1918, vol. i, pp. 179, 180, 191, 221.
[4] Behrend: *As from Kemmel Hill*, p. 77.

The battle continued inexorably. Day by day casualties mounted, more ground was lost, and a situation developed for the Allies which was more serious than any since the calamitous Battles of the Frontiers in August 1914. In this statement alone resides the most serious possible indictment of the British Government: it was the dramatic fulfilment of the Army Council's warning in January that the Government was 'taking an unreasonably grave risk of losing the War and sacrificing to no purpose the British Army . . .'.[1] It was a sad result of all the suffering endured during the previous four years, all the experience gained, all the effort put into the mobilization of Britain. Yet it was a fact, a fact that had to be dealt with: it was the crisis of the War. And once again, as in 1914, despite the tension and the drama, the pain and the heroism of the rolling battle, the true point of decision lay inside the minds of the generals who had to cope. The first to meet the test was General Gough. His single infantry division in Army reserve was immediately sucked into the battle, and with it the two G.H.Q. divisions behind his front. That gave him fourteen divisions in all with which to oppose the forty-three against him; his prospects were not agreeable:

> From the British Army I could expect one division in three days, and one more the following day. From French sources, one division would be with me ready to take its place in the battlefield after two days, and then I might hope for two more after three days; a total of five divisions in action by the fifth day of battle, a help certainly, but—when a front of over forty miles had to be reinforced—still quite insufficient to bring to a standstill the German masses which would also be receiving reinforcement. We must look forward to maintaining the struggle for at least eight days. Our losses in the Forward Zone, where our battalions had so faithfully and steadfastly fought it out, and had been almost annihilated in doing so, had proved what the result of a decisive battle would be.[2]

It was now that Haig's understanding with General Pétain was put to the acid test. All his arrangements were based on the promises of mutual aid in the event of such an emergency as had now arisen:

> . . . I have arranged as a preliminary measure with the Commander-in-Chief of the French Armies for all preparations to be made for the rapid despatch of a force of from six to eight British divisions with a proportionate amount of artillery and subsidiary services to his assistance.

[1] See pp. 140–141.
[2] Gough, p. 265.

L

General Pétain *has made similar arrangements* for relief or
intervention of French troops on the British front. These arrangements, both French and British, *are now being completed*, and
zones of concentration opposite those fronts which are most
vulnerable and likely to be attacked are being provided.[1]

Gough, fully aware of this understanding, now naturally turned to
his ally, and looked for the intervention of General Humbert with
his Third French Army; he was in for a rude awakening:

Humbert came in to see me, and when I said something to the
effect that it was a desperate struggle and that I was glad to see
him with his Army, he replied, 'Mais, je n'ai que mon fanion',
referring to the little pennant on his motor with the Army colours.
This, however, was not exactly the aid that we were looking for at
that moment.[2]

There was worse to follow, but this time it was Haig who sustained
the impact. It was bad enough that the French Army which was to
have supported his right flank did not exist. It was far worse to discover, by the fourth day of battle, that General Pétain was convinced
that the British had been thoroughly defeated; that therefore it was
no longer a prime object to keep the Allied armies in touch; and that
the chief task of the French Army must now be the defence of Paris,
while the British made such withdrawal as they could upon the
Channel Ports. The spectre thus arose of a gap forming and widening
between the Allies, through which the Germans would pour their
reserves and destroy their enemies in detail. This alarming frame of
mind was disclosed to Haig at a meeting with Pétain at 11 p.m. on
March 24th:

Pétain struck me as very much upset, almost unbalanced and most
anxious. ... In my opinion, our Army's existence in France
depends on keeping the British and French Armies united. So I
hurried back to my Headquarters at Beaurepaire Château to
report the serious change in *French strategy* to the C.I.G.S. and
Secretary of State for War, and ask them to come to France ...
in order to arrange that General Foch or some other determined
General who would fight, should be given supreme control of the
operations in France.[3]

So ended, under the hammer of dire events, an old story dating
back to the War's beginnings. If the failure of the British Govern-

---

[1] O.A.D. 770: Haig to the British Military Representative, Supreme War
Council, March 2nd. (My italics.)
[2] Gough, p. 266.
[3] See Terraine: *Douglas Haig: The Educated Soldier*, pp. 420–425.

ment to grip the problem of man-power had created one set of conditions for defeat in the field, the failure of the Allies to evolve effective strategic unity undoubtedly did the rest. What March 21st revealed was what Britain's responsible military leaders had already pointed out with some emphasis—that the question of strategic control was intimately bound up with the vital matter of Reserves.

All through the War, the Central Powers had enjoyed two inestimable advantages: their central position, which made possible a flexible strategy based on interior lines of communication; and the firm effective control exercised by the German General Staff. There were frictions, naturally—both national and personal; there were divided aims and opinions. Very early indeed, in a bitter moment, some Germans spoke of the Austrian Alliance as being 'fettered to a corpse'. A series of Austrian disasters on the Eastern Front, coupled with fire-eating Austrian ambitions on the Italian Front, often brought German Staff Officers to the edge of frenzy. They themselves had their 'Easterners' and 'Westerners' with inevitable clashes of personality. In 1915 and 1916 there was little love lost between Falkenhayn, Chief of the General Staff, and the Hindenburg-Ludendorff combination in the East, which succeeded him. The rôle of the Kaiser, and the galaxy of minor royalty which constituted the German Empire, also made for difficulties. Yet, by comparison with the tribulations of the *Entente*, the German position was excellent. At least the two main partners of the Triple Alliance spoke the same language (an advantage well appreciated by the British and Americans from 1941–1945). And the sheer mass and quality of the German Army always provided the General Staff with the leverage it required against any serious recalcitrance of its allies. Indeed, it had been the constant dream of every forward-looking person on the Allied side to find some means of matching this powerful weapon of unity.

In a Coalition of more or less equal partners, however, true unity is the most elusive of goals; much lip-service is paid to it, without a corresponding intellectual effort to understand its foundations. At sea, for example, there was almost perfect unity from beginning to end of the 1914–1918 war—in the sense that there were no great inter-Allied disputes about the conduct of the war at sea, nor any discords over supreme command among the admirals such as those which occurred from time to time among the generals. There was a perfectly good reason for this, which might have been recognised as a lesson to be applied to the land fronts. The simple and rather daunting truth, of course, was that 'unity of direction' at sea was founded upon the absolute supremacy of the Royal Navy. This perfectly matched the 'unity of direction' among the Central Powers founded upon the absolute supremacy of the German Army. In the

same way, there was, until well into 1916, a degree of 'unity of
direction' among the Allies on the Western Front. This was founded
upon the unquestionable supremacy of the French Army until about
the middle of that year—a fact recognised by Haig and clearly
stated by him on becoming Commander-in-Chief. On January 1st
1916 he spoke to the Head of the French Mission at G.H.Q., General
des Vallières:

> I showed him the instructions which I have received from the
> S. of S. for War containing the orders of the Govt. to me. I
> pointed out that I am *not under* General Joffre's orders, but that
> would make no difference, as my intention was to do my utmost
> to carry out General Joffre's wishes on strategical matters, as if
> they were orders.[1]

This was the price of junior partnership, not always easily perceptible
in Whitehall, but very clear to the man on the spot. But this kind of
unity, informal and limited, and brought about by the compulsions
of sheer necessity, was never what the visionaries had in mind.

One of the loudest and most persistent advocates of 'unity' throughout the War (until he had to operate within it) was Sir Henry Wilson,
who became C.I.G.S. in February 1918. His definition of 'Superior
Direction', as he called it, was the most comprehensive:

> Such a Body will be above all Sectional Fronts, it would view the
> War as a whole, it would treat the line of battle from Nieuport to
> Mesopotamia as one line, and it would allot to each of the Allies
> the part which it would play.[2]

There is no doubt that phrases such as 'from Nieuport to Meso-
potamia' held out attractions to amateur strategists which were not
to be measured by any reality which they might express. There was
something grand about them, suggesting that one's thoughts were
on a superior scale; politicians liked that, and Henry Wilson took
care not to disappoint them. But that apart, it is worth spending a
moment on a further inspection of his ideas.

By the time Wilson had arrived at the concept outlined above,
Russia had dropped out of the War. One wonders whether, at any
time while she remained a belligerent, there was any possibility of
her accepting such a scheme. Russia was never backward in demanding Allied help—and it must be stated that she was never backward
in sacrificing her men in support of the Allies. But Unity? Is it

[1] Terraine: *Douglas Haig*, p. 182.
[2] Memorandum to the War Cabinet, Oct. 20th 1917; qu. Lloyd George,
War Memoirs.

believable that the most autocratic government in the civilised world, secretive and always more than a little xenophobic, would ever have permitted foreigners to 'allot the part which it would play'? And if one entertains this doubt about the government of the Tsar, how much more so of the neurotically suspicious Bolsheviks who followed him! The very fact of Russia's existence as a major Ally made true unity impossible. And when America emerged in place of Russia as the man-power reservoir of the Alliance, it was soon discovered that she, too, had the profoundest reservations about unity.

Yet, within limits, Henry Wilson's 'Superior Direction' became a fact, and played its brief but significant part in the conduct of the War. On November 7th 1917, a Supreme War Council, consisting of political and military representatives of France, Britain, Italy and America, was created, with the duty 'of continuously surveying the field of operations as a whole, and, by the light of information derived from all fronts and from all Governments and Staffs, of co-ordinating the plans prepared by the different General Staffs, and, if necessary, of making proposals of their own for the better conduct of the war'.[1] The curious defects in the structure of this body; the peculiarities surrounding the position of the British military representative (Wilson himself) who was expected by the Prime Minister to supply an 'alternative strategy' to that of the Government's responsible advisers, need not be gone into here.[2] What we are concerned with is the direct influence of the 'Superior Direction' on the battle of March 1918.

On February 2nd, on the proposal of Mr. Lloyd George, the Supreme War Council decided on the creation of a General Reserve for the Western, Italian and Balkan (Salonika) Fronts. An 'Executive Committee', consisting of the Permanent Military Representatives of Britain, Italy and America, with General Foch for France, was set up with

the following powers to be exercised in consultation with the Commanders-in-Chief of the Armies concerned:

(a) to determine the strength in all arms and composition of the General Reserve, and the contribution of each national army thereto;

(b) to select the localities in which the General Reserve is normally to be stationed;

(c) to make arrangements for transportation and concentration of the General Reserve in the different areas;

---

[1] Lloyd George: Speech in the House of Commons, Nov. 14th 1917.
[2] See Terraine: *The Western Front*, pp. 100–106.

(d) to decide and issue orders as to the time, place and period of employment of the General Reserve . . .

(e) to determine the time, place and strength of the counter-offensive, and then to hand over to one or more of the commanders-in-chief the necessary troops for the operation . . .

(f) until the movement of the General Reserve begins, it will for all purposes of discipline, instruction and administration, be under the orders of the respective commanders-in-chief, but no movement can be ordered except by the Executive Committee. . . .[1]

It was also decided that the President of the Executive Committee should be General Foch.

This outcome satisfied many of those present as a day's work well done; others were less pleased. Haig commented with perspicacity: 'To some extent it makes Foch a "Generalissimo" '. This was, of course, true—but within limits which Haig expressed in a letter to his wife on February 5th:

. . . although it was decided to form an Inter-Allied Reserve, before the Committee can handle it they must form it. Now I cannot part with any of my troops—so if they want a Reserve it must be found from French and British troops in Italy—the five divisions I sent there are really the Reserves of the British Forces in France—or bring troops from Salonika or elsewhere.[2]

General Pétain was equally opposed to the idea. On February 6th Repington, in his new *Morning Post* capacity, dined with the French C.-in-C. at Compiègne:

On the question of the Higher Command, Pétain said that he did not mean to allow Foch and Co. to interfere with his reserves. If they like to handle the Anglo–French divisions in Italy this was another matter, but I said their ambitions went much further, whereupon Pétain said that if they interfered with him he would not remain in command. He was sure that Haig and he would agree and could carry on.[3]

The Army Council, first pointing out that 'he who controls the reserve controls the whole', and that this meant that 'the Committee will in fact exercise the powers of a Generalissimo' (echoing Haig's thought), then went on to indicate certain constitutional difficulties arising:

[1] Official History, 1918, vol. i, pp. 77–78.
[2] Blake, p. 283.
[3] Repington, ii, p. 222.

The effect of this arrangement will be that the Executive Committee will be invested with powers over the British Forces in France, Italy, and the Balkans, although *it has no constitutional responsibility for their safety*, which is directly affected by the composition, strength, location and employment of the Reserves.

Constitutionally the Army Council are responsible for the safety and welfare of the British Army. The powers conferred on the Executive Committee, however, *will enable it to disregard the Army Council*, in that it is allowed to interpose directly between the Council and the Commanders-in-Chief.

In regard to the position of Commanders-in-Chief, it must be remembered that they are responsible, through the Army Council, for carrying out the policy of His Majesty's Government, while under the system now established *they would be given orders affecting their operations by two different authorities*, the Executive Committee and the Army Council. This system could not fail to cause dangerous confusion and complication in the conduct of the operations.

The Army Council therefore consider that the constitution of the Executive Committee as it now stands would not only place Commanders-in-Chief in an impossible position, but would also deprive the Council of the responsibility entrusted to them under the Constitution of the Realm, and that any such abrogation of that responsibility would be a violation of the trust reposed in them.[1]

Once again, the views of the Army Council were brushed aside; the Supreme War Council itself was to a large extent Lloyd George's creation, and any extension of its powers at the expense of Haig and Robertson seemed to him a most desirable consummation. He was not to be put off by words or considerations of constitutional theory. What killed the idea was fact: the hard fact of Pétain and Haig refusing to risk the safety of their armies by parting with any troops. 'That, in effect,' wrote Robertson, 'put an end to the Executive Committee as an organ of command, for as no general reserve was constituted the Committee was left with no executive functions to perform.'[2]

The still-birth of the Committee, however, meant also the non-existence of an Allied Reserve on the day of battle—with what fatal consequences we have seen. It is necessary, therefore, to examine a little further what the basis of the military opposition to the Execu-

[1] Army Council Memorandum 1/S.W.C./73; author's papers. (My italics.)
[2] Robertson, ii, p. 292.

tive Committee was. It was a reasoned opposition, not merely the instinctive conservatism of professional soldiers at work again. In Pétain's case it was founded upon a wrong Intelligence appreciation of German intentions, about which we shall have more to say. Here it need only be noted that he told Repington on February 6th that 'He had identified 172 (enemy) divisions for certain on his front'— which was nonsense, since according to G.H.Q., there were on that date only 174 German divisions altogether in the West.[1] Right or wrong, however, Pétain would act by what he believed. In the case of Haig and the British General Staff, every consideration was dominated by the sheer shortage of troops. The *idea* of a General Reserve was not challenged—every lesson of military history taught its value. (Furthermore, paper after paper issued by G.H.Q. at this time emphasised the importance of reserves in the coming battle.) What it was found impossible to accept was the manner of creating the proposed Inter-Allied Reserve. A G.H.Q. paper of March 12th sets out the argument, and is worth quoting in full:

> The theory that a reserve should be maintained in the hands of every *Commander* is correct, since every Commander must have the means at his disposal for:—
> (a) Maintaining and influencing the battle.
> (b) Renewing the battle either on the same front or elsewhere.
> (c) Meeting unforeseen contingencies.
> It is essential, however, that unity and homogeneity should be preserved in the formation of a reserve, and that such a reserve should be appointed and handled by a responsible Commander.
> To weaken Armies in order to place a general reserve wanting in homogeneity in the hands of a Committee composed of members of different nationalities is a complete misunderstanding of the rôle of a reserve in great modern battles. The modern battle between Armies equally trained and armed and of equal resolution is not generally an affair of two or three days, but is a prolonged struggle lasting for weeks and perhaps months.
> Into this struggle are drawn first the reserves of Armies and then the reserves of the supreme Commander. The latter, however, are not thrown suddenly into the vast arena of the modern battlefield and, in the first instance, do not produce any decisive effect in the battle, which in its preliminary stages is simply a 'bataille d'usure' —a wearing down of the enemy's forces. The reserves of the supreme Commander are therefore used not only to influence the battle and meet the unforeseen, but also to secure a rotation of divisions in the combat, so that, as formations become exhausted,

[1] See p. 130.

they may be withdrawn, rested, and refitted. To do this effectively, reserve divisions must be at the immediate and absolute disposal of the Commander who alone is responsible for the conduct of the operations, and who alone has sufficient local knowledge of the conditions to decide how and when these reserve divisions are to be employed.

It is recognised, however, that in the conditions which prevail in France, it may be well to vest in some central authority the power to order one or other of the Commanders-in-Chief to move a portion of his forces to the assistance of another Army, or to attack as a means of relieving the pressure on his neighbour. In the case of a divergency of opinion between the Commanders-in-Chief, such an authority may be necessary, but to vest in a Committee the power to handle troops, even if such were available, which is not now the case, would be to create, in fact, a Generalissimo in the form of a Committee. History affords numerous examples of the failures of such forms of authority.[1]

This, then, was the considered position of the British Commander-in-Chief and his Staff; their paper reveals considerable prescience of future events, and it is interesting to note in it the germ of the idea which so powerfully possessed Haig twelve days later, when the battle reached its first perilous climax: a central authority with power to give orders to the Commanders-in-Chief. For the time being, however, the implications of the paper were negative to the Reserve as proposed; it no doubt fortified Haig in his conversation with Sir Henry Wilson (who had now replaced Robertson as C.I.G.S.) the following day:

Douglas Haig . . . said that, if I wanted a General Reserve, I must make some more divisions and I must get more man-power. I could not get him to see the problem in any other light. I impressed on him the fact that by refusing to contribute to the General Reserve he was killing that body, and he would have to live on Pétain's charity, and he would find that very cold charity. But I was quite unable to persuade him. . . . At this juncture I am clear that, if we have to choose between a General Reserve and Haig, we must choose Haig, wrong as I believe him to be.[2]

Wilson, for once, was right: it was Pétain's 'cold charity' which Gough first encountered when Humbert arrived without an Army; it was the extremity of the chill that Haig encountered on March 24th, when Pétain announced his intention of abandoning the right

[1] *Note on the General Reserve* (*O.A.D. 776*) March 12th; author's papers.
[2] Wilson Diary, March 13th 1918.

wing of the British Army. The shock must have been severe. Haig
liked Pétain and always got on well with him (indeed, their personal
relations survived even this abysmal moment). But he had failed to
take two things into account. For the first he cannot be blamed: it
was simply that a German deception plan, calculated to make Pétain
believe that whatever happened on the Somme, the main blow would
be delivered against the French in Champagne, had succeeded brilliantly. At their meeting on March 24th, Pétain told Haig that 'he
expected every moment to be attacked in Champagne and he did
not believe that the main German blow had yet been delivered'.[1]
Yet G.H.Q. Intelligence had already identified over fifty German
divisions in battle (and four days later had identified seventy-eight)—
a reasonable indication of a 'main blow'. French Intelligence was
seriously at fault.

Haig's second error was quite simply his assessment of Pétain's
character. All through the summer and autumn of 1917, Pétain had
been free with promises of support for his British allies in their ill-
starred Flanders offensive—but always he was slow and slight in
fulfilment. Yet Haig continued to trust him; not until this bleak
interview revealed it, did he perceive the fundamental pessimism
beneath Pétain's mask of cool, ironic realism. Haig himself did not
contemplate defeat; he could not enter the mind of a man who did.
But now he knew about Pétain, and his thoughts turned at once to
General Foch, because with all his faults—and both Haig and Sir
John French before him had good opportunities of knowing these—
Foch, also, was a man who did not contemplate defeat.

On March 26th Haig's solution was adopted. A vital Allied conference assembled at the little town of Doullens, some 20 miles north
of Amiens, now clearly an objective of the German thrust. M.
Poincaré, President of the French Republic, was the conference
chairman; supporting him were the Prime Minister, M. Clemenceau,
the Minister of Armaments, M. Loucheur, General Pétain, and
General Foch, Chief of Staff of the French Army. The French
Ministers, in their turn, had been made aware of the nature of their
problem. Just before the conference began, Clemenceau took
Poincaré aside, and reported something Pétain had said to him:
' "The Germans are going to beat the English in the open field,
after which they will beat us too." Should a general speak—or even
think like that?'[2]

On the British side of the table sat Lord Milner, Minister without
Portfolio[3]; Sir Henry Wilson, C.I.G.S.; Sir Douglas Haig; Haig's

---

[1] Blake, p. 297.

[2] Raymond Poincaré: *Au Service de la France*.

[3] Milner became Secretary of State for War just under a month later.

Chief of Staff, Sir Herbert Lawrence; and Major-General A. A.
Montgomery, Chief of Staff of the Fourth Army, who took notes.
Haig opened the proceedings by stating the situation, the details of
which he had ascertained at a meeting with his Army Commanders
just before the conference began. As Haig spoke, there were interjec-
tions by Pétain, in keeping with the frame of mind which he had
displayed to Clemenceau. Pétain, remarked Haig, 'had a terrible
look. He had the appearance of a Commander who was in a funk and
has lost his nerve.' When Pétain's turn came, he concluded: '. . .
everything possible must be done to defend Amiens'. Foch, who
had been looking increasingly impatient, broke in: 'We must fight
in front of Amiens, we must fight where we are now. As we have not
been able to stop the Germans on the Somme, we must not now
retire a single inch.' This was in characteristic vein, and Haig took
it as his cue: 'If General Foch will consent to give me his advice,
I will gladly follow it'. The Ministers conferred briefly; then
Clemenceau produced a formula, charging Foch with 'the co-
ordination of the action of the British and French Armies in front
of Amiens'. 'This proposal,' wrote Haig,

> seemed to me quite worthless as Foch would be in a subordinate
> position to Pétain and myself. In my opinion, it was essential to
> success that Foch should control Pétain; so I at once recom-
> mended that Foch should *co-ordinate the action of the Allied
> Armies on the Western Front*. Both Governments agreed to this.[1]

Poincaré remarked, when all was settled: 'Je crois, messieurs, que
nous avons bien travaillé pour la victoire'.[2] Henry Wilson commented: 'Douglas Haig is ten years younger tonight than he was
yesterday afternoon', and congratulated himself as a chief architect
of the unity of command which had at last been achieved. As the
years passed, many claims were advanced for this honour; in the
immediate sense, as the instigator of the Doullens Conference, and
as the one who guided it along the right lines, Haig's claim is the
best. But there is sound sense in the final comment of Field-Marshal
Sir William Robertson: 'A moment's reflection will suffice to show
that it was due to no particular individual—unless it be to General
Ludendorff—but to force of circumstances'.[3]

And so, after nearly four years of war, formal Unity of Command
was achieved by the Allies on the Western Front. In practical terms,
under Foch, it meant that the Allies, though they might be defeated,

---

[1] Terraine: *Douglas Haig*, p. 424. (Haig's italics.)
[2] This and other details of the Doullens Conference are from the British
Official History, based on Loucheur's notes.
[3] Robertson, p. 295.

would not be divided. This was the meaning of his appointment—
significant enough, but this was almost its whole meaning. Foch
himself has made clear the limitations of his office:

> What . . . was known by the term 'unified command' gives a false
> idea of the powers exercised by the individual in question—that
> is, if it is meant that he commanded in the military sense of the
> word, as he would do, for example, in the French Army. His
> orders to Allied troops could not have the same characteristic of
> absolutism, for these troops were not his, especially in the sense
> that he could not inflict punishment in case this became necessary.
> But by persuasion he could stimulate or restrain their Com-
> manders-in-Chief, decide upon the policy to follow, and thus
> bring about those concerted actions which result in victory, even
> when the armies concerned are utterly dissimilar.
>
> If, at some appropriate moment, an official mandate is drawn
> up which clearly specifies for all the allies the functions of this
> person, nothing is more to be desired. But it must be on condition
> that the man thus designated can quickly justify the concession.
> For the greatness of a title will not long protect him from criticism,
> opposition or divergence of views and of efforts, on the part of
> armies which, in spite of everything, remain foreign armies for
> him. But they will willingly recognise his authority once they have
> seen and favourably judged his manner of exercising it.
>
> Supreme Command narrowly exercised divides the efforts of a
> coalition; confidence unites and strengthens them.[1]

It was a fortunate chance that what was needed above all at the
moment of Foch's appointment was an over-ruling of the *French*
Commander-in-Chief, and not some other, for it was precisely this
that Foch was able to do, by virtue of his rank and seniority in the
French Army. For any larger purpose, the Doullens arrangement
was quickly seen to be unsatisfactory. In Foch's own words: 'The
simple rôle of *co-ordinator* was not sufficient for the larger programme
which would certainly have to be undertaken shortly'. Eight days
later the Doullens formula was revised at another conference at
Beauvais, and the position clarified in the terms which would remain
operative until the end of the War:

> M. Clemenceau desired that General Foch's powers as stated in
> the DOULLENS agreement should be more definitely laid down.
> That document gave General Foch authority to 'co-ordinate the
> action of the allied armies on the Western Front'.

[1] Foch: *Memoirs*, translated by Col. T. Bentley Mott; Heinemann 1931,
pp. 210–211.

After some discussion, the three Governments concerned agreed to entrust to General Foch 'the strategical direction of military operations. The Commanders-in-Chief of the British, French and American Armies will have full control of the tactical action of their respective armies. Each Commander-in-Chief will have the right of appeal to his Government if, in his opinion, his Army is endangered by reason of any order received from General Foch.'[1]

So Foch got his larger powers—with built-in safeguards for each of the national contingents. But the Supreme Command of 1918 remained a very flimsy edifice. Foch himself was an anachronism, a survival of epochs of 'La Gloire'; he worked by intuition and inspiration; he did not make use of a modern Staff structure; he was never at home in the new age of increasingly mechanistic war. But he was dauntless, which was what mattered on March 26th.

His influence on the battle then surging over the fields of Picardy was slight. Already, at the Army Commanders' gathering which immediately preceded Foch's appointment, General Byng had been able to report to Haig:

In the south, near the Somme the enemy is very tired and there is no real fighting taking place there. Friend and foe are, it seems, dead beat and seem to stagger up against each other.[2]

Already the lack of an arm of exploitation was robbing the Germans of the fruits of victory; and already the fatal opportunism which passed for strategy in the mind of Ludendorff was having its effect. To Crown Prince Rupprecht, enquiring at one stage of the battle what his strategic objective was, Ludendorff replied: 'I forbid myself to use the word *strategy*. We chop a hole. The rest follows. We did it that way in Russia.'[3] This was not the way to win the War. Now, in face of that eternal perplexity of war, partial success, Ludendorff was at a loss. In his original intention, the main axis of his advance, once off the mark, would be westward and north-westward, to roll up the British line. It was precisely along this axis that the Germans had made the least progress; on the other hand, the astonishing success of what had originally been intended merely as a vast covering operation, the south-westward attack on the British Fifth Army, now offered glittering prizes, chief of them the rail-centre of Amiens. The question was, whether to continue to push towards Arras, the original main axis, or to snatch at Amiens while the chance existed; strong as it was, the German Army could

[1] Official record of Beauvais Conference, April 3rd 1918.
[2] Haig's Diary (author's papers).
[3] Quoted in the British Official History, 1918, ii, p. 464.

not manage both, and a choice had to be made. Ludendorff could not bring himself to the agonising decision. On the 27th and 28th of March the Germans attacked both towards Amiens, and northward towards Arras. It was on the Arras front, held by the British Third Army, that they met their first clear defeat. A British officer wrote:

> Quite suddenly the smoke cleared; and there, barely 200 yards in front, were the enemy in full view bearing down on us in a compact huddled mass that somehow, for its lack of colour, in the cold grey of dawn, reminded one forcibly of a cinematograph picture . . . I have never been able to estimate the numbers . . . but, as the smoke lifted . . . I counted five lines, each, I calculated, five deep, so deep, in fact, that I had to rub my eyes to make sure that they were not new belts of wire grown up in the night! Out of the dugout poured the thirty or forty survivors of B Company. In an instant the rattle of rapid fire, a fire sustained almost continuously for an hour till rifles were red hot and bolts jammed, broke out from every fire bay. . . . Rapid fire, intense, concentrated, sustained, never before had I realised so vividly its terriffic potentialities![1]

Clumsy German tactics, recalling the mass onslaughts of 1914, broke the strength of the German Army, and contributed to the smashing of this attack; on the 28th it was formally abandoned by O.H.L. Ludendorff's mind was already turning to Flanders, which had been the most favoured battle-ground from the first, and where ground conditions were now becoming acceptable. Nevertheless, his opportunism compelled him to make a final desperate attempt on Amiens in the interval required to switch his artillery to the north. But it was too late. The German impetus was dying. Field-Marshal von Hindenburg wrote:

> Our advance became slower and slower. The hopes and wishes which had soared beyond Amiens had to be recalled. Facts must be treated as facts. . . . We ought to have shouted in the ear of every single man: 'Press on to Amiens. Put in your last ounce. Perhaps Amiens means decisive victory. Capture Villiers-Bretonneux whatever happens, so that from its heights we can command Amiens with masses of our heavy artillery!' It was in vain; our strength was exhausted.[2]

The 'March Offensive' ended on April 5th. This was the sixteenth day of terrible battle, and on it Ludendorff concluded: 'The enemy's

---

[1] *The War History of the 1st Battalion, Queen's Westminster Rifles,* by Major J. Q. Henriques; Medici Society 1923, p. 222.
[2] Hindenburg: *Out of my Life;* Cassell 1920, p. 350.

resistance was beyond our powers ... O.H.L. was forced to take the extremely hard decision to abandon the attack on Amiens for good'.[1] The German achievement had been great: a vast bulge had been driven into the Allied line; immense quantities of munitions had been destroyed or captured; nearly a quarter of a million casualties had been inflicted. The majority of these, of course, were sustained by the British Army: a total of 178,000, of whom over 70,000 were prisoners. The French had lost 77,000, which indicates that they, too, must have been doing something, even if their performance was sometimes disappointing to their hard-pressed allies. This rate of loss is staggering, and if one adds to it the German casualties (about the same as the Allies) it is easy to see why this event towers above all that had preceded it since the very blackest moments at the very opening of the War, in 1914. It represents a human wastage of 31,000 a day. All that can be said in mitigation is that, by the very nature of this warfare, because it was the forward movement of a victorious mass for much of the time, many of the men represented in these dreadful figures were, in fact, prisoners, and thus survived alive. But many did not.

For the British Army, the ordeal was by no means over; Haig's fears—and his strategy inspired by them—were now seen to be fully justified: the German offensive in Flanders opened on April 9th on the sector of the British First Army, and quickly extended to the front of the Second Army too. Because of the prodigious consumption of German resources on the southern front, the attack was on a reduced scale. Nevertheless, at the point of impact, the Germans once again achieved a menacing local superiority—the unfortunate Portuguese Division in the front line, for example, was attacked by no less than four German divisions. Moreover, a number of the British divisions in Flanders had come up from the south, where they had been severely battered, and were by no means yet battle-worthy.[2] The chronic British shortage of reserves was, of course, as

---

[1] Ludendorff: *My War Memories.*

[2] 'The 34th Divn (Third Army) had been pulled out for rest on 26th March; the 40th (Third Army) on 28th March; the 50th (Fifth Army) on 2nd April; the 51st (Third Army) on 28th March. They then had to travel north. En route, they received drafts of recruits, with a few old soldiers, which raised battalions from a strength of under 200 to 500 or 600, but with very few officers; some drafts, e.g. 150 for the 120th Bde., who had never been under fire before, joined on the 9th during the battle. There were, more-over, the gaps in the ranks of the officers and N.C.O.s to fill; clothing, boots and rifles to issue; transport to repair, new horses to replace casualties to be drawn; machine gunners and Lewis gunners to train; the guns to cali-brate; and a hundred and one other things to do. The 50th Divn had just three clear days to carry out all these tasks; the other divns but a little

acute as ever; and Flanders presented the added difficulty that here
there was no room to manoeuvre in retreat.[1] Every position had to
be held to the last, so that this engagement, whose official title is the
Battle of the Lys, was from the first a 'soldiers' battle'—another way
of saying that it was very grim indeed.

The severity of the fighting and the dangers of the situation were
reflected on April 11th by a very unusual gesture on the part of the
Commander-in-Chief: the issuing of the famous 'Backs to the Wall'
Order. It was most unlike Haig to do such a thing. The sad fact is
that, as far as the fighting was concerned, there was very little more
that he could do; the day-to-day direction of the battle was in the
hands of his Army Commanders, General Sir Henry Horne, the
artilleryman commanding the First Army, and General Sir Herbert
Plumer, commanding the Second. General Plumer was the most
reliable and competent of them all, which was one consolation at
least. Haig's real battle was behind the lines, trying to extract from
Foch sufficient French reinforcements in time to prevent the destruction of the British Army.

Throughout the battle, Haig never lost sight of his difficult
double task:

> The most important thing is to keep connection with the French.
> With this object in view I must be strong at and south of Arras.
>
> I must also cover Calais and Boulogne. . . .[2]

For an army in the weakened condition that his was in in April, this
was a formidable proposition, a dangerous stretching of limited
resources. On April 10th Haig told Foch:

> It is vitally important, in order to enable us to continue the battle
> for a prolonged period, that the French Army should take im-
> mediate steps to relieve *some part* of the British front, and take an
> active share in the battle.[3]

---

longer. Many of the brigadiers saw their re-formed brigades for the first
time on the march up to the battle. The 34th and 40th Divns were without
their artillery; the staff of the 34th Divn artillery was in the act of taking
over from that of the 38th on the night of the 8th/9th. These divns were
supported in the battle by the batteries of the 38th and 66th Divns. The
50th Divn had no artillery until that of the 34th Divn, which had just
arrived, came to its support about 4 p.m. The artillery of the 51st Divn
did not arrive until the evening of 9th April.'
(Official History, 1918, ii, p. 160 f.n.)
[1] See p. 146.
[2] Haig Diary, April 11th; author's papers.
[3] Haig to Foch; author's papers. (Haig's italics.)

Two days later Haig pursued the same matter with the French Prime Minister, Clemenceau, with whom, fortunately, he was always on excellent terms:

> I next pointed out the urgent necessity of the French reinforcing the British, and of getting the latter on to a shorter line *in order to be able to continue the battle*. My troops are fast getting worn out.[1]

But, as his biographer Duff Cooper wrote:

> To Haig's urgent requests for reliefs on account of the tiredness of his troops (Foch) would reply that there must be no relief during a battle; and to the suggestion that the line might be shortened by a withdrawal on the left he answered monotonously that there must be no withdrawal.[2]

To these unhelpful dogmas, Foch added the irritation of ill-founded optimism. On April 15th he gave it as his opinion that the battle in Flanders was 'finie'. Haig was moved to retort:

> I find it necessary to place on record my opinion that the arrangements made by you are insufficient to meet the present military situation.[3]

So far from the battle being 'finie', it still had fifteen days to run— days of great strain, hardship and danger to the Allied cause. By the time it ended, Haig had obtained the presence on his front of fourteen French Infantry divisions and three of cavalry; but he was never able entirely to overcome Foch's reluctance to commit these troops to the battle in progress, and sometimes, when they were committed, their performance was disconcerting, as on April 25th, when the French lost the pivotal position of Mount Kemmel. A further price that Haig had to pay for the degree of support which he received from the French was the sending of worn-out British divisions to 'recuperate' on a 'quiet' French sector—the sector in question being the Aisne. This was not merely a bad administrative arrangement, but later it proved to be a tragedy for the troops concerned, when the Germans launched their next attack, upon the French Army, precisely at this point.

Meanwhile, once again, clumsy tactics, exhaustion and frustration in the face of a stubborn British defence brought the Germans to a halt. The battle of the Lys ended without their gaining one single major strategic objective. It had, of course, been costly: the price to

---

[1] Haig Diary, April 12th; author's papers. (Haig's italics.)
[2] Duff Cooper: *Haig;* Faber 1935.
[3] Haig to Foch, April 15th; author's papers.

the Allies was a further 76,300 British casualties, and 35,000 French. Taken in conjunction with the losses of the 'March Offensive', the totals provide a grim commentary on the then prevailing (in Government circles) and persistent belief that the defensive was less costly than attack. British casualties, in the 41 days from March 21st to the conclusion of the German offensives at the end of April, were

239,793.

In 105 days of offensive during the Third Battle of Ypres (Passchendaele) they were

244,897.

Allied casualties, during the 'March Offensive'—only 16 days— totalled 230,493: a rate of loss which makes 'Passchendaele' seem like child's play. Fortunately for the Allies, the clumsy mass tactics of the Germans, ruthlessly pushed home in their desperate attempt to snatch victory at any price, produced a loss practically equal to that of the Allies. The two figures are:

Allies	351,793
German	348,300.[1]

It is permissible to wonder how the myth of the 'cheap' defensive, as opposed to the 'costly' offensive has been able to persist for so long in the face of these facts. It appears that what happened was the simple, disastrous statistical error of not comparing like with like. Churchill, for example, or Lloyd George, would set *known British* losses on, say, the Somme in 1916, against *unknown German* losses. No-one *knows* to this day, and it is unlikely that anyone ever will know, what the German losses on the Somme were; high or low, every figure given is a calculation based on estimates. For March– April 1918, the German figures are clear. But in any case, the imponderables are too great in comparing British and German performances: factors such as the quality of the armies, or their equipment,[2] or their methods have to be taken into account. On the other hand, to compare *known British* losses in attack with *known British* losses in defence offers indisputable evidence. But in 1918 this was the hard way to re-learn old truths.

So ended the great German attacks on the British Army in 1918. They had failed in every respect: failed to break the British, failed to divide them from the French, failed even to obtain the consolation prize of some important centre such as Amiens or Hazebrouck.

---

[1] Brig.-Gen. Sir J. E. Edmonds: *Short History of World War I.*
[2] How does one allow, for example, for the approximately 30% of bad British artillery ammunition in the opening phases of the Somme in 1916?

Nevertheless, their efforts had constituted a severe trial of Allied nerves. The impact of war, during these dreadful weeks, took the form of a gigantic human catastrophe, and was seared into the consciousness of tens of thousands of men on both sides of the front line. If one among them could be singled out as a particular recipient of that impact, it was the British Commander-in-Chief. On Haig fell an overwhelming, continuing moral responsibility; the safety of his army and of his country were at stake time after time. The knowledge that he did not have the confidence of the Government added to his burden. If, at the end of the ordeal, his head was somewhat bowed, this was not to be wondered at; but it was not bowed very low—almost immediately his robust mind began again to concentrate on the subject which had preoccupied him even before he became Commander-in-Chief: how the War might be most quickly brought to an end.

XII

England was beastly in 1918; it was in the hands of the dismal and incompetent. Pessimism raged among those who knew nothing of the war; 'défaitisme', the desire to stop the war at all costs, even by the admission of defeat, broke out among the fainthearts; while those at home who still had the will to fight preferred to use the most disgusting means—to fight by lying propaganda, and by imitating the bad tradition of the German army which consistently made war against civilians. No wonder that a genuine and silent pacifism was rising in the breast of the war-weary populations. Envy, hatred, malice and all uncharitableness, fear and cruelty born of fear, seemed the dominant passions of the leaders of the nations in those days. Only in the trenches (on both sides of No Man's Land) were chivalry and sweet reasonableness to be found.[1]

Such were the sentiments of a soldier returning from the Western Front to serve at home during the last year of the War; he found, as so many found, that a great gulf had opened between himself and his comrades on the one side, and the people for whose sakes they were risking their lives on the other. Army and people alike were bruised by the impact of the German spring offensive. The heavy casualties suffered by the Army were slowly replaced. Whole divisions were reduced to skeleton formations, some of them scheduled to be broken up altogether. Even with the reinforcements now belatedly brought in from other theatres of war (the fields of action which the Government and the Supreme War Council had persisted in regarding as more 'profitable' than the Western Front—until the enemy taught them the truth) the Army remained for a long time pitifully weak. Its chief reinforcement would necessarily be the men raised for it at home, and we have already seen how inadequate Government policies were in that respect. Much attention focussed on the 'boy soldiers', the 18-year-olds, who were flung into the furnace of the German attacks. It is well to recollect that the age-limits of recruitment had been pushed up as well as down, and that perhaps even

Charles Edmonds: *A Subaltern's War;* Peter Davies 1929, p. 188.

greater suffering was inflicted on the older men now going out in large numbers. An infantry corporal makes this telling comment:

> I have no complaint about the courage displayed by these elderly soldiers—it was just that the kind of life they were called upon to live was so wildly outside anything they could have imagined that they couldn't get on terms with it. . . .
>
> The sort of men we got were those senior clerical and retail employees who had for years past gone home every evening to find their slippers in the fender, and the wife shush-shushing the kids with the admonition 'You must be quiet now, dears—poor Daddy's tired'. It was sheer, abominable cruelty to hurl such men as these into the brutal, amphibious life of the front-line infantry. Their days and nights were an endless round of misery, bewilderment and discomfort. Their clothes and boots were painful to wear—and they often had to wear them constantly for several days on end, and wet-through at that. They did not get enough to eat. Their teeth (natural or artificial) were quite incapable of dealing with the hard-tack biscuits that were the staple diet for the front line. We youngsters ate the biscuits—dry. We gave the jam to the old chaps to eat by the spoonful; it made some nourishment for them. . . .[1]

With an army severely mauled in battle, and compelled to recoup with doubtful material, there were considerable doubts at the highest command levels about the moral state of the troops. What *were* they thinking? What *could* they be thinking, after such experiences and in such conditions? The Censorship Department at G.H.Q. made a close study of letters from soldiers to their families at home during April, May and June. Their report was presented to Haig for his secret information in July, and makes strange reading to modern eyes. It may be that the Censorship Department itself was somewhat surprised at what it discovered, because it prefaced a substantial section of the extracts quoted with this statement:

> War weariness and over-strained nerves are largely responsible for letters exhibiting bad moral (sic), frequently accentuated by local shortage of food during the fighting. A disproportionate number of extracts is given to illustrate varying points of view. . . .[2]

It is to be noted that the Censorship staff, so far from wanting to paint rosy pictures or decorate with whitewash, preferred to give *disproportionate* weight to the letters indicating disaffection in some

---

[1] W. C. Glazebrook, D.C.M.: letter to the author, Nov. 11th 1964.
[2] Censorship Dept. Report to the C.-in-C., July 1918; author's papers.

degree or other. It is only possible now to reproduce a small number of the extracts shown to Haig, and the need for such disproportion no longer exists—rather the contrary. But we will begin with some of the 'bad' letters—letters which, in fact, only say exactly what later generations might expect men to be saying in such circumstances.

On April 22nd a man in the Third Army (37th Division) found time to philosophise a little:

> I hate the war more every day, to bow and scrape to those who in other days you would not condescend to know makes my blood boil. And yet we must put up with it and all for what? Money, Money. I don't believe there is any real principles being fought for. It is money grabbing, money—and we are the mugs.

The 63rd (Royal Naval) Division, also in the Third Army, was heavily punished during the 'March Offensive', losing 4,137 officers and men, of whom 1,946 were 'missing'. An artilleryman of the division, writing home in May, said:

> You will probably have seen a few bits in the newspapers about us (Glorious deeds!). If you ever hear anybody say that the troops are in excellent spirits just refer them to this battery. The sooner one side wins the better and we know who will win (*not us*).

A soldier of the South Staffordshire Regiment was in a somewhat similar mood at the beginning of June:

> I am sure we are on the wrong side, what do you think about it? I think we get worse off every day for food, and it's a misery to be under the officers that are coming out now.

From the First Australian Division, which had hard fighting on the Lys with over 1,700 casualties, comes a statement in familiar terms (June 8th):

> Things are not too good over this side, they are sticking the dirt into the Aussies a treat. It's a barstard in the line and it's a barstard out. A man would be better off in the clinc doing a couple of years.[1] Nothing would please me more than to see our blokes jib. We used to go crook in Egypt about the discipline, it was nothing there to what it is here.

Another Australian at the beginning of July, when the Australian Corps was certainly busy, wrote:

[1] According to Haig (Diary, March 3rd 1918) the Australians had 9 men per thousand in prison, compared with 1·6 per thousand Canadian, New Zealand, South African, 1 per thousand British.

I won't soldier any more for them as long as I am in France as they are treating us like dogs, all the boys are fed up with it as they won't give us any rest, I think they want to kill all the Australians.

Two more extracts will suffice to display the Army's discontents; the first is dated (June 15th) but unattributed:

We are expecting Fritz over any time now. I think the quicker he drives us out of France the better, it is quite time to end it somehow or other . . . everybody is fed up with the war out here and don't care who wins so long as we can get it over.

Finally, from the 17th Division on the same day:

Good luck I say to anyone who can keep out of this hell. I am surprised to hear that you have joined the W.L.A.[1] Do you realize Maggie you are helping to prolong the war? I suppose you did not think. What does it matter whether we win the war or not? We shall never get it over so long as the women and girls keep relieving men for the Army. That is like fighting our own mothers and our own sisters. Only when there are no men left will the war finish, that is the way the lads look at it out here.

Without apologies I propose to offer the other side of the story at its proper length; it is necessary to understand how the majority of men felt, in order to understand what the majority of men did. With two disenchanted Australians fresh in mind, let us start with another one (March 30th):

The Hun has had the best of us for the last week or so—not because he is a better man, but because in places he outnumbered us by four to one and we had to give ground rather than sacrifice precious lives to no account. We'll get back all we have lost off him again in good time whenever we feel we want it again. The German generals are wasting the lives of their men recklessly whilst our Generals are taking the utmost care of their men and resources. We need not have the slightest doubt about the downfall of the damnable German nation in the end. And I would cheerfully give up my life rather than be in the shoes of any one of the cowardly curs, who hang back in Australia while the fate of the English speaking race is being decided here in France.

The 8th Division was one of the unluckiest divisions on the Western Front: time after time it found itself in the very thick of horrible

[1] Women's Land Army.

occasions, taking high casualties. Time after time it repaired itself, and wonderfully rebuilt its morale. In the spring battles of 1918 the division lost 390 officers and 8,210 other ranks—appalling figures. An 8th Division soldier wrote on April 29th:

> Ours is a nation whose spirit cannot be broken. To read some of the deeds accomplished by our boys makes one proud to be an Englishman.

As the Battle of the Lys came to its end on April 30th, a man in the 4th Division wrote:

> Well we have given Fritz something to go on with these last few weeks. You cannot step for his dead, and we have been swiping out Battalions of his at a time. It has been jolly fine sport.

Whatever else one may think about that last remark, it was scarcely the effect that the German General Staff had intended to produce. From the 63rd Division, whose depressed gunner we have quoted earlier, came something in a different vein, presumably a reply to a gloomy letter from home:

> Cheer up we shall whack him yet. The heads of affairs have got things well in hand. We must keep persevering. Faith and good sound tackling will do him in yet.

A moving passage comes from the letter of a King's Own Scottish Borderer on May 8th:

> The night previous to our departure from the billet for the trenches we were all singing and a chap just remarked 'You would think we were going home instead of going into the arena', but this is where we beat Fritz; in dark days or bright, we don't lose heart, 'Jerry' may give us a smack today, but he will get a harder one tomorrow. Really I am so proud to be a British soldier and to be able to fight to the bitter end for British interest and it is the same with us all here.

Haig's 'Backs to the Wall' Order on April 11th received a mixed reaction according to the circumstances of the men addressed. The corporal of the East Surreys quoted on page 171 dryly remarked:

> His famous 'backs to the wall' message did not encourage us—we never received it. We to whom it was addressed, the infantry of the front line, were too scattered, too busy trying to survive, to be called into any kind of formation to listen to orders of the day. When I read it in the newspapers my own reaction was that had I heard it on the day it was issued I should have longed for anything

as solid as a wall behind us. So far as we could see, all there was
behind us was a diminishing strip of France and the cold, wet
English Channel.

A soldier in the 32nd Division, however, remembered the Order
when he wrote home on May 19th:

> They may attack any day, but we shall obey our chief's command
> and have our backs to the wall, and not one inch will we retire.
> No one knows it better than the Huns.[1]

It was small wonder that Haig himself, many of his generals, fretting
in their back positions, many politicians, many journalists and others
who visited the Army in their varying moods of despondency at
different times, invariably found themselves encouraged and up-
lifted by contact with the troops. It was small wonder that Sir
William Robertson echoed the Duke of Wellington by saying, when
it was all over, 'that no one but a perfectly damned fool *can* lose a
campaign with a British Army to back him'. But it was an army
that took a little knowing, and later generations have often found the
exercise difficult. They might take a lesson from a man in the Royal
Warwicks, writing on May 22nd:

> I can bear testimony to the splendid qualities of our troops, they
> are perhaps the biggest lot of growsers under the sun, but they
> have their growse and finish with it and always fight well. No task
> is too great for them to undertake, but they must have their growse
> with it, it is part of their lives. I really believe as you say that
> Jerry will not digest the lump he has bitten, on the contrary I
> think he will receive a severe attack of indigestion from us before
> long.

Depressing letters from home—not infrequent in these days of
rationing and air raids—sometimes received short shrift, as in this
case from a man in the IV Corps:

> It is no use being pessimistic Clara for I tell you we are bound to
> win with the men we have got. I have just seen a Battn. of them
> going into the trenches. They look into the gates of Hell and
> laugh, this every night and day, and I tell you the boys of Britain
> cannot be beat.

Planning the counter-strokes which so soon occupied his mind, Haig
did not have the comfort of knowing yet what his Army's feelings
were about such matters; when he received this report in July it

---

[1] For an astonishing Australian echo of Haig, see Terraine: *Douglas Haig*,
pp. 433–434.

must have been a vast support to him in carrying out the plans he had laid. At any rate, he could count on one backer, in the 231st Brigade (June 6th):

> There is no getting away from the fact that we are in for a gruelling time and plenty of severe fighting in the near future and may possibly have to give ground in places, but *please do not be alarmed* as Tommy Atkins is on his metal and *all will be well*. We are preparing something for Fritz and very soon it will be our day, and then it will be God help the Huns for they will get *Hell*.

The brave letters of these simple-minded, patriotic, self-sacrificing men are often almost incomprehensible by modern standards of thought and feeling; one perceives a departed race of unassuming heroes—and the modern world professes not to like heroes. Even at the time, in mid-1918, after all that they had endured, in the light of their immediate future prospects, I suggest that there was something breathtaking about the sentiments expressed. But they do help us to understand how it was that an army which had passed through such a trial, in which its fortunes sank to such a low ebb, was able after only a few weeks to begin upon one of the most glorious passages in our military history. They help us also to understand why so many soldiers, like Charles Carrington (Edmonds), found England 'beastly' at that time. Too often we find in the extracts from their letters that these hard-tried soldiers were having to fight, not only the tough enemy in the field, but also the defeatism of their people at home; thus, from the 73rd Brigade (May 7th):

> For God's sake don't talk about us being beat. Fancy if a letter like that fall into German hands they would think we were really beaten and we are far from that yet. You must not think about being beat. Never mind what you hear we will win yet. I would rather see you all in the grave as see the Bosche win.

From the 41st Brigade (June 13th) the same unshaken, indestructible quality:

> Well we are not downhearted and never will be. Never be under the impression that we are beaten and never let people talk to you on that matter, but I can assure you that every one of our lads are bound to win never mind how long it takes.

From the 231st Brigade again (possibly the man already quoted above) on May 21st:

> One thing you can certainly rely on. Our Army will do its duty. It is therefore the work of those at home to do theirs.

How sad it was that such an admonition should be needed—but it *was* needed. Equally sad, in a different way, is the spectacle of the means by which the despondent public at home maintained its war spirit. As Charles Carrington said, this was all too often done by the most disgusting means—disgusting, that is to say, to those who knew the realities of war. Determination to defeat the Germans in the field was one thing; but only rarely was this expanded by the fighting soldiers into anything resembling hate. Yet hate, deliberately inculcated, was one of the desperate 'cures' adopted by civilians for the flagging of the spirit as the war dragged on. Important public figures lent themselves to this business. Sir Arthur Conan Doyle is to be found writing to the *Times* in December 1917 on the subject of German outrages against British prisoners of war. Conan Doyle demanded 'implacable hatred' against the perpetrators of these deeds. When reproved by the Dean of Manchester, he retorted on January 16th 1918:

> The Dean of Manchester speaks of 'implacable hatred' and 'in-vincible resolve' as if they represented alternative courses. My whole point was that hatred, or, if my critics prefer it, righteous wrath, is the means to attain invincible resolve and it is as such that I have recommended it. Luke-warm feelings can give only half-hearted results. If our workers could actually see the vile things which have been perpetrated upon our people they would be filled by such feelings, call them what you may, that they would work with redoubled heart and vigour. Since they cannot see them they should be brought home to them in every way, verbal or pictorial, that is possible. I cannot understand how it is that reverend ecclesiastics go out of their way to reprove me for what they judge, rightly or wrongly, to be an excess of anti-German feeling on my part, while they have not a word of public reproba-tion for those of their own number who have depressed the national spirit or hampered military counsels by their published utterances.

This drew from the Dean an answer which, if dignified, may be thought mild in view of the doctrine which Conan Doyle was advocating.

> . . . Sir Arthur Conan Doyle need not, I think, fear that the Church has fallen or will fall behind him in the moral reprobation of German criminality. But personal or national hatred is one thing; it is, I am afraid, the temper of Germany. Righteous indignation is another thing; it is, or is coming to be, the temper of Great Britain. Has there been in Great Britain any parallel to the insults and injuries which prisoners of war have suffered in Germany?

If there are, as Sir Arthur says 'reverend ecclesiastics' who have 'depressed the national spirit or hampered military counsels by their public utterances', they must be very few; for the clergy, like Churchmen and Christians generally, so far as I know them, while they hate militarism in itself, are grimly determined to spend and be spent without reserve in the prosecution of a righteous war to its only proper and final goal, a righteous peace.[1]

Righteous indignation is dangerous material; like certain others, it has its 'critical bulk'—too much of it can cause a very nasty explosion. By July 1918 the sundry shocks of war had produced just such a state in Britain. On July 3rd the *Times* published a letter addressed to it from the Olympus of the Reform Club. The writer, Mr. T. B. Napier, pronounced:

At last . . . the view of Germany as she really is, is dawning on the British people. They are finding her to be a great heathen nation, ruthless, a worshipper of pure force, hacking her way with deeds of devilish cruelty and with a never-ending stream of lies and chicanery to what she hopes will be European hegemony. They are beginning to think that with a nation so polluted and polluting, whose ideals are so false and whose human feeling is so dead, no people acknowledging the morals of Christianity, or even of civilization, ought, as it values its own soul, to have truck or dealing or even speech. But the British people find no expression, not even an echo, of their growing conviction from the lips of their leaders. To the people the war is becoming a holy war—a war of right against wrong, of Heaven against Hell. . . . Let the Prime Minister, Mr. Bonar Law and Mr. Asquith say not once, but often . . . that if we are victorious we will vindicate the laws of right and wrong, by exacting full and adequate punishment for this defilement of human nature; and that in any event we will do our utmost in the councils of the Allies to deprive Germany of the benefits of civilization until she has, by repentance and amendment, become worthy of sharing them. Then there will cease to be an alien enemy question of any difficulty.

Few documents could so vividly illustrate the analysis made by the late Major-General J. F. C. Fuller:

War by propaganda is pre-eminently a democratic instrument, fashioned to dominate the mass-mind—Rousseau's 'general will'. Its purposes are: (1) to stimulate the mass-mind on the home front;

[1] The *Times*, Jan. 18th 1918.

(2) to win to one's support the mass-minds of neutral nations; and
(3) to subvert the mass-mind on the enemy's inner front.

The first is accomplished by awakening the tribal instincts latent in man, and, in order to focus these instincts, to *transform the enemy into a devil*.[1]

It is all too clear that, in the case of Mr. T. B. Napier, composing his wrathful sermon in the Reform Club, propaganda had succeeded brilliantly: for him the issues of the War were already 'Heaven against Hell'—a bad omen for the Peace which was now only five months off. Unfortunately, there were many who, in varying degrees, shared his views. His last sentence may appear puzzling at first sight, but it is full of significance: 'there will cease to be an alien enemy question. . . .'

Only two days before the *Times* published Mr. Napier's letter, the House of Commons witnessed an extraordinary scene. The central actor in it was Mr. Pemberton-Billing, Independent Member for East Herts, and it was, in truth, only the climax to other extraordinary scenes in which he had recently played the lead. At the beginning of June the country was rocked by the case of what was known as the 'Black Book'. Pemberton-Billing was sued for libel by a dancer, Maud Allan, whom he had accused, in his weekly paper *Vigilante* (formerly *The Imperialist*) of sexual perversion. (The accusation was founded on a dance which she performed, 'The Vision of Salome', in private Sunday performances of Oscar Wilde's banned play *Salome*.) Pemberton-Billing was tried before Mr. Justice Darling at the Old Bailey, and conducted his own defence by methods all his own. Michael MacDonagh of the *Times* was among those who witnessed the ensuing spectacles:

> For the defence it is alleged there is a Black Book containing the names of 47,000 English men and women, compiled by Germany's secret service agents in this country during the last twenty years, with records of their moral weaknesses and sexual vices, and that from these English men and women, it is suggested, the German agents extract valuable information by threats of exposure. It is further alleged that the names include persons distinguished in society and politics—members of the Royal Household, Privy Councillors, Cabinet Ministers and their wives, diplomats, poets, novelists, bankers, proprietors and editors of newspapers, and that among these would be found those who were called the depraved patrons of the obscene *Salome*.[2]

[1] Fuller: *The Conduct of War, 1789–1961;* Eyre & Spottiswoode 1961.
[2] *In London During the Great War.*

The joke question of the hour was, 'Well, is your name in the Black Book?' But it could be a serious matter, in view of the manner in which Pemberton-Billing conducted his defence. He called a Mrs. Villiers-Stuart, who claimed that she had actually seen the Black Book. Here is part of his examination of this witness:

'Has your life ever been threatened in this connection?'

'I have.'

Mr. Justice DARLING: 'No, no. You know, Mr. Billing, I have allowed you a great deal of latitude, but you are putting questions which I should not have allowed any counsel to come near putting. If you undertake to conduct your own case you must conduct it according to the rules of evidence.'

Mr. BILLING: 'I know nothing about evidence and I know nothing about law. I come to this Court in the public interest to prove what I propose to prove.'

Mr. Justice DARLING: 'I say that any questions which are not permissible ——'

At this point Mr. Billing raised his arm, and pointing dramatically at the Judge shouted to the witness: 'Is Mr. Justice Darling's name in that Book?'

The witness immediately replied, 'It is'.

In the same loud voice, and still with his hand out-stretched, Mr. Billing demanded of the witness: 'Is Mrs. Asquith's name in that Book? Is Mr. Asquith's name in that Book? Is Haldane's name in that Book?'

Mrs. Villiers-Stuart announced 'It is' in each instance.

Mr. Billing, his face white with anger, paused, and the Judge quietly asked him: 'Have you finished asking questions of that character?'

Mr. BILLING: 'I have not.'

Mr. Justice DARLING: 'I have not the least objection to your having put the question about myself, but I am determined to protect other people who are absolutely defenceless. You must obey my ruling as to that, or you will not be allowed to continue this examination.'

The witness interposed with the remark: 'The Book is in Germany and it can be produced. It will have to be produced.'

After a few moments of intense silence, the Judge bade Mr. Billing to resume the witnesses' examination, and remember the warning he had given.[1]

All this would be merely comic relief, were it not for the fact that,

[1] MacDonagh.

after a six-day trial, Pemberton-Billing was acquitted by the jury.
Not only that, but, remarked MacDonagh:

> Hardly ever has a verdict been received in the Central Court with
> such a demonstration of approval. The crowd in the gallery sprang
> to their feet and cheered—the women waving their handkerchiefs
> and the men their hats. ... Has 'P.-B.' achieved, at last, his
> ambition of being a National hero? It looks like it.

British Law embodies a slowly-acquired but deeply entrenched
notion of justice and fair play. The Pemberton-Billing verdict and
accompanying demonstration showed how this, together with many
other fundamental decencies, can become a casualty of war through
fear and propaganda. Pemberton-Billing, flushed with his triumph
in the Law Courts, carried his campaign to the House of Commons.
On July 1st he staged a scene there which is sufficiently unusual to
warrant full quotation from Michael MacDonagh, who witnessed it.
It began when Pemberton-Billing, entirely out of order, tried to raise
the question of, as he put it, 'the number of damned Germans that
are running free about the country'.

> The Speaker called upon Mr. Billing to withdraw, in accordance
> with the decision of the House; but the hon. member retained his
> seat on the front bench below the gangway on the Opposition side,
> saying 'I'll not leave. I am doing what I consider to be my duty.'
> The Serjeant-at-Arms was then directed by the Speaker to remove
> the hon. member, and approaching Mr. Billing had a brief talk
> with him, after which he came to the Table, and addressing the
> Speaker said, 'The hon. member continues to dispute your ruling,
> sir'. 'Then,' said the Speaker, addressing the House, 'I will
> suspend the sitting until such time as the hon. member has left,'
> and, speaking to the Serjeant-at-Arms, he added, 'Call in the
> officers and have him removed while the House is suspended.'
> The Speaker thereupon left the Chamber, but most of the
> members remained in their places. Those sitting near Mr. Billing
> on the front bench and on the bench immediately behind removed
> some distance away. Then, at a signal from the Serjeant-at-Arms,
> four of the attendants came in and seizing Mr. Billing by the arms
> and legs lifted him from his seat with some difficulty, owing to the
> resistance he offered, and carried him struggling out of the House.
> Some members loudly cheered, a few hissed, and there was a cry
> of 'Silence!' as if in depreciation of both expressions of feeling.

But Pemberton-Billing had accurately judged the country's mood.
The middle months of 1918 saw a resurgence of the anti-alien

agitation of 1914 which, in fact, exceeded the hysteria of that time.
To its credit, the Government, backed by the majority of Members
of the House of Commons, tried to soft-pedal this public outcry.
Lloyd George expressed private contempt of the whole thing, but
did little to mend matters by saying in the House on July 11th:

> There is never a case of a British set-back when I do not get
> anonymous letters written by Germans in this country crowing
> over it. The letters have British post-marks upon them. They are
> obviously written by Germans and the writers say they are
> Germans. Where are they? I feel that that sort of thing has got
> to be stopped.

By this time the public mood was definitely ugly: local authorities
and other bodies urged the Government to take severe measures with
enemy aliens. The *Times* itself (June 10th) considered the Government's critics' case 'constructive, decided, and in our opinion altogether convincing'. A sane and moderate report on the alien problem
by a House of Commons Committee merely annoyed the agitators,
and caused them to redouble their efforts. On July 13th the London
Chamber of Commerce, in its wisdom, was urging stronger action.
On July 15th the *Times* carried this report:

ENEMY ALIENS
MEETING IN TRAFALGAR SQUARE
DEMAND FOR IMMEDIATE INTERNMENT

> There could be no more signal proof of the earnestness with which
> the general public of London regard the danger of allowing
> Germans to be at large in our midst than the demonstration in
> Trafalgar Square on Saturday afternoon. *It was the biggest crowd
> seen in the square since the outbreak of the war*.[1] In spirit and
> temper it was also the most determined. On each side of the
> plinth of the Nelson Column ... were two large placards in-
> scribed:—'A Clean Sweep' and 'Intern Them All'. These mottoes
> well expressed the sentiments of the great throng that filled the
> square.

'Intern Them All' now became the watchword; against the background of this national temper the Government had to prepare new
legislation. Evidence was invited, and the hysterics were not slow in
providing what they called evidence. The Manchester Free Trade
Hall, where Liberalism had so often been so loudly proclaimed, was
the scene of the next mass meeting demanding total internment.
That was on July 24th; not to be outdone, on the next day the

---

[1] My italics.

Liverpool City Council held an 'animated debate' on the by now obsessive subject. Ealing Town Council went even further; on July 29th a Committee of Public Safety was set up 'the duty of which will be to collect reliable information relating to every known enemy alien in the district'. On July 30th there was a meeting in the Albert Hall. On the 31st Hendon reeled at the discovery that there were 105 aliens in its midst, and felt that 'it has an unnecessary proportion of them among its inhabitants'. On August 1st there was alarm about aliens in the ports, and Newcastle joined the chorus demanding immediate internment of one and all.

The Government's problem, of course, was to find any real action worth taking. The problem may have seemed real enough in the fevered minds of those who demanded action; time after time investigation showed that it did not exist. Yet by August 30th it could be announced that 300 unfortunates had been rounded up. To the fire-eaters, this was ludicrous. Michael MacDonagh wrote on August 24th:

A monster petition to the Government forthwith to intern every enemy alien without distinction of any kind, and take drastic steps to eradicate German influence in Government circles and society, was adopted at a meeting in Hyde Park this afternoon, which I reported, and was brought to 10 Downing Street. . . .

The petition had 1,250,000 signatures. It was over two miles in length. Rolled up like a big drum it was carried from Hyde Park to Downing Street in a lorry decorated with the Union Jack, the Stars and Stripes, the French Tricolour and the flags of the other Allied Nations. It was escorted by a procession with bands and banners almost as long as itself and of so diversified a composition as to be possible only in London in War-time. In the marching ranks were thousands of discharged soldiers and sailors, and groups of Dominion soldiers on furlough. There were representatives of branches of the British Empire Union, members of Trade Unions with their big allegorical banners, deputations from the Committees of Public Safety which have been formed in cities and towns throughout the country for the special purpose of hunting down German spies. At the end was a long array of the general public, men and women, which included many representative City men of the Baltic and the Stock Exchange—an impressive array of silk hats and frock coats. The route lay through Oxford Street, Regent Street and Cockspur Street to Trafalgar Square, where the procession waited until the return of the deputation who went with the petition to Downing Street. Lloyd George was out of town. One of his secretaries conveyed to the deputation the

Prime Minister's regrets that he was unable to receive them personally, and assured them that he would give the petition serious consideration on his return.[1]

This response, reported back by the deputation to the waiting demonstrators in Trafalgar Square, was not at all well received. A resolution promptly passed declared that it 'clearly indicates that His Majesty's Government do not appreciate the deep national feeling in regard to the great peril of the enemy alien at large'. The meeting dispersed with vows to badger their M.P.s incessantly, and otherwise keep up the demand for cruel measures. All in all, it was a fine example of mob passion. The Government of the day—not the most distinguished of British governments for good sense and decency—deserves all credit for deliberate procrastination and refusal to stampede. In this it was well supported by the officials at the Home Office; Michael MacDonagh went there during the week of the great demonstration to try to establish some facts:

They say there are many pitiful cases of Germans long years in this country, married to English wives and having sons fighting in the British Army. Some came to this country in infancy and have not since been back to Germany. A large number did not know they were of German nationality until the issue of the alien regulations when the War began; and at the present time there are 234 of this class serving in the Army, who joined as Volunteers in the full belief that they were British. The officials say that the agitation 'intern them all' is promoted by sour and vindictive 'Die-Hards' and is productive of much hardship and injustice.

So the passions of the Home Front in 1918 directed themselves against the easy enemies (insofar as they existed at all!)—the weak, the helpless, the bewildered victims of the 'storm of the world'. The Army in the field had other things to think about, other things to do. Week by week, through August and beyond, the Army gave the British public something else with which, hesitantly, doubtfully at first after so many disappointments, to occupy its mind.

On August 12th the *Times* headlined:

GREAT ALLIED ADVANCE

August 22nd:

ATTACK ON THE ANCRE

August 23rd:

NEW BRITISH STROKE

[1] *In London During the Great War.*

August 24th:

BRITISH FRONT ABLAZE

August 28th:

ALLIES SWEEP FORWARD

August 30th:

THE FLOWING TIDE

The Army in the field was winning the War.

XIII

THE REPLY OF FOCH
BRILLIANT FRENCH COUNTER-STROKE
ADVANCE ON FRONT OF 27 MILES
THREAT TO SOISSONS

With these headlines to the lead story on its news page, The *Times* announced, on July 19th, the first of the great Allied counter-offensives of 1918. The first editorial commented, with some pre-science:

> It is already realized that the counter-stroke is one of the most brilliant operations of the war. It may even prove to bear comparison with the famous battle of the Ourcq, fought in September 1914, by General Maunoury, which led to the great victory on the Marne. . . .

The official designation of the battle which Foch so dramatically transformed with this counter-stroke is, in fact, the Second Battle of the Marne. It had begun on July 15th with a German offensive— the last of the War; by the 17th this was clearly seen to have failed (indeed, the German heavy artillery was already beginning to move to Flanders for another attack on the British). At 4.35 a.m. on the 18th the French struck back, with brilliant early success. On July 20th the *Times* was able to report 16,000 German prisoners; the first editorial stated:

> . . . If the direct military value of Thursday's counter-stroke is very great, its moral value is even greater. The thing which has delighted the Allied nations is not so much the important positions secured and the heavy repulse of the enemy, but rather the proof that, in his own good time, General Foch now feels strong enough to assume the offensive when opportunity offers. But we must be careful not to magnify the results of his counter-stroke until they are complete. . . .

> . . . the latest investigations show that Prince Rupert sent very few units to support the Marne offensive. He is still solidly arrayed, and we have by no means heard the last of him . . . it is

186

inconceivable that the attacks east and west of Reims constitute the whole of the German plan. Germany is approaching a grave crisis in the war and in her political fortunes, and it would be absurd to suppose that she has staked her destinies upon a limited offensive. . . . The Allies may soon feel her strength elsewhere. . . .

Even with good news continuing to flow in (by July 22nd the French were claiming over 20,000 prisoners and over 400 guns) it was hard to see that this was the watershed of the War. The *Times*'s references to Prince Rupprecht's Army Group reflected the pre-occupations of the British Commander-in-Chief. From the moment the German attacks on the Lys had died away at the end of April, two thoughts had guided Haig's mind. The first (to which he had clung through all the vicissitudes of March and April) had been succinctly expressed by G.H.Q. Intelligence as far back as January: 'If Germany attacks and fails she will be ruined'. She *had* attacked— and she had failed everywhere; the message of July emphasised that. It was therefore now a question of making certain of her ruin. But throughout the intervening months before the French counter-attack—apart from the serious weakness of his own army, which needed the interval for rest and recuperation—Haig's offensive intentions were tempered by his second thought: his persisting fear that the Germans might renew their attacks on him in Flanders.

There is no doubt that this anxiety on Haig's part was irritating to Foch, who was already suffering from his lack of a properly constituted Staff to advise him. It also annoyed some of Haig's own Army Commanders, when they began to have the feel of a weakening enemy in front of them. The Australians in General Rawlinson's Fourth Army won a brilliant little victory at Le Hamel on July 4th. On July 5th Haig wrote in his diary:

> Sir H. Rawlinson . . . wished me to approve of him making another attack south of the Somme to advance his line still further. I did not approve of his proposal, because it would result (if successful) in extending our line at a time when reserves are very small. . . .

It was not that Haig did not want to attack (Le Hamel proved that); it was that he still did not dare to displace his exiguous reserves from the northern sector facing Rupprecht. His strategy was absolutely correct, as German sources demonstrate. Summing up the courses open to Germany at the end of the Battle of the Lys, Ludendorff wrote:

> The most favourable operation in itself was to continue the attack on the English Army at Ypres and Bailleul; but on that front the enemy was now so strong in numbers that it was impossible, even

with rested troops. Before we could attack here again the enemy must become weaker. . .[1]

It was precisely to weaken the British Flanders front by forcing the French to withdraw their forces there that Ludendorff launched his devastating attack in Champagne in May. With Paris herself soon once more threatened, it was hard to grasp that the German objective was not really the French capital but the ruined Belgian town of Ypres and the Channel Ports behind it. In Champagne Ludendorff was not concerned with geographical objectives:

How far the attack would take us could not be foretold. I hoped it would lead to such a heavy drain on the reserves of the enemy as would enable us to resume the attack in Flanders.[1]

Right up to the very eve of the French counter-attack on July 18th, Ludendorff adhered to this intention:

G.H.Q.[2] still clung to the idea of an attack in Flanders by the Army Group of Crown Prince Rupprecht, although the hoped-for weakening of the enemy had not come about.[1]

As the French passed through crisis after crisis between May 27th (a grim day for the British divisions 'resting' on their front) and July 18th, sharp disputes arose between Haig and Foch over German intentions and the handling of Allied reserves. The pressures on Foch were acute: one German attack was signalised by their deepest advance on any single day of the War on the Western Front. But Haig was adamant; his Intelligence Branch, under Brigadier-General E. W. Cox, kept a vigilant eye throughout all this time on the state of Prince Rupprecht's reserves. On May 16th Cox reported that he had identified 208 German divisions on the Western Front; on May 29th he had established 70 battleworthy divisions in Rupprecht's Group, of which 39 were in reserve. The fluctuations thereafter reflected the sway of battle in the south:

May 31st	35 divisions in Rupprecht's reserve
June 3rd	32 divisions in Rupprecht's reserve
June 8th	42 divisions in Rupprecht's reserve
June 17th	30 divisions in Rupprecht's reserve
June 25th	28 divisions in Rupprecht's reserve
July 16th	23 divisions in Rupprecht's reserve.[3]

So the figure was declining, but still remained formidable—and

[1] *My War Memories.*
[2] *German* G.H.Q., of course: O.H.L.
[3] From Haig's diary entries.

might increase again. It was on the last date mentioned, July 16th, that Haig asked himself:

> Will the enemy go on with his attacks about Rheims, or will he withdraw such of his reserves as are left and add them to Rupprecht's reserves for a blow against the British? Evidence seems to be accumulating of an attack against the Hazebrouck–Ypres front about the 20th. . . .

It was a good question; the evidence was correct. It was on that very day, according to Ludendorff, that

> The railway transport of artillery, trench-mortars and planes from the Rheims district had begun according to plan. . . . In the night of the 17th–18th I myself went to the Headquarters of the Army Group of Crown Prince Rupprecht, to review once more the state of their preparations. The attack was intended as a continuation of that which had been suspended at the end of April . . . its objectives being the possession of the commanding heights between Poperhinghe and Bailleul, as well as the high ground round Hazebrouck.

Rarely has a commander read his opponents's mind so clearly as Haig read Ludendorff's at that juncture. But it was on the very next day that Foch launched his counter-stroke, and Ludendorff was caught off balance:

> A crisis lay before us for the next few days, and until it was over no great strategical decisions could be taken. The Army Group of Prince Rupprecht *continued its preparations for attack*.[1] It had to relinquish certain divisions, but *even then an offensive was still possible*.[1]

In fact, it was not until July 22nd that the German High Command definitely gave up the idea of renewing the Flanders attack.

This decision, when it at last became apparent, freed Haig's mind for the pursuit of his own offensive schemes. These he had matured, in his resolute, deliberate manner, for two months. They dated, in fact, from a visit which Foch had paid to him on May 16th:

> (He) explained to me an offensive project which he wishes me to carry out if the enemy does not launch his big attack within the next few weeks. I agreed with his general plan, and said I would study my share of the undertaking, and let him know. But he must not write his plan nor allow the French commanders to talk about it. Success will depend mainly on secrecy.[2]

[1] My italics.
[2] Haig Diary; see Terraine: *Douglas Haig*, pp. 438–439; also Duff Cooper: *Haig*.

The next day Haig visited Rawlinson:

> I told R. to begin studying in conjunction with General Debeney[1]
> the question of an attack eastwards from Villers Bretonneux in
> combination with an attack from the French front south of Roye.
> I gave him details of the scheme.

In these two diary entries Haig traces the outlines of what was to be
the decisive action of the War: the beginning of the end. By the time
it could take place, however, much had happened to divert Foch's
attention from his own proposals to Haig in May: the French had
been driven back to the Marne, their Army severely mauled, Paris
threatened again. Through all this Haig never lost sight of the enter-
prise which he and Foch had agreed on, and he prepared steadily
for it. He resisted demands from Foch for more British reserves to
be sent south; he resisted demands for other diversionary action;
and he resisted Foch's later suggestions that the locale of the big
attack should be changed:

> I see no object in pushing forward over the flat and wet country
> between Robecq and Festubert. . . . The operation which to my
> mind is of the greatest importance, and which I suggest to you
> should be carried out as early as possible, is to advance the allied
> front east and south-east of Amiens so as to disentangle that town
> and the railway line. . . .[2]

Haig's view prevailed. Foch acknowledged the force of his ideas and
placed the First French Army directly under him for the occasion.

While the date of it approached, the British public and Government digested the apparent turn in the fortunes of war in their several
fashions. Munitions workers in Coventry, Birmingham and elsewhere
went on strike, and were warned by the Government that, if they did
not go back to work, they would 'become liable to the provisions of
the Military Service Act. The men on strike were only granted
exemption because their services were considered of more value to
the State in the workshops than in the Army.' The *Times* echoed the
disgust of many in its editorial on July 27th:

> In stricken France men began to breathe again last week, and upon
> that very instant came the news that English workmen were about
> to suspend work on munitions.

Two days later, however, the paper was able to report:

REASON PREVAILS

NO GENERAL STRIKE

and on July 30th:

[1] Commanding the First French Army on Rawlinson's right.
[2] Haig to Foch, July 17th.

STRIKE ENDED

The impetus of the Allied[1] counter-stroke which began on July 18th had evidently declined. The 'threat to Soissons' which the *Times* had headlined on that day was not fulfilled until August 2nd. The report on the capture of Soissons in the paper next day was sub-headed

ENEMY IN FULL RETREAT

This was something of an exaggeration. The truth was that the Allied offensive was over; but it had done its work. Nearly 30,000 Germans had been taken prisoner, 793 guns had been captured, and the German High Command found itself under the painful necessity of breaking up ten divisions. Foch was rewarded with the baton of a Maréchal de France on August 6th.

Too often disillusioned, badly shaken by the impact of the German offensives, distrustful of its military advisers, but too unsure of itself to challenge them again, the British Government displayed at this stage of the War a startling degree of nonentity. Its mental confusions were well expressed by Lord Rothermere, one of the three Press barons whom Lloyd George had felt it convenient to include in his Administration.[2] Writing in his newspaper *The Sunday Pictorial* on August 4th, Lord Rothermere held out to his readers the comforting prospect of a 'Seven Years' War'. After four years of war, he told them, 'we are still very far, indeed, from our goal, and we ought soberly to confront the situation as it now exists'. This he proceeded to do, beginning with the happy thought that the importance of the Second Battle of the Marne might well be exaggerated.

Lord Rothermere and Lord Northcliffe were brothers; the *Times* consequently found the Air Minister's article worth reproducing at some length for its readers, who might otherwise not have sought inspiration in *The Sunday Pictorial*. Hopes of an early peace, wrote Lord Rothermere, appeared to be based on 'something or other' happening in Germany, but, said the *Times*, he 'believes all such expectations to be unwarranted'. It then quotes very fully the interesting conclusions which Lord Rothermere drew from that belief:

> It is a mistake to suppose that the throne of the Hohenzollerns is in any real danger. Why should it be? . . . No nation, certainly not Germany, has been so prodigal of man-power in the battle line as Great Britain has been. France learned her lesson early. We have not learned it thoroughly even now. . . .

[1] British, American and Italian forces took part beside the French.
[2] Lord Rothermere, Air Minister; Lord Northcliffe, Director of Propaganda in Foreign Parts; Lord Beaverbrook, Minister for Propaganda.

That a Minister responsible for one of the Armed Services could hold such views at such a time is staggering. Germany's prodigality of man-power had never been so unmistakably displayed. Lord Rothermere could not know the figures revealed after the War from German sources: 688,341 admitted casualties from March 21st to the end of June, with another 196,000 in July.[1] But every eye-witness account of the fighting tells of the awful losses which the Germans sustained in their mass attacks in 1918. As to France, her casualties had brought her Army to mutiny. But no such considerations could halt a Press baron in the pursuit of the nation's military leaders—for it is they who were the real target of Lord Rothermere's article. He continues:

> . . . The British tradition appears to be that while admirals and commanders of ships must suffer for grievous blunders, generals can do no wrong. This should not continue. . . . In the fifth year of the war it is time that British generalship was not necessarily taken for granted. It should be submitted when necessary to close, competent and ruthless scrutiny, in the interests of the real fighting men. The range of selection for the highest commands should be widened. . . .

This was encouraging stuff indeed from a Service Minister at the turning-point of the War. It is to be noted that Lord Rothermere had suffered two personal bereavements through the War which un-doubtedly clouded his mind. Yet he *was* a Minister, and the silence of his colleagues at what can only be understood as an open attack on the British High Command is indicative. The fact that the attack was repeated in the *Times* is equally so. Certainly it is more significant than the strange cures for the nation's ills with which the Air Minister concluded his article:

> Comb out the Army at the back of the front and in this country as it has never yet been combed. We ought to raise 1,000,000 coloured troops for service in the fighting line on the Western Front. . . . Moreover I hold that mercenaries should be employed where possible. . . .

And he finally wound up with this rousing (if baffling) clarion-call:

> Civilian control of the Army must be completely restored in this country. . . .

We do not know whether Haig read Lord Rothermere's article. The *Times's* version of it was probably drawn to his attention; he

[3] Edmonds: *A Short History of World War I.*

could scarcely be unaware that the malignant Harmsworth brothers were out for his blood[1] and he had known for some time that the Government would have liked to replace him. But it did not matter. Only four days elapsed between Rothermere's idiotic outburst and Haig's greatest triumph. The stage was set, everything was ready, and on August 8th the curtain rose.

The Battle of Amiens, which opened on that day, was one of the great surprises of the War—a military classic. Zero hour for Rawlinson's Fourth Army was 4.20 a.m.; for the French First Army on his right it was three-quarters of an hour later. The preparations had been carried out with meticulous secrecy;[2] they involved the assembly of over 500 tanks—the largest concentration yet achieved—on the British front; Rawlinson also deployed over 2,000 guns, 684 of them heavies; the Allies between them massed 1,900 aircraft for the occasion. An outstanding achievement of surprise was the concealment of the whole Cavalry Corps—a dangerously conspicuous unit. But the peak of all was the secret transfer of the four divisions of the Canadian Corps, nearly 100,000 strong, from the Ypres front, their insertion behind the right wing of the Australian Corps, and unsuspected entry into the battle. The skills required for such arrangements were great; their smooth completion was a due reward for the slow, arduous process of professionalisation which the British Army had been undergoing in the midst of war. Not since the compact, Regular Expeditionary Force of 1914 had quietly mobilised, embarked and deployed at Mons, had such cool efficiency been seen.

On August 8th Nature favoured the Allies, as she had favoured the Germans on March 21st: a thick mist covered the battlefield, neutralising the effect of the defending machine guns. Tanks and infantry loomed upon the Germans suddenly out of this mist, over-running their defences. By 1.30 p.m. the day's main fighting was over. By then the Canadians had advanced 8 miles; they took over 5,000 prisoners and 161 guns. The Australians were on all their objectives, except on their extreme left; they took nearly 8,000 prisoners and 173 guns. The total German losses for the day were about 27,000. Their Official Monograph states:

> As the sun set on the battlefield on 8 August the greatest defeat which the German Army had suffered since the beginning of the war was an accomplished fact.

[1] For an excellent (though appalling) account of the Harmsworth brothers in the full flight of intrigue against Haig, see Andrew Boyle: *Trenchard;* Collins 1962, pp. 249–253.

[2] For a more detailed account of this battle, see Terraine: *The Western Front*, pp. 156–175.

Ludendorff wrote:

> August 8th was the black day of the German Army in the history
> of the war. This was the worst experience I had to go through. . . .
> 8th August made things clear for both army commands, both for
> the German and for that of the enemy.

The battle continued until August 11th. Allied progress slowed
up perceptibly, although another French Army joined in on the right
of General Debeney. Once again there was a clash of opinion and of
will between Haig and Foch. Carried away by Rawlinson's early
success, Foch wanted the British Fourth Army to maintain its
pressure. Rawlinson demurred, pointing out that the Allies were
now approaching the wilderness of the 1916 Somme battlefields,
which would be bound to make progress difficult unless some
leverage could be applied. This fitted with Haig's declared plans for
extending the battle northward into the sector of the British Third
Army; but he felt obliged to support the Supreme Commander as
far as possible. Rawlinson became forthright: 'Who commands the
British Army? You or Foch?' he asked. Haig then tackled Foch again,
and Foch gave way: 'I definitely came around to the opinion of
Field-Marshal Haig . . .'.[1] The strategy of the ensuing final offensives
of the Allies was thus decided: alternating blows, successively loosen-
ing up one sector of the German front after another, rising to
crescendos of simultaneous attacks as and when possible.

Meanwhile the impact of war on the field of battle had become
unmistakable. A German reserve division entering the line met other
troops 'falling back in disorderly flight, among them drunken
Bavarians, who shouted to the 9th Regiment, "What do you war-
prolongers want? If the enemy were only on the Rhine—the war
would then be over!" ' Another regiment was greeted with shouts of:
'We thought that we had set the thing going, now you asses are
corking up the hole again!' Faced with all the symptoms of disaster,
the German leaders met at Supreme Headquarters at Avesnes on
August 11th. The Kaiser was present. He listened to the gloomy
tale of three days of defeat. Ludendorff offered his resignation, but
this was not accepted. Nevertheless, the Kaiser was sufficiently
impressed to utter historic words

> I see that we must strike a balance. We have nearly reached the
> limit of our powers of resistance. The war must be ended.

Three days later he ordered his Foreign Secretary, von Hintze, to
try to open peace negotiations. 'Thus,' comments the British Official
History,

[1] Foch: *Memoirs*.

the collapse of Germany began not in the Navy, not in the Home-
land, not in any of the sideshows, but on the Western Front in
consequence of defeat in the field.

So much for Rothermere; so much for the querulities of the British
Government.

Even now, those who had fallen into the habit of doubting the
capacity of the British Army and its leaders found it hard to see the
great hope which had been born. On August 10th, under the heading:

THE NEW ALLIED OFFENSIVE

the *Times* wrote editorially:

> The new Franco–British offensive initiated under the command
> of Sir Douglas Haig . . . is one of the greatest and most gratifying
> surprises of the war. It surprised the British public just as much
> as the enemy. . . .

Perhaps the surprise was too much to swallow. Speaking at Newport
the next day, Lloyd George made his own analysis of the victory:

> It is due undoubtedly to the brilliant qualities of our troops, and
> of the French troops, who are also in. It is due to the very
> courageous leadership of Sir Douglas Haig and General Rawlinson
> and of the French generals. I must say I think a large share of the
> triumph is to be attributed to the unity of command. . . . Every-
> body had combined and you have had one great directing mind. . . .[1]

Lloyd George clung ever after to the institution of Supreme Command to escape or mitigate the necessity of praising Haig. In his *War
Memoirs* he dismissed Haig's victories with the simple sentence:

> He did well in the concluding stages of the 1918 campaign—under
> Foch's supreme direction.

We have already seen how wide of the mark this notion is, but it may
be as well to bury it under the crushing comment of one who had
every opportunity of perceiving the truth: General Sir John Monash,
whose Australian Army Corps was the spearhead of the Battle of
Amiens and of many of the successes which followed:

> It has come to be an article of faith that the whole of the successive
> stages of the great closing offensive of the war had been the subject
> of most careful timing, and of minute organisation on the part of
> the Allied High Command, and of our own G.H.Q. Much eulo-
> gistic writing has been devoted to an attempted analysis of the
> comprehensive and far-reaching plans which resulted in the

[1] The *Times*, Aug. 12th 1918.

delivery of blow upon blow, in a prescribed order of time and for the achievement of definite strategical or tactical ends.

All who played any part in these great events well know that it was nothing of the kind; that nothing in the nature of a detailed time-table to control so vast a field of effort was possible. All commanders, and the most exalted of them in a higher degree even than those wielding lesser forces, became opportunists, and bent their energies, not to the realisation of a great general plan for a succession of timed attacks, but upon the problem of hitting whenever and wherever an opportunity offered, and the means were ready to hand.[1]

General Monash's remarkable soldiers continued the process of 'hitting wherever and whenever an opportunity offered'. The Australians did not attach grandiloquent names to their tactical prowess. What the Germans called 'infiltration', the sardonic Australians called 'peaceful penetration', and by this method kept the Fourth Army front fluid. A German divisional commander in August described the Australian tactic with a distinct tone of grievance:

> The enemy, who has grown up in the Australian bush, wriggles to our posts with great dexterity from flank and rear in the high crops in order to overwhelm them. It has often happened that complete pickets have disappeared from the forward line without trace. . . .[2]

So the Fourth Army continued to make progress; but for the time being the emphasis of battle shifted elsewhere.

The Battle of Amiens passed into history; the Battle of Albert (which the French called the Battle of Bapaume) now followed. It opened on August 21st with a small advance by the British Third Army, making good use of tanks and aircraft. This was only a preliminary, masking a much larger intention. But on that day Haig received an important visitor—Winston Churchill, Minister of Munitions, who came to discuss production programmes for the future. Once more the gap between Government thinking and the realities of the War was revealed; Haig wrote in his diary:

> He is most anxious to help us in every way. . . . His schemes are all timed for 'completion in *next June*'! I told him we ought to do our utmost to get a decision this autumn. . . . In reply I was

[1] Monash: *The Australian Victories in France in 1918;* Angus & Robertson 1936.
[2] Commander of the 41st Division, quoted in The *Times*, Aug. 19th.

told that that the General Staff in London calculate that the decisive period of the war cannot arrive until next July.

The 'General Staff in London', of course was headed by Sir Henry Wilson, whom Lloyd George had brought in in preference to Robertson. Wilson had already given one signal demonstration of his strategical insight by persuading the Government, on the eve of the great German offensive in the West, that the best course for the Allies would be to concentrate against Turkey! The views which Churchill now reported were not unfamiliar to Haig, though it must have been depressing to find how much significance the Government attached to them. He was already in possession of a 33-page document from Wilson entitled 'British Military Policy 1918–1919'[1] on which he had written the comment:

> Words! Words! Words! lots of words and little else. Theoretical rubbish! Whoever drafted this stuff would never win any campaign.

Winning the campaign was now his sole object: he wanted to end the War—in 1918. He told his Army Commanders: 'Risks which a month ago would have been criminal to incur, ought now to be incurred as a duty'.

The Battle of Albert gathered momentum. On August 23rd the *Times* announced:

NEW BRITISH STROKE
ALBERT TAKEN

Three days later a Special Correspondent wrote:

> These are great days. It surely must be that they will even loom greatly in history, but they are certainly great to live in. . . . The sweep of our advance is so rapid that no man can say where our advanced line as a whole may stand at any given moment, for every half-hour brings news that this or that village is in our hands, or that an airman has seen the khaki figures somewhere where we never dreamed that they had reached. . . . When one remembers what the names of Thiepval and Fricourt and Mametz and Contalmaison meant in the old days of 1916, and Le Sars and Warlencourt, it is difficult to realize that we have again swept over all that ground between Friday night and Sunday morning. . . .

The Third Army was now at the outskirts of Bapaume, the mocking goal never reached during the long-drawn-out battles of the Somme in 1916. This, said the *Times* editorial (August 26th):

---

[1] See Duff Cooper: *Haig*, chap. xxv.

set the seal on a wonderful weekend, and brought into view possibilities which were certainly not in sight a week ago. To the north of the Somme the Germans are retreating before the British at such a pace that people are beginning to ask whether they will be able to stand on the old Hindenburg Line. . . .

This ominous name was now to be heard on many lips, and was present in many thoughts.

On August 29th the New Zealand Division entered Bapaume. Further south, on the night of August 30th/31st, the 2nd Australian Division startled even General Monash by its swift storming of the strong defensive position of Mont St. Quentin, opening the way to Péronne. On September 1st this great battle officially ended; in eleven days the British had taken 34,000 prisoners and 270 guns. The First Army, on the left of the Third, had entered the fighting on August 26th, and its battle, officially designated the Battle of the Scarpe (August 26th–September 3rd) produced another 16,000 prisoners and 200 guns. The tide was flowing indeed. One more thrust by the Third and Fourth Armies (the Battle of Havrincourt and Epêhy, September 12th–18th) brought in 12,000 more prisoners and 100 guns. Yet the Germans were never easy to beat; August cost the British Army heavy casualties. The results, however, were clear to see: all three Armies engaged (First, Third and Fourth) were by now right up to the Hindenburg position. The Germans were not going to abandon it. It was evident that a great climax was at hand.

The Hindenburg Line was the most massive and elaborate system of defences constructed during the War. Each section of it was given a code name, drawn from the Nordic mythology; the vital portion between Cambrai and St. Quentin was called the 'Siegfried' sector. The very existence of the Line was a monument to the British victory won at such cost on the Somme in 1916. It was precisely to avoid having to fight another such battle that Ludendorff ordered the construction of these works, and in the spring of 1917 he retired to them in the face of another impending Allied offensive. In the 'Alberich' sector, between St. Quentin and Laon, this withdrawal had had a disconcerting effect on the French attack. With the deep German advances of the spring and summer of 1918, the Hindenburg Line had fallen far behind the battle-front. But now, in September, the German Army was back on it again.

What was the Hindenburg Line—what kind of obstacle? Major-General Sir Frederick Maurice describes the sector which the British were now about to assault:

. . . the Siegfried system . . . was as much as ten miles deep. The most elaborate wire entanglements were provided in front of each line of trenches. They were often arranged in geometrical patterns, so that the angles could be swept by machine gun fire, and there were, in places, as many as eight or nine belts of barbed wire in front of the trenches. Standing, after the great battle had been won and the Siegfried system had been pierced, on the ridges east of the St. Quentin Canal, in the heart of the system, one looked over miles of dense entanglements running in every direction, and was filled with amazement that it should have been possible for flesh and blood to storm a way through such obstacles.[1]

Flesh and blood had already done well-nigh superhuman deeds. Between August 8th and September 26th the British Army had sustained 189,976 casualties. At home, Lloyd George and his Government, still prey to gloomy doubts, could not bring themselves to believe that the victory which had so long eluded the military leaders —at such a cost, and despite many promises—was at last in sight. On September 1st Haig received a telegram from Sir Henry Wilson, marked 'Personal'. It said:

> Just a word of caution in regard to incurring heavy losses in attacks on Hindenburg Line as opposed to losses when driving the enemy back to that line. I do not mean to say that you have incurred such losses but I know the War Cabinet would become anxious if we received heavy punishment in attacking the Hindenburg Line without success.

This was, no doubt, part of that 'close, competent and ruthless scrutiny' to which Rothermere had advocated that British generalship should be submitted. It evoked from Haig the reply:

> My dear Henry,
>
> With reference to your wire re casualties in attacking the Hindenburg Line—what a wretched lot! and how well they mean to support me! What confidence! Please call their attention to my action two weeks ago when the French pressed me to attack the strong lines of defence east of Roye-Chaulnes front. I wrote you at the time and instead of attacking south of the Somme I started Byng's attack. I assure you I watch the drafts most carefully.

In his diary he gave fuller vent to his feelings:

> It is impossible for a C.I.G.S. to send a telegram of this nature to a C.-in-C. in the field as a 'personal' one. . . . The object of this telegram is, no doubt, to save the Prime Minister . . . in case of any failure. So I read it to mean that I can attack the Hindenburg Line if I think it right to do so. . . . If my attack is successful, I

[1] Maurice: *The Last Four Months;* Cassell, 1919, pp. 133–135.

will remain on as C.-in-C. If we fail, or our losses are excessive, I can hope for no mercy! . . .

Once again, neither the Government nor, this time, its chief adviser, the C.I.G.S., appear to have grasped that the assault on Germany's main line of defence might involve more than the personal whim of the British Commander-in-Chief. On this occasion, however, there *was* a co-ordinated Allied strategy, which Foch and Haig had worked out together. It involved French, American and Belgian armies, though the main rôle was undoubtedly British. To have removed their contribution at this stage would have been like depriving an orchestra, performing Wagner's 'Ring' cycle, of all its brass. But in the event, of course, the sole effect of the Government's intervention was to plant the credit for the greatest victory of the War squarely on Haig. This time the impact of war, directed at one man, treated him fairly; for what followed was a triumph.

The battle began on September 26th, with an American and French attack far away in the Argonne. This was America's hardest battle of the War, the one in which the young American Army sustained the bulk of its war casualties—and proved once more, the hard way, that the War's hardships were not the fault of individuals, or class systems, or national characteristics, but were a universal symptom in which West Point was as much at a loss as St. Cyr, Potsdam or Sandhurst. However, the chief object of the Franco–American attack was diversion, and the losses which the Germans incurred in the Argonne fighting certainly provided that.

On September 27th the British First and Third Armies launched their attack on the Hindenburg Line itself. By the evening of the 28th they had bitten in to a depth of six miles. On the 29th the Fourth Army joined in and completed the break. On this day the outstanding feat was the crossing of the St. Quentin Canal by the 46th (North Midland Territorial) Division. Officers swam across first with ropes; their men followed, using life-belts from Channel steamers, rafts and portable boats; pontoon bridges were quickly thrown across to bring in reserves.

The sector which had been considered in some ways the most formidable part of the Hindenburg Line on the (Fourth) army front had been captured at small cost. . . . The enemy's defences had been penetrated by a deep wedge to a maximum depth of some 6,000 yards. . . . Over 5,100 prisoners, 90 guns, and many hundreds of machine guns and trench mortars were captured, the 46th Division alone accounting for 4,200 prisoners and 70 guns.[1]

[1] Major-General Sir Archibald Montgomery: *The Story of the Fourth Army;* Hodder & Stoughton 1919.

The losses of the 46th Division in this brilliant action were only 800.

Yet the main issue had been decided even before this feat of arms was completed. Sir Philip Gibbs, War Correspondent, wrote:

> I saw the Second German Guards coming along in batches like companies, and after they had been put in barbed wire enclosures they laughed, and clapped at the sight of other crowds of comrades coming down as prisoners. I thought then, 'Something has broken in the German spirit'. For the first time the end semed very near.[1]

The collapse of morale was no less palpable in the German High Command. Already Ludendorff had reached the bitter conclusion that 'we must plainly sue for peace if peace could be had'. Fortified by the stubborn qualities of the German soldiery, and finding little disposition among the Allies to seek for any compromise, the tentative German peace feelers after August 11th had produced nothing. While the Hindenburg Line remained intact, it was possible for Germany to go on hoping that the worst might not happen; but now the picture had been transformed. Ludendorff continues:

> At six o'clock on the afternoon of the 28th of September, I went down to the Field-Marshal's room, which was one floor below mine. I explained to him my views as to a peace offer and a request for an armistice. ... The Field-Marshal listened to me with emotion. He answered that he had intended to say the same to me in the evening, that he had considered the whole situation carefully, and thought the step necessary. ... The Field-Marshal and I parted with a firm handshake, like men who have buried their dearest hopes, and who are resolved to hold together in the hardest hours of human life as they have held together in success. ...[2]

The next day Hindenburg informed the Kaiser and Secretary of State von Hintze that 'the situation demanded an immediate armistice in order to save a catastrophe'. On October 1st, at 1 p.m., Hindenburg demanded that an appeal for an armistice must be made by the next morning. The leaders of the Reichstag were told that 'the war is lost'. Chancellor Hertling resigned, and was replaced by the Liberal, Prince Max of Baden. On October 4th, German and Austrian Notes were sent to President Woodrow Wilson, proposing Armistice terms.

Officially, the storming of the Hindenburg Line was completed on October 5th; in nine days the British had taken 35,000 prisoners

[1] Gibbs: *Realities of War.*
[2] *Memoirs.*

and 380 guns. But the true effect lay in more than these spoils of war; as General Maurice wrote:

> The victors . . . looked out over rolling, wooded and well-watered country with something of the joy and wonder which filled the soldiers of Xenophon when at the end of their great march they first saw the sea. The leafy trees, the harvested fields, the green meadow lands and the valleys were to an army which had lived and fought for four years surrounded by hideous devastation, with the stink of the blood-soaked, battle-torn ground ever in their nostrils, more convincing evidence of achievement than tens of thousands of prisoners and hundreds of guns.[1]

In Flanders, on September 28th, the British Second Army had joined in the general battle under the overall command of the King of the Belgians. On the ruined fields of 'Passchendaele' a similar triumph was enacted to that on the Somme in August. A few days before the advance, an officer who had led a battalion at Third Ypres in 1917 noted sadly:

> The bones of most of my officers and many of the other ranks lie between here and Zonnebeke. . . .[2]

Now a brigadier, this officer went forward on the 28th immediately behind his battalions, anxiously hoping that his memories of 1917 would not be repeated. Zero hour was 5.30 a.m.:

> Soon walking wounded trickle back along the Menin Road; then prisoners, and wounded on stretchers. . . . It always makes me sick to see so many fine fellows mangled and bloody from this God-forsaken war.
>
> In action the first reports of progress—or failure—usually come from wounded; junior commanders are far too busy to write messages until there is a pause in the operations. I am informed that the attack started well. . . .[2]

As it started, so it continued:

> By about 11 o'c the 28th Brigade is established on its Final Objective, with patrols well forward. . . . The day's success has been astonishing: an advance of over five miles (more than in four months' bloody fighting last year).[3]

The Germans were going back everywhere; but their rearguards fought obstinately; the weather was turning—there could be no swift pursuit. On October 6th the British First, Third and Fourth

---

[1] Maurice: *The Last Four Months.*
[2] *General Jack's Diary.*
[3] Ibid., pp. 272–274.

Armies began the Second Battle of Le Cateau. While it was still in progress, grudgingly and belatedly, prompted by Marshal Foch, the Prime Minister sent a telegram to Haig acknowledging that the offensive 'is the greatest chapter in our military history'. What he could not bring himself to do, either then or later, was to acknowledge equally frankly the rôle of the man who, in Foch's words, had 'made easy a great combination, and sanctioned a prolonged and gigantic effort'—Haig himself. The dangers of this frame of mind went far beyond the mere personal spite and churlishness with which it displayed itself. Already in September, when Lloyd George had been speaking in Manchester, *The Spectator* had percipiently drawn attention to his silences on Haig:

> We regret the omission of any graceful acknowledgement of Sir Douglas Haig's services, not merely because a great soldier is receiving less encouragement than he has earned—to find a parallel for the frigidity displayed towards Sir Douglas Haig, and the indifference towards his advice we think we should have to go back to the treatment of Wellington by the Perceval Ministry during the Peninsular War—but because official praise of Sir Douglas Haig would stand in the public view for a recognition of the strategy of Westernism.

This was the crux of the matter: the great victorious offensive on the Western Front was now palpably winning the War: Bulgaria surrendered on September 30th; Turkey was in a state of collapse; Austria could do no other than join Germany in the approach to President Wilson for an armistice. When Germany could no longer support them—when it was seen that she herself was struggling for survival—her allies fell away. This was what the British General Staff (until the advent of Henry Wilson) had always predicted. Lloyd George had persistently argued the opposite policy (under the attractive but entirely misleading title of 'knocking away the props'—it was always Germany that did the 'propping') and he could not forgive the soldiers for being right.

Meanwhile, as statesmen and diplomats conferred and considered peace terms to which they had given altogether insufficient thought, the War dragged on. The British Army still had two more great battles to fight, two more convincing demonstrations of conclusive victory: the Battle of the Selle (October 17th–25th: 20,000 prisoners, 475 guns) and the Battle of the Sambre (November 1st–11th: 19,000 prisoners, 450 guns). The condition of the German Army was now pitiable:

> Every road was littered with broken-down motor trucks, guns, machine guns and trench mortars. Great stacks of supplies and

military stores of all kinds were abandoned. Every railway line
was blocked with loaded trucks which the Germans had been
unable to remove. The sixty miles of railway in the valley of the
Meuse between Dinant and Mézières was filled from end to end
with a continuous line of German freight trains carrying guns,
ammunition, engineering equipment and other paraphernalia. On
the Belgian canals alone over eight hundred fully charged military
barges were found. It is beyond dispute that on November 11th
the lines of communication immediately behind the German
armies had been thrown into complete disorder by the streams of
traffic which were converging on the Meuse bridges, disorder
greatly intensified by the attacks of the Allied airmen. The German
armies, unable to resist on the fighting front, could no longer
retreat in good order. . . .[1]

At last, on November 11th, at 11 a.m., the roar of battle died
away; the Armistice came into effect along the whole of the Western
Front. Turkey and Austria–Hungary had already stopped fighting.
The last phase of the War in the West, from September 27th to
November 11th had cost the British and Dominion forces another
158,000 officers and men; victory over such a fine fighting instrument as the German Army could never be cheaply won—as a second
war would prove. But the British achievement, since August 8th,
had been astonishing; in that time the five British Armies on the
Western Front had taken:

188,700 prisoners   2,840 guns.

The achievements of the other Allies were:

French	139,000 prisoners	1,880 guns
American	43,200 prisoners	1,421 guns
Belgian	14,500 prisoners	474 guns.
	196,700	3,775.

Well might Foch say:

> Never at any time in history has the British Army achieved greater
> results in attack than in this unbroken offensive.

And Haig, in his Despatch of December 21st 1918 paid tribute to
those who had sustained the cruellest impact of war throughout—
the troops themselves:

> Their courage and resolution rose superior to every test, their
> cheerfulness never failing, however terrible the conditions in
> which they lived and fought. By the long road they trod with so
> much faith and with such devoted and self-sacrificing bravery we
> have arrived at victory, and today they have their reward.

[1] Maurice: *The Last Four Months.*

XIV

If History were a kinder teacher, it might have been possible to end this book on the warm note of Haig's tribute to his army. It would have been pleasant indeed to record that the troops who had endured so much had received their true reward: a just and lasting peace. But we know that it was not so. Neither the people behind the Army nor the Government which ruled it were in the right mood to make real peace. The spirit of revenge—or, as some would have preferred to call it, 'righteous indignation'—had been awakened in the British people. The Germans, with characteristic ineptitude, succeeded in fanning the flames right up to the end by the torpedoing, on October 10th—long after their U-boat campaign had militarily failed—of the Irish mail-boat *Leinster*, with the loss of 527 lives.

The Government, taken unawares by a victory the whole strategy of which it had opposed, was now found incapable of giving a right lead to the nation, or of giving it the voice due to it in peace-making. The Prime Minister's distrust (shared by many of his colleagues) of Britain's military leaders, and their consequent unwillingness to proclaim the achievement of the Army under those leaders, duly produced the ill results which might be expected. It is an astonishing fact that at the Armistice negotiations which began on November 7th in Marshal Foch's famous railway-carriage in the Forest of Compiègne, the army which had done most to bring about the Armistice was unrepresented. Neither its Commander-in-Chief, nor his Chief of Staff, nor any other officer representing him and his men was there; Britain's representative was the First Sea Lord, Admiral Wemyss. It was understandable that the Navy of what was still, in 1918, the world's leading Sea Power should have its say; yet it remains astounding that an army which, on November 1st, numbered 1,966,727 officers and men, the largest military force ever known in the history of the British Empire, an army which had just won nine successive victories unparalleled in British military history, should have no voice at all. The worst of it was that a precedent was set which would shortly lead to even direr consequences.

The Armistice had no sooner been obtained than the Government itself proceeded to dissolve. On November 2nd Lloyd George wrote to Bonar Law, Deputy Prime Minister and Leader of the Conservative Party:

> . . . I believe it is essential that there should be a fresh Parliament, possessed of the authority which a General Election alone can give it, to deal with the difficult transitional period which will follow the cessation of hostilities. If there is to be an election, I think it right that it should be a Coalition Election. . . .

To this Bonar Law agreed. The machinery was set in motion. The will of the people would now be tested: a satisfying democratic procedure. On the day after the Armistice, November 12th, Lloyd George addressed the Coalition Liberals:

> We must not allow any sense of revenge, any spirit of greed, any grasping desire, to over-ride the fundamental principles of righteousness. Vigorous attempts will be made to hector and bully the Government in the endeavour to make them depart from the strict principles of right, and to satisfy some base, sordid, squalid ideas of vengeance and of avarice. We must relentlessly set our faces against that.[1]

Four days later, at a great Coalition meeting in the Central Hall Westminster, Lloyd George struck an even loftier note:

> I want to so build that when we are forgotten dust, in ages to come, men will look back at what we have done during the last four-and-a-half years, and what will be done during the next four-and-a-half years, and say of the men and women of this generation—'They builded well'.[2]

And so, on Monday, November 25th, Parliament was dissolved; nominations were received by December 4th; Polling Day was fixed for December 14th; votes would be counted by December 30th; the 'Khaki Election' was in full swing. Now the temper of the people would be shown—and the capacity of their leaders to guide them. This is not the place for a full account of the 1918 Election; many accounts in any case exist. But it is necessary to catch at least a whiff of the frame of mind of the British people at the end of the War. It was well summed up by Winston Churchill:

> . . . when the Election came it woefully cheapened Britain. The Prime Minister and his principal colleagues were astonished and to some extent overborne by the passions they encountered in the constituencies. The brave people whom nothing had daunted had suffered too much. Their unpent feelings were lashed by the popular Press into fury. The crippled and mutilated soldiers

[1] Thomas Jones: *Lloyd George;* O.U.P. 1951.
[2] The *Times*, Nov. 18th 1918.

darkened the streets. The returned prisoners told the hard tale of bonds and privation. Every cottage had its empty chair. Hatred of the beaten foe, thirst for his just punishment, rushed up from the heart of deeply injured millions. Those that had done the least in the conflict were, as might be expected, the foremost in detailing the penalties of the vanquished.[1]

It will be sufficient here to note how this inflamed condition of Public Opinion affected Lloyd George himself, and how far it drew him from the ringing phrases of his earlier speeches. He very quickly became aware that the cost of the War—the material cost, as well as the cost in blood—was much in the public mind. A letter in the *Daily Mail* on November 27th put the matter succinctly:

Is a British Government going to show tenderness to the Hun?

Two days later, at Newcastle-on-Tyne, Lloyd George said:

... When Germany defeated France she made France pay. That is a principle which she herself has established ... that is the principle we should proceed upon—that Germany must pay the costs of the war up to the limit of her capacity to do so. ...[2]

The next day he told Lord Riddell:

They must pay to the uttermost farthing.

But he added, ruefully:

... the question is how they can be made to pay beyond a certain point. ...

This glimpse of the intractable difficulties inherent in the concept of 'Reparations' was not vouchsafed to many. And there was another matter; on November 30th the Trade Unionist G. N. Barnes addressed a meeting at Netherton:

I have heard the Kaiser mentioned. Well, I am for hanging the Kaiser. ... It would be a monstrous thing if the greatest culprit and murderer in history escaped the just penalty of his crimes.[2]

On December 6th Lloyd George issued a statement to the Press:

The war was a hideous and abominable crime, a crime which has sent millions of the best young men of Europe to their death and mutilation, and which has plunged myriads of homes into desolation. Is no one responsible? Is no one to be called to account? Is there to be no punishment? Surely that is neither God's justice nor Man's? The men responsible for this outrage on the human race must not be let off because their heads were crowned when

---

[1] Churchill: *The Aftermath;* Thornton Butterworth, 1929.
[2] *Times* reports.

they perpetrated the deed. The British Government referred the
question of the criminal culpability of the Kaiser and his accomplices to their Law Officer some weeks ago. They invited a body
of jurists in England to investigate the matter, and they have
unanimously come to the conclusion that the Kaiser and his
accomplices in the making of this war ought to be tried by an
international Court. . . .[1]

On December 10th speaking in London, Lloyd George went somewhat further:

Those who are responsible for the atrocities of this war must be
made responsible. The higher, the more exalted they are, the
more necessary that they should be made to suffer. . . . But the
German people who sanctioned the war, who went into the war
with a full and enthusiastic mind, who would now have been
acclaiming the victory if there had been one—they must be held
responsible too.[1]

So the nation's loudly-expressed desires for retribution and vengeance
swayed the minds of its leaders. Lloyd George won his Election with
a majority of 262, and with this assurance of popular backing marched
into the Peace Conference in January 1919. 'He reached the Conference,' said Churchill,

somewhat dishevelled by the vulgarities and blatancies of the
recent General Election. Pinned to his coat-tails were the posters,
'Hang the Kaiser', 'Search Their Pockets', 'Make them Pay'; and
this sensibly detracted from the dignity of his entrance upon the
scene.

The Army's influence was no more acknowledged at the Paris
Peace Conference than in the Armistice talks. The Army itself was
reticent about its triumphs; the men returning were only too eager
to forget this dreadful war, only too thankful still to be alive. Demobilisation was the order of the day: the troops desired nothing
better,[2] the Government desired nothing better than to forget about

---

[1] Ibid.

[2] 'When this blasted war is over,
No more soldiering for me.
When I get my civvy clothes on,
Oh, how happy I shall be!
No more church parades on Sunday,
No more asking for a pass,
I shall tell the Sergeant-Major
To stick his passes up his —— . . . etc.'
Soldiers' song, to the tune of the hymn: 'Take it to the Lord in prayer'.

the Army. Certainly the views of the Commander-in-Chief were not sought. And yet those views were not irrelevant. On October 26th, as the Battle of the Selle ended (this was also the day on which Ludendorff resigned) Haig had written to his wife:

> . . . it is important that our Statesmen . . . should not attempt to so humiliate Germany as to produce a desire for revenge in years to come.

On November 1st, with the Armistice delegation due to cross the lines in only six days' time, he wrote again:

> I am afraid the Allied Statesmen mean to exact humiliating terms from Germany. I think this is a mistake, because it is merely laying up trouble for the future, and may encourage the wish for revenge in the future.

Such thoughts might have had a sobering effect in Paris in 1919. But the Military Adviser of the Conference was the Allied Generalissimo, Marshal Foch, and no-one else. Yet Marshal Foch was, and could never cease to be, a French soldier, French to the core of his being. Foch remembered, as a young student in Metz in 1871, jumping to his feet with the others of his class as the crash of artillery salvoes shook the windows: German gunners 'announcing to the occupied city that its permanent bondage was decreed'.[1] Foch would be a French general, obeying the dictates of French policy. When the Allies found French policy difficult to accommodate, they would be at a disadvantage in having only a French military adviser. In the event, it was General (later Field-Marshal) Plumer, who became Commander-in-Chief of the British Occupation Forces on the Rhine at the end of the War, who galvanised the Peace Conference into action with a telegram in March 1919 depicting the wretched state of the German population as a result of the continuation of the Allied blockade:

> Perhaps the most impressive passage in his telegram was that in which he pointed out how bad was the effect produced upon the British Army of the spectacle of the sufferings of German women and children. When the Prime Minister had finished reading this dispatch he remarked, with some emphasis: 'Gentlemen, you cannot say that General Plumer is a pro-German'.[2]

Plumer's telegram was the voice of sanity and decency belatedly heard; Haig's views, if heard in time, might have averted this cruelty,

[1] Liddell Hart: *Foch: Man of Orleans*, 1931.
[2] General Sir Charles Harington: *Plumer of Messines;* John Murray 1935.

and other misfortunes besides. But Haig's view was not heard at any time.

So the miseries of Peace replaced the miseries of war: the war which had begun with the assassination of the heir to the Austrian throne—and now there was no Austrian throne; the war which had been about the cynical disregard of a 'scrap of paper', a scrap of paper intended, with others, to ensure national security—and for four and a half years security had been translated into the bloody devastation of nations; the war which had turned into a life-and-death struggle between powerful, modern empires—and now saw the death of four empires, the grave weakening of others; the war which had drawn in the masses as no previous war ever had—and in order to do so had become, for far too many people, what Mr. T. B. Napier of the Reform Club called a war 'of Heaven against Hell'. By that assessment, the British Army might be said to have overcome the legions of Hell; but it was hard to discern either the British Government or the British people on the side of the angels.

The Government's failure to acknowledge and convey to the public, at the time, the supreme achievement of the British Army in 1918 was never corrected, and was fatal. The sense of having won a major victory *in the field* over a mighty enemy, obtained by absolute military prowess, hard-won professionalism, remained lacking. Propaganda stories of gallant deeds could not be a substitute. Soon they would, in any case, begin to be supplanted by the literature and propaganda of denigration and 'disenchantment'. The horrors of the Somme and Passchendaele made better 'copy' than the 'Hundred Days' Campaign' of 1918 with its nine cumulative victories. And yet, in peace-making, the Government, urged on by the Press, adopted attitudes which could only be based on the assumption of such victories:

> During the early stages of the Conference the Northcliffe Press divided its energies between 'The impudent Hun' and 'How to smash Lenin'. They clamoured for the occupation of Moscow and Petrograd. They at the same time clamoured for demobilisation. In April they raised the panic of 'surrender'. 'It is,' they exclaimed, 'not our business to ask what Germany will think of the terms. Our duty is to dictate such terms as shall give a material guarantee for security, and let the Hun think what he likes about them.' And still they clamoured for demobilisation. From then on the *Daily Mail* inserted in a neat little 'box' upon the front page the epigraph 'The Junkers will cheat you yet'. This little slogan appeared each day at the head of their leading article. When the Germans actually reached Versailles this warning was supple-

mented by another 'box' which ran as follows: 'Lest we forget. Killed 670,986. Wounded 1,041,000. Missing 350,243.' And still they clamoured for demobilisation.[1]

Demobilisation of the Army (two million men by mid-April 1919) and disregard of its work made a poor foundation for the dictation of doctrinaire peace terms. Germans could hardly interpret these otherwise than as hypocritical and harsh. Nor could they be expected, if the Government whose army had done most to defeat them in the closing stages of the War chose not to assert this fact, to remedy the omission. They felt themselves tricked, betrayed. Philip Gibbs, reporting from the Occupation Zone, 'became aware of a myth which persisted in the minds of most Germans, and which nothing would alter.

"Our armies, of course, were never defeated in the field," I heard. "It was a stab in the back which betrayed them. Revolution from behind by Communists and Jews." '[2]

So a legend was born—the legend on which National-Socialism fed and grew. General Ludendorff, one of Hitler's earliest supporters, naturally lost no time in making use of it:

The proud German Army, after victoriously resisting an enemy superior in numbers for four years, performing feats unprecedented in history, and keeping our foes from the frontiers, disappeared in a moment.[3]

The German Army did not 'disappear in a moment'; it had been steadily ground down by defeat in battle; almost 400,000 prisoners in three months take a lot of explaining away. That is the significance of the Hundred Days' Campaign. That is why it was a fatal omission not to dwell upon it. That campaign makes nonsense of the idea of 'futility'; it reveals that it was in the field that German militarism was beaten in 1918. From this it might have been deduced that, if revived (and nothing was more certain to revive it than a dictated peace) German militarism would have to be beaten in the field again. And so the true futility might have been avoided: having to lay Europe in ruins to destroy that militarism a second time.

---

[1] Harold Nicolson: *Peacemaking;* Constable 1933.
[2] Gibbs: *The Pageant of the Years.*
[3] Ludendorff: *My War Memories;* published in 1919.

CHRONOLOGY OF CRISIS

1899 (Oct.)	Outbreak of South African War
(Dec.)	'Black Week'
1900	Invasion scare (Jan., Feb., Mar.)
(June)	2nd German Navy Law aims at 38 battleships in 20 years
1902 (Jan.)	Anglo–Japanese Treaty
(May)	Peace of Vereeniging ends S. African War
1903	Russian naval 'scare' (Jan., Feb.)
(May)	Edward VII visits Paris
1904 (Feb.)	Outbreak of Russo–Japanese War
(Apr.)	The *Entente Cordiale*
(Oct.)	Admiral Fisher becomes First Sea Lord
1905 (Jan.)	Outbreak of revolution in Russia; 'Bloody Sunday'
(Mar.)	Kaiser visits Tangier; Moroccan Crisis begins
(Sept.)	End of Russo–Japanese War
(Dec.)	Liberal Ministry formed; Haldane Secretary of State for War; Army reforms begin
1906 (Jan.)	Anglo–French secret military and naval conversations
	General Election: Liberal landslide
	Algeçiras Conference on Morocco opens
(Feb.)	Launching of H.M.S. *Dreadnought* makes all other battleships obsolete, sets off new arms race
(April)	German diplomatic defeat at Algeçiras
(June)	3rd German Navy Law
1907 (Aug.)	Anglo–Russian Agreement establishes Triple *Entente*
1908 (Oct.)	Austria annexes Bosnia and Herzegovina
	Kaiser's *Daily Telegraph* interview
1909 (Mar.)	Naval Scare: ('We want Eight . . .')
(April)	Abandonment of Two-power Standard
1911 (July)	Agadir Crisis begins; Lloyd George's Mansion House speech
(Aug.)	Kaiser refers to Germany's 'place in the sun'
(Oct.)	Churchill becomes First Lord of Admiralty
1912 (Feb.)	Haldane's visit to Germany
(Oct.)	Lord Roberts's Manchester speech
	First Balkan War
1913 (June)	Second Balkan War
(Nov.)	Zabern incident
1914 (June)	Sarajevo

APPENDIX II

MARCHING SONGS BY 'A.C.A.'

I.   Air, 'Keel Row'

1 He tore the scrap of paper,
    The Belgian scrap of paper,
    He tore the scrap of paper,
      And bade the bullets fly.

Chorus

      So now we're off to Berlin,
      To Berlin, to Berlin,
      So now we're off to Berlin,
        To ask the reason why.

2 He shot the wives and children,
    The wives and little children,
    He shot the wives and children,
      And laughed to see them die.

3 He sacked the shrines of Louvain,
    Of Senlis, Reims, and Louvain,
    He sacked the shrines of Louvain,
      They flamed against the sky.

4 He swore his heart was bleeding,
    His tender heart was bleeding,
    He swore his heart was bleeding
      And winked his wicked eye.

5 He tried the road to Paris,
    The blood-stained road to Paris,
    He tried the road to Paris—
      It only was a try.

6 He talked of German culture,
    Of blood and iron culture,
    He talked of German culture,
      And every word a lie.

II.   Air, 'Cheer, Boys, Cheer'

1 March, boys, march, along the road to Berlin,
    Singing, and cheering, and seeking all the way
  A wild cat, whose moustaches want uncurling,
    A man-eating tiger, brought at last to bay.

2 Although he swore his tender heart was bleeding
    For shrines he'd burnt, and womenfolk he'd slain,
  He knew to what his cruel words were leading,
    When he bade his Uhlans recall the Huns again.

3 By all the blood, that stained the Belgian waters,
  By all the dead, that strewed the Belgian fields,
By children slain, by outraged wives and daughters,
  We'll show no mercy, till the tyrant yields.

4 Down for ever down with the blood and iron culture,
  Down for ever down with the Prussian Kaiser's pride,
Wring the eagle's neck—he's changed into a vulture,
  Gorged with the flesh of the thousands who have died.

III.   Air, 'John Brown's Body'

1 Belgium has been harried with fire and with sword,
Belgium has been harried with fire and with sword,
Belgium has been harried with fire and with sword,
But the Kaiser's got to pay.

Chorus

  Glory, glory, Hallelujah (ter.)

2. The women and the children lie dead upon the ground, (ter.)

3. The shrines of God Almighty are shattered with the shells, (ter.)

4 Our comrades in their thousands have fallen on the road, (ter.)

5 From all the world alike there comes the same tremendous voice, (ter.)

IV.   Air, 'Massa's in the Cold Ground'

1 Think of the friends who marched beside us,
  Think of the graves wherein they lie,
Think of the Kaiser who began it,
  And swear that his might shall die.

2 Think of the homes we've left behind us,
  Sisters, mothers, wives, and kids and all,
Think of the Kaiser who began it,
  And swear that his throne shall fall.

3 Think of the ruined Belgian homesteads,
  Think of the churches flaming high,
Think of the Kaiser who began it,
  And swear that his might shall die.

4 Think of the men who came to help us,
  Think how they answered to the call,
Think of the Kaiser who began it,
  And swear that his throne shall fall.

V.   Air, 'John Peel'

1 D'ye ken John French, with his khaki suit,
  His belt and gaiters, and stout brown boot,
Along with his guns, and his horse, and his foot,
  On the road to Berlin in the morning.

Chorus

> Yes we ken John French, and old Joffre too,
> And all his men to the Tricolor true,
> And Belgians and Russians, a jolly good few,
>   On the road to Berlin in the morning.

2 The Prussian Kaiser must be made to kneel,
  The Prussian Eagle must be made to feel
  The force of the bullet and the good cold steel,
    On the road to Berlin in the morning.

3 For the mothers they slew, and the kids as well,
  And for sundry things it's not fit to tell,
  We've got to catch 'em and give 'em hell,
    On the road to Berlin in the morning.

VI.   Air, 'Here's to the Maiden'

1 Here's to the health of the King and the Queen,
    Ever at work for a living,
  Morning and evening and all that's between,
    Cheering and helping and giving—
      Give them a shout,
      Lengthen it out,
    Tell friends and enemies what we're about.

2 Here's to Lord Kitchener, brown with the sun,
    Gentle, persuasive, and balmy,
  Giving his orders and getting them done,
    All that he wants for the Army—
      Give him a shout, etc.

3 Here's to John Jellicoe, first in command,
    Watchful afar on the ocean,
  Keeping an eye upon Heligoland,
    Keeping the raiders in motion—
      Give him a shout, etc.

4 Here's to Lord Roberts at three score and ten
    Still patriotic and sprightly,
  Asking for money and asking for men,
    Asking for both of them rightly—
      Give him a shout, etc.

5 Here's to all Britishers under the sky,
    Dwellers in hot land or cold land,
  Ready to march, or to fight, or to die,
    All for the sake of the old land—
      Give them a shout, etc.

Of course, some of those familiar old tunes were actually used by the soldiers; thus, to the last one ('Here's to the Maiden') they sang 'What did you join the Army for?' which we have already quoted (see p. 174). To 'John Brown's Body' they set many verses, among them this beauty:

P

John Brown's baby's got a pimple on his—shush!
John Brown's baby's got a pimple on his—shush!
John Brown's baby's got a pimple on his—shush!
    The poor kid can't sit down.

APPENDIX III

Winston Churchill's reply to Prince Louis of Battenberg's letter of resignation:

October 29, 1914

My dear Prince Louis,

This is no ordinary war, but a struggle between nations for life or death. It raises passions between races of the most terrible kind. It effaces the old land-marks and frontiers of our civilization. I cannot further oppose the wish, you have during the last few weeks expressed to me, to be released from the burden of responsibility which you have borne thus far with so much honour and success.

The anxieties and toils which rest upon the naval administration of our country are in themselves enough to try a man's spirit; and when to them are added the ineradicable difficulties of which you speak, I could not at this juncture in fairness ask you to support them.

The Navy of to-day, and still more the Navy of to-morrow, bears the imprint of your work. The enormous impending influx of capital ships, the score of thirty-knot cruisers, and destroyers and submarines unequalled in modern construction which are coming now to hand, are the results of labours which we have had in common, and in which the Board of Admiralty owes so much to your aid.

The first step which secured the timely concentration of the Fleet was taken by you.

I must express publicly my deep indebtedness to you, and the pain I feel at the severance of our three years' official association. In all the circumstances you are right in your decision. The spirit in which you have acted is the same in which Prince Maurice of Battenberg has given his life to our cause and in which your gallant son is now serving in the Fleet.

I beg you to accept my profound respect and that of our colleagues on the Board.

I remain,
Yours very sincerely,
Winston S. Churchill.

It only remains to be noted that Prince Louis was promoted to Admiral of the Fleet in August 1921, a bare month before his death.

APPENDIX IV

Extract from General Smuts's Memorandum to the War Cabinet, following his visit to the Western Front, Jan. 21st–Jan. 26th 1918 with Hankey.

(N.B. Hankey: *The Supreme Command, 1914–1918*, Allen & Unwin, 1961, vol. ii, p. 760: 'Then we returned to Amiens and Boulogne, where I wrote a report for Smuts strongly opposing the extension of the British line to the south as desired by the French'.)

I am satisfied that the morale of the Army is good. The bearing of the troops coming in and out of the line and in large working parties all along the front is in every way satisfactory. The Army is well found and in good fettle. There is no question, however, that the men are tired. This applies more especially to the infantry. ... A defensive system that amply sufficed for an Army continuously on the offensive, does not meet the defensive needs of the existing situation, and behind the elaborate system of the main battle zone, reserve defences are being constructed. The preparation of this vast, but absolutely essential scheme of defence, requires an immense amount of labour. As the greater part of the work has to be done within the zone of artillery fire, native and prisoner labour cannot be employed to any considerable extent. The burden falls in the main on the infantry. Consequently, divisions which have completed their term in the defensive line have, almost immediately, to be turned to the construction of defence works. The result is that they suffer in regard both to rest and training. In the circumstances, the surprising feature is not that they are fatigued but that their spirits are so good. ...

The point, however, to which I wish to draw attention is that this need of rest is a psychological factor of the utmost importance in relation to the question of the extension of the line for which the French are pressing. It is my deliberate opinion, as the result of a most careful study of the question, that, if the Army is compelled at the present time to take over any further portion of the line beyond that already agreed to, and nearly completed, we shall be running serious risks. We shall be straining the Army too far. Either the defences will not be completed in time, or the essential rest will not be obtained, and the Army will not be in the state in which it ought to be to resist an attack. Moreover, any further extension of the front will cause great discontent among all ranks.

BIBLIOGRAPHY

Original and Official Sources:

In this book a number of documents included in the extensive Haig papers appear in print for the first time, notably the extracts from the Censorship Report on Army morale prepared for G.H.Q. in the early months of 1918.

The files of *The Times* and other newspapers are freely quoted. The Official History of the First World War, *Military Operations, France and Belgium*, compiled by Brigadier-General Sir J. E. Edmonds, has, as always, provided an important bedrock.

The *Statistics of the Military Effort of the British Empire During the Great War, 1914–1920*, published by H.M.S.O. in 1922, has supplied many significant and startling figures.

I have also consulted the Report of the Royal Commission on the War in South Africa (Elgin Commission, 1903), with its Minutes and Appendices, a most valuable source of evidence about the pre-1914 Army and the leaders of the 1914–1918 war.

Published Works Quoted or Referred to in the text:

Balfour, Michael: *The Kaiser and His Times*; Cresset Press, 1964.
Behrend, Arthur: *As from Kemmel Hill*; Eyre & Spottiswoode, 1963.
Blake, Robert: *The Private Papers of Douglas Haig*; Eyre & Spottiswoode, 1952.
Bonham-Carter, Victor: *Soldier True: The Life and Times of Field-Marshal Sir William Robertson*; Muller, 1963.
Briggs, Asa (Ed.): *They Saw it Happen*; Blackwell, 1960.
Brophy, John (and Eric Partridge): *Songs and Slang of the British Soldier, 1914–1918*; Scholartis Press, 1931.
Buchan, John: *Memory Hold the Door*; Hodder & Stoughton, 1940.
Callwell, Sir C. E.: *Experience of a Dug Out, 1914–1918*; Constable, 1920.
    Field-Marshal Sir Henry Wilson: His Life and Diaries (2 vols.); Cassell, 1927.
Carrington, Charles: *Soldier from the Wars Returning*; Hutchinson, 1965.
Charteris, Brig.-Gen. J.: *At G.H.Q.*; Cassell, 1931.

Churchill, Winston: *The World Crisis*, Odhams Edition, 1938.
  The Aftermath; Thornton Butterworth, 1929.
Clarke, Basil: *How the Progress of the War was Chronicled by Pen and Camera*; Amalgamated Press, 1919.
Cooper, Duff: *Haig*; Faber, 1935.
  Old Men Forget; Hart-Davis, 1954.
Crozier, F. P.: *A Brass Hat in No Man's Land*; Cape, 1930.
Edmonds, Charles: *A Subaltern's War*; Peter Davies, 1929.
Edmonds, Sir J. E.: *A Short History of World War I*; O.U.P., 1951.
Esher, Lord: *Journals and Letters* (4 vols.); Nicolson & Watson, 1934.
Foch, Marshal: *Memoirs* (translated by Col. T. Bentley Mott); Heinemann, 1931.
Frankau, Gilbert: *The City of Fear* (poems); Chatto & Windus, 1917.
French, Field-Marshal Viscount: *1914*; Constable, 1919.
Fuller, Major-General J. F. C.: *The Conduct of War, 1789–1961*; Eyre & Spottiswoode, 1961.
Gibbs, Philip: *Realities of War*; Heinemann, 1920.
  The Battles of the Somme; Heinemann, 1917.
  The Pageant of the Years; Heinemann, 1946.
Gorce, P.-M. de la: *The French Army*; Weidenfeld & Nicolson, 1963.
Gough, General Sir Hubert: *The Fifth Army*; Hodder & Stoughton, 1931.
Grey, Viscount: *Twenty-Five Years*; Hodder & Stoughton, 1925.
Guinn, Paul: *British Strategy and Politics 1914–1918*; O.U.P., 1965.
Haldane, Lord: *Before the War*; Cassell, 1920.
  Haldane; Hodder & Stoughton, 1919.
Hankey, Lord: *The Supreme Command, 1914–1918* (2 vols.); Allen & Unwin, 1961.
Harington, Gen. Sir Charles: *Plumer of Messines*; John Murray, 1935.
Henriques, J. Q.: *The War History of the 1st Battalion, Queen's Westminster Rifles*; Medici Society, 1923.
Hindenburg, Field-Marshal von: *Out of My Life*; Cassell, 1920.
Huguet, General: *Britain and the War: A French Indictment*; Cassell, 1928.
Isselin, Henri: *The Battle of the Marne*; Elek Books, 1965.
Joffre, Marshal: *Memoirs*; Geoffrey Bles, 1932.
Jones, Thomas: *Lloyd George*; O.U.P., 1951.
Liddell Hart, B. H.: *Foch: Man of Orleans*; 1931.
Lloyd George, David: *War Memoirs*; Odhams Edition, 1938.
Ludendorff, General: *My War Memories*; Hutchinson, 1919.
MacDonagh, Michael: *In London During the Great War*; Eyre & Spottiswoode, 1935.
Magnus, Sir Philip: *Kitchener*; John Murray, 1958.

Marder, A. J.: *Anatomy of British Sea Power, 1880–1905*; Frank Cass & Co., 1940.

From the Dreadnought to Scapa Flow; O.U.P. (4 vols.).

Maurice, Sir Frederick: *The Last Four Months*; Cassell, 1919.

Monash, General Sir John: *The Australian Victories in France in 1918*; Angus & Robertson, 1936.

Montgomery, Sir A. A.: *The Story of the Fourth Army*; Hodder & Stoughton, 1919.

Nicolson, Harold: *King George V: His Life and Reign*; Constable, 1952.

Peacemaking; Constable, 1933.

Oliver, F. S.: *Ordeal by Battle*; Macmillan, 1915.

The Anvil of War: Letters Between F. S. Oliver and His Brother, 1914–1918; Macmillan, 1936.

Orpen, Sir William: *An Onlooker in France*; Williams & Norgate, 1921.

Pack, S. W. C.: *Matapan*; Batsford, 1961.

Repington, Colonel: *The First World War*; Constable, 1920.

Vestigia; Constable, 1919.

Robertson, Field-Marshal Sir William: *Soldiers and Statesmen* (2 vols.); Cassell, 1926.

Rogers, Col. H. C. B.: *Tanks in Battle*; Seeley, Service & Co., 1965.

Rogerson, Sidney: *The Last of the Ebb*; Arthur Barker, 1937.

Seymour, W. W.: *The History of the Rifle Brigade in the War of 1914–1918*; The Rifle Brigade Club, 1936.

Sitwell, Sir Osbert: *Laughter in the Next Room*; Macmillan, 1949.

Steinberg, Jonathan: *Yesterday's Deterrent: Tirpitz and the Birth of the German Battle Fleet*; Macdonald, 1965.

Stumpf, Richard (Ed. Daniel Horn): *The Private War of Seaman Stumpf*; Leslie Frewin, 1969.

Swinton, Sir Ernest: *Eyewitness*; Hodder & Stoughton, 1932.

Eyewitness's Narrative of the War; Edward Arnold, 1915.

Torraine, John: *Douglas Haig: The Educated Soldier*; Hutchinson, 1963.

General Jack's Diary (Ed.); Eyre & Spottiswoode, 1964.

Mons: The Retreat to Victory; Batsford, 1960.

The Life and Times of Lord Mountbatten; Hutchinson, 1968.

The Western Front; Hutchinson, 1964.

Thomson, G. M.: *The Twelve Days*; Hutchinson, 1964.

Trevelyan, G. M.: *Grey of Falloden*; Longmans, Green & Co., 1937.

Verity, William: 'Haldane and Asquith'; article in *History Today*, July, 1968.

Watt, R. M.: *Dare Call it Treason*; Chatto & Windus, 1964.

Wheeler-Bennett, Sir John: *Brest-Litovsk: The Forgotten Peace*; Macmillan, 1938.

Woodward, Sir Llewellyn: *Great Britain and the War of 1914–1918*; Methuen, 1967.

Wyrall, Everard: *The History of the 19th Division, 1914–1918*; Edward Arnold.

INDEX